Discovery Travel Adventures

BACKCOUNTRY TREKS

Judith Dunham
Editor

John Gattuso
Series Editor

Discovery Communications, Inc.

Distribution
United States
Langenscheidt Publishers, Inc.
46–35 54th Road, Maspeth, NY 11378
Fax: 718-784-0640

Worldwide
APA Publications GmbH & Co.
Verlag KG Singapore Branch, Singapore
38 Joo Koon Road, Singapore 628990
Tel: 65-865-1600. Fax: 65-861-6438

Discovery Communications produces high-quality nonfiction television programming, interactive media, books, films, and consumer products. Discovery Networks, a division of Discovery Communications, Inc., operates and manages the Discovery Channel, TLC, Animal Planet, Travel Channel, and Discovery Health Channel. Visit Discovery Channel Online at www.discovery.com.

Although every effort is made to provide accurate information in this publication, we would appreciate readers calling our attention to any errors or outdated information by writing us at: Insight Guides, P.O. Box 7910, London SE1 1WE, England; fax: 44-20-7403-0290;
e-mail: insight@apaguide.demon.co.uk

Printed by Insight Print Services (Pte) Ltd,
38 Joo Koon Road, Singapore 628990.

Library of Congress Cataloging-in-Publication Data
Backcountry treks / Judith Dunham, editor.
p. cm.—(Discovery travel adventures)
Includes bibliographical references and index.
ISBN 1-56331-926-8
1. Backpacking—United States—Guidebooks. 2. Hiking—United States—Guidebooks. 3. Outdoor recreation—United States—Guidebooks. I. Dunham, Judith. II. Series.

GV199.4.B23 2000
917.304'929—dc21

00-020084

About This Book

B*ackcountry Treks* combines the interests and enthusiasm of two of the world's best-known information providers: **Insight Guides**, whose titles have set the standard for visual travel guides since 1970, and **Discovery Communications**, the world's premier source of nonfiction entertainment. The editors of Insight Guides provide both practical advice and general understanding about a destination's history, culture, institutions, and people. Discovery Communications and its website, www.discovery.com, help millions of viewers explore their world from the comfort of their home and encourage them to explore it firsthand.

This guidebook reflects the contributions of many knowledgeable editors and writers who share an enthusiasm for North American wilderness. Series editor **John Gattuso**, of Stone Creek Publications in New Jersey, worked with Insight Guides and Discovery Communications to conceive and direct the series. Gattuso chose **Judith Dunham**, a San Francisco Bay Area writer and editor with many books to her credit, including others in this series, to serve as project editor. "Every part of the backcountry experience is compelling," she says, "from poring over maps and assembling all the necessary gear to embarking on an adventure you'll always remember. Readers will feel the excitement as soon as they take their first steps into this book."

Heading into the backcountry even for an overnight stay demands preparation, and two seasoned travelers help get readers off to the right start. **Justin Cronin**, an avid camper, cyclist, and flyfisher living in Philadelphia, offers advice on planning a trip and describes the infinite options for enjoying the wilderness. Californian **Peter Jensen** has backpacked the John Muir Trail and sailed along the Pacific Coast, among many other adventures. He brings this extensive background to chapters on the essential matters of equipment selection and outdoor skills.

For travel advice both inspiring and reliable, the best sources are writers who know their destinations intimately. **Steve Kemp** has spent more than a decade exploring Great Smoky Mountains National Park on foot – and on paper as publications director of the park's natural history association. His chapter brims with detailed knowledge of Great Smoky's natural treasures. **Stephen Jermanok** branches out from his Massachusetts home on treks throughout the Northeast. He covers Adirondack Park, where he has canoed and hiked since childhood and still spends part of each summer. World traveler **Diane Marshall**, who has been to more than 30 countries, is also a dedicated paddler. For a favorite local adventure, she launches her kayak into her "backyard" – Everglades National Park. She journeys through the park's Ten Thousand Islands for this book.

Lawrence Cheek writes about North Cascades National Park, an easy drive from his home outside Seattle. "I can no more imagine living without mountains on my horizon than breathing on the moon," he says. "I love plodding the North Cascades, being receptive to the infinite variety of large and small miracles around me." Sharing this passion for mountains is **Jeremy Schmidt**, who enjoys backpacking, climbing, and skiing in his local range, the northern Rockies. He relished covering the Bob Marshall Wilderness for "its ability to offer a wilderness experience that's no less than profound."

Mel White introduces readers to backcountry not far from his front door in Little Rock, Arkansas – the Ouachita National Forest, a place he visits time and again to hike the trails and float the rivers. He also takes readers to Big Bend National Park in Texas, one of his favorite destinations outside his home range. North Carolina native **T. Edward Nickens**, who writes about natural history and outdoor sports for national magazines, shares his experiences hiking, biking, and skiing in West Virginia's Monongahela National Forest.

Whether she is skiing, snowshoeing, hiking, or scuba diving, **Claire Walter** is an enthusiastic backcountry traveler who has written about her home state of Colorado, as well as distant tropical locations, for dozens of publications. For this book, she takes readers backpacking in the San Juan Mountains. San Francisco Bay Area environmental writer **Glen Martin** hoists a backpack and heads for Sequoia and Kings Canyon National Parks. Other projects have taken him to Alaska and down the Sacramento River by kayak.

Living in Duluth, Minnesota, gives **Michael Furtman**, who specializes in writing about wildlife, access to great backcountry destinations throughout the upper Midwest. He gladly accepted assignments to write about two very different places, Theodore Roosevelt National Park in North Dakota and Isle Royale National Park in Michigan. **Rose Houk**, a Flagstaff-based author of several books on nature travel, rides on horseback through Arizona's Mazatzal Wilderness. "This is some of the last great unspoiled terrain in the country," she says, "with a true western flavor."

Nicky Leach, based in Santa Fe, New Mexico, and a veteran of other titles in this series, has authored many travel books, including an award-winning guide to Southwest parks. Her in-depth knowledge of the region's geology and wildlife enriches her chapter on Grand Staircase-Escalante National Monument. She also covers wilderness navigation and leave-no-trace ethics. **David Rains Wallace**, recipient of the prestigious John Burroughs Medal for Nature Writing among many other honors, has published more than a dozen books on the natural history of North and Central America. He brings his astute perceptions to his chapter on Joshua Tree National Park.

"The best part of setting off into the woods," **Wayne Curtis** says, "is getting the chance to let the landscape come to life, to notice how intricate and interwoven the ecosystems around us really are." Curtis's treks have taken him from his home on the Maine coast throughout New England and maritime Canada. He welcomed the opportunity to write about Gros Morne National Park and White Mountain National Forest. Few writers know arctic Alaska as well as **Nick Jans**, who lives outside Gates of the Arctic National Park, the destination he penned for this book. By his own estimation, he has logged close to 75,000 miles in his travels throughout the area since settling there in the late 1970s.

Thanks to the many park rangers and naturalists who reviewed the text. Thanks also to members of Stone Creek Publications' editorial team – **Edward A. Jardim, Nicole Buchenholz, Sallie Graziano,** and **Enid Stubin**.

Oxeye daisies (above) show off their blossoms.

A rock climber (opposite) works a fissure in a cliff face in the Colorado Rockies.

Mountain biking (below) has become one of the most popular ways to penetrate the backcountry.

Preceding pages: Expert mountaineers from around the world climb the pinnacles and walls of Colorado's Eldorado Canyon.

Following pages: From a belay on an overhang, a climber surveys a breathtaking view of the Grand Canyon.

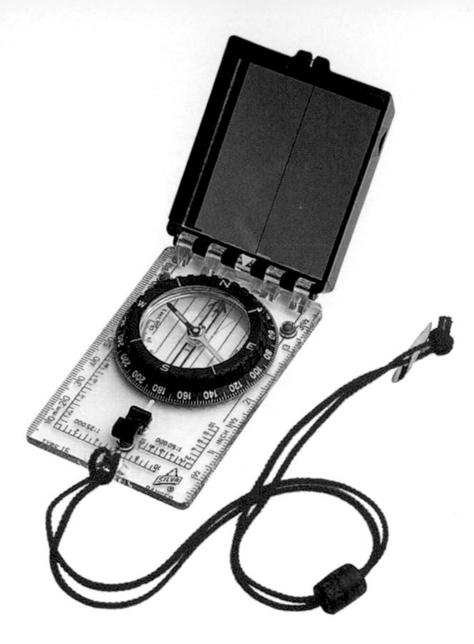

Table of Contents

INTRODUCTION

In Search of Wilderness 16
by Judith Dunham

SECTION ONE: PREPARING FOR THE FIELD

1 **Planning a Trip** 22
by Justin Cronin

2 **Getting Equipped** 28
by Peter Jensen

3 **Survival Basics** 36
by Peter Jensen

4 **Seeking Challenges** 44
by Justin Cronin

SECTION TWO: BACKCOUNTRY DESTINATIONS

5 **Gros Morne National Park, Newfoundland** 54
by Wayne Curtis

6 **White Mountain National Forest, New Hampshire** 62
by Wayne Curtis

7 **Adirondack Park, New York** 70
by Stephen Jermanok

8 **Monongahela National Forest, West Virginia** 80
by T. Edward Nickens

9 **Great Smoky Mountains National Park, Tennessee–North Carolina** 88
by Steve Kemp

10 **Ten Thousand Islands, Florida** 96
Diane P. Marshall

11 **Ouachita National Forest, Arkansas–Oklahoma** 104
by Mel White

12 **Isle Royale National Park, Michigan** 112
by Michael Furtman

13 **Theodore Roosevelt National Park, North Dakota** 120
by Michael Furtman

14 **Bob Marshall Wilderness, Montana** 128
by Jeremy Schmidt

15 **Grand Staircase–Escalante National Monument, Utah** . . . 138
by Nicky Leach

16 **San Juan Mountains, Colorado** 148
by Claire Walter

17 **Big Bend National Park, Texas** 158
by Mel White

18 **Mazatzal Wilderness, Arizona** 166
by Rose Houk

19 **Joshua Tree National Park, California** 174
by David Rains Wallace

20 **Sequoia and Kings Canyon National Parks, California** . . . 184
by Glen Martin

21 **North Cascades National Park, Washington** 192
by Lawrence W. Cheek

22 **Gates of the Arctic National Park and Preserve, Alaska** . . . 202
by Nick Jans

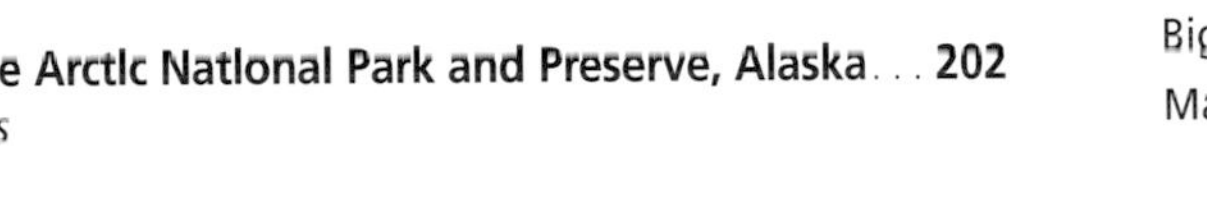

Resource Directory 212

Index 220

MAPS

Gros Morne National Park, Newfoundland 56

White Mountain National Forest, New Hampshire 64

Adirondack Park, New York 72

Monongahela National Forest, West Virginia 82

Great Smoky Mountains National Park, Tennessee–North Carolina 90

Ten Thousand Islands, Florida 99

Ouachita National Forest, Arkansas–Oklahoma 106

Isle Royale National Park, Michigan 114

Theodore Roosevelt National Park, North Dakota 122

Bob Marshall Wilderness, Montana 130

Grand Staircase–Escalante National Monument, Utah 140

San Juan Mountains, Colorado 150

Big Bend National Park, Texas 160

Mazatzal Wilderness, Arizona 168

Joshua Tree National Park, California 176

Sequoia and Kings Canyon National Parks, California 186

North Cascades National Park, Washington 194

Gates of the Arctic National Park and Preserve, Alaska 205

CAMELBAK

INTRODUCTION

In Search of Wilderness

Weeks of methodical preparation have led you to this moment. You tug at the straps of your backpack in an effort to settle the 30-pound load on your hips. After one last check of your water bottle and the laces of your hiking boots, there's nothing else to do but walk. You try to set a comfortable pace that will take you to the first night's camp, and you wonder, Why am I out here when I could be relaxing at a beachfront resort? ◆ The question evaporates almost immediately. You know why you're here – to retreat from the routines of everyday life, find solitude and solace, embrace the unknown, learn about yourself by exploring the outdoors. ◆ An afternoon hike in the wilderness just isn't enough to reach these noble goals. Getting there requires full immersion in the sort of places where nightfall unveils stars so plentiful that they nearly obscure familiar constellations, and where the dawn chorus of birds is a reliable wake-up call. ◆ Wilderness travel, with all its pleasures and challenges, has never been so popular. Every year and in all seasons, millions of people hike, pedal, or paddle into North America's sprawling backcountry regions. It wasn't always so. A century ago, most Americans regarded wilderness as an impediment to "progress." It was an obstacle to be endured on the way to a better place or an exploitable storehouse of natural wealth. ◆ By the early 20th century, when naturalist and writer John Muir declared that "wildness is a necessity," a handful of prescient

Step into the backcountry, leave your mundane stresses behind, and discover nature's grand and subtle wonders.

The stunning formations of Coyote Butte (left) are preserved in Utah's Grand Staircase-Escalante National Monument.

Preceding pages: A backpacker traverses a high-country ridge in the North Cascades, Washington; a mountain biker shoulders his bike in Baja California; a kayaker skirts icebergs in the Stikine-LeConte Wilderness, Alaska.

Camping overnight (left) allows backpackers to savor Washington's Olympic National Park, from the majestic scenery to the wildflowers and wildlife.

A hiker (bottom) enjoys a moment of solitude and reverie at Arches National Park in Utah.

The peak of Mount Stuart (opposite) towers over trekkers in the Alpine Lakes Wilderness of Washington.

activists had realized the merit of preserving entire ecosystems for their own sake, rather than for their economic value. The message was spread over the decades by one voice after another – from John Muir to such other notable wilderness advocates as Theodore Roosevelt, Bob Marshall, Aldo Leopold, and Rachel Carson. Step after hard-won step – from the establishment of the first national park in 1872, to the passage of the Wilderness Act in 1964 and the Endangered Species Act in 1966, to the efforts of today's environmentalists – has ensured that you can find expanses of wild country within a day's drive of home. The definition of progress, we now know, must encompass preservation of wilderness and all of its inhabitants.

The desire to experience the backcountry arises partly from a wish to experience a simpler way of life. The only possessions you take along are those you can carry on your back, paddle in a canoe, or load on a llama or packhorse. You gain confidence from relying on your ability to navigate through the arctic tundra, hike over a 10,000-foot pass, or make camp in the snow. Being outdoors day after day, night after night, also transforms your sense of time. There's little need for a man-made timepiece when you are constantly made aware of the arc of the sun, the movement of shadows, the phases of the moon, and the coming and going of the tide.

The isolation and pace of backcountry travel encourage you to examine your surroundings in detail, from the smallest of nature's creatures to the grandest of landscapes. You can probe the depths of geologic time in a sandstone canyon in southern Utah, gaze into the eyes of a bottlenosed dolphin while kayaking in the Everglades, watch a twilight gathering of creatures at a Mojave Desert waterhole, or stand at the foot of a mighty glacier in the North Cascades.

The journey starts here as you explore the pages of this book, whose words and pictures will kindle your yearning for adventure.

SECTION ONE

◆

Preparing For the Field

◆

Getting ready for a trek is one of its many pleasures. You'll find satisfaction in choosing a place to go, assembling all your gear, and learning wilderness skills. And the adventure itself still lies ahead.

CHAPTER 1

Planning a Trip

Wilderness travel is predicated on a kind of plunge, an immersion into the unknown as clarifying as the waters of a mountain lake. Planning seems anathema to its restless and spontaneous spirit, like scheduling a surprise. And yet, here's the paradox – preparing for a backcountry excursion requires as much, if not more, advance preparation than other forms of travel. ◆ It's the very unpredictability of the wilderness – the reason most of us seek it in the first place – that demands an extra measure of thoroughness when we contemplate a trip off the beaten path. As inhabitants of the civilized world, we are experts; we can jet into a strange city with nothing more than a guidebook and a credit card, and live to tell the tale. But in the backcountry, lack of preparation and experience is an invitation to disappointment or, worse, disaster. ◆ Planning for your trip need not be onerous, however. Done right, getting ready for a backwoods excursion for a weekend, a week, or a month is part of its pleasure, just as reading a restaurant menu sharpens the delight you take in the meal itself. Nor should taking a well-planned trip be an exercise in following a lockstep itinerary. Why not stop to shed your hiking boots and dip your toes in an alpine stream, or take a side trip to camp overlooking an inspiring view? The best preparation leaves room for such improvisation and discovery. ◆ Though it may sometimes seem that the landscape is solid pavement from coast to coast – a continent-sized clutter of highways and strip malls, subdivisions, and skyscrapers – a substantial percentage of North America remains as ruggedly beautiful as it ever was. Compared

Deciding where to go is more than a practical exercise. It's a chance to savor the journey to come.

A backpacker and her canine companion have found the perfect campsite overlooking a Colorado canyon.

Preceding pages: A climber ascends a big wall in Utah's Canyonlands National Park.

with Europe, this continent is still a spacious place, and many of its most ravishing locales are distinguished by their inclusion in a vast network of national, state, and provincial preserves to keep them wild.

In the United States, national parks (54 and counting) and more than 300 national monuments, seashores, lakeshores, trails, and rivers designated wild and scenic provide backcountry opportunities in abundance. More immense and more rugged still are national forests and grasslands, which fall under the authority of the U.S. Forest Service. They account for some 184 million acres – an impressive 8.5 percent of the nation's total land area. Located mainly in the West, this land is mostly open country.

Some of the best (and most challenging) backcountry can be found in wilderness areas, which sometimes straddle several national forests. The 2.3-million-acre Frank Church–River of No Return Wilderness, one of the largest, contains parts of six different national forests in Idaho, as well as two wild and scenic rivers: the Salmon and its Middle Fork. Others, such as the North Absaroka Wilderness in Wyoming on the northeastern boundary of Yellowstone National Park, press to the edge of national parks and monuments, offering adventurers many of the same experiences without the crowds.

State parks, though generally smaller, tempt wilderness travelers with untrammeled beauty and outdoor challenges of their own. Some, such as New York's Adirondack Park and Maine's Baxter State Park, are within easy striking distance of major cities. Across the border, the Canadian national and provincial park system mirrors that of the United States – and is even larger.

Making Priorities

While finding wilderness is easy, choosing among the options can be overwhelming. When it comes to planning a trip, many people think exclusively about where they want to go instead of what they want to do. It's equally important to ask yourself: What do you want from your trip? What sorts of landscapes and experiences entice you?

There are nearly as many reasons to seek the wilderness

Horseback riding through Nevada's rugged Jarbridge Wilderness (left) is an option for adventurers who don't want to carry backpacks.

Hikers (opposite) view a panorama of peaks more than 7,000 feet high in Washington's Olympic National Park.

Backcountry travel has its physical challenges, like carrying a mountain bike between steep trails (below).

as there are seekers. For some, the attraction lies in physical challenge – the chance to trade the comforts of the modern world for the heart-quickening thrill of something more raw and pure. Others prefer to commune quietly with nature: to stand in the shade of giant trees in an ancient forest, or float past canyon walls etched by the patient forces of time, or observe nature's rhythms in the comings and goings of wildlife around a desert spring. Still others yearn simply for the "other," the experience of a place vastly different from what they've ever seen before: a glacial bay by moonlight, or a high-country meadow spangled with spring wildflowers, or a prairie grassland where elk and bison graze.

Whatever intrigues you, research possible destinations. Every park and wilderness has its particular attractions. Interested in geology? Consider Grand Staircase-Escalante National Monument in Utah, or the badlands of Theodore Roosevelt National Park in North Dakota, or the Ouachita National Forest in Arkansas. Woodland habitats? The ancient redwood stands and misty rain forests of the Pacific Northwest deserve their reputation for grandeur, but don't rule out the East and destinations such as the Adirondack Mountains or the Great Smoky Mountains, which promise spectacular fall foliage as well. Birding? Few destinations can touch Texas's Big Bend National Park, which draws thousands of birders (though not enough to make the place seem crowded). Desert landscapes? At California's Joshua Tree National Park, you'll find not one desert, but two – the cooler, higher Mojave and the sun-scorched, low-lying Colorado – presided over by the region's signature tree, an enormous yucca whose striking profile reminded early Mormon pioneers of the prophet Joshua, leading them to a promised land.

Consider, as well, the time of year. Many prized destinations are also the most sought after; at high season, they can be less like wildernesses than wilderness theme parks. To avoid the crowds, select a less popular

destination or itinerary, or a time of year that scares fainter hearts away. Though about three-quarters of a million people descend on Yellowstone in July, fewer than 20,000 visit in March.

Assess Your Abilities

For most people, backcountry travel means hiking, and foot power is often the best way to explore the wilderness. But for those who want to try something different or free themselves from the burden of carrying their gear, other options await, including wheel, hoof, and paddle power.

Wheels mean mountain bikes, a relatively recent invention that is fast becoming one of the most popular ways to penetrate the backcountry. Abundant old logging and mining roads and trails that allow mountain bikes give bikers quick (and sometimes pulse-quickening) access to miles of open country. Packing in your gear by horse or llama can make easy work of difficult, high-country terrain and enable you to cover lots of ground. Kayaks, canoes, and inflatable rafts offer both the neophyte and the experienced paddler a similar experience of freedom. In Florida's Ten Thousand Islands, for example, it's possible to strap your belongings to a kayak and travel for days without once lugging a heavy backpack.

Backcountry trekking by most means is more arduous than other forms of travel, and that is part of its appeal. Technical advances in outdoor gear have made the wilderness a much more comfortable (and stylish) place. But all the expensive gear in the world can't substitute for brain and body power.

When planning a trip, gauge your level of fitness and experience, and be honest. Slick-rock hiking in Utah with a 40-pound backpack may sound like fun, but is your body up to it? If not, perhaps a less challenging excursion, on a friendlier landscape, would be a better choice; you can always train for the more difficult trip next year. Even for the physically fit, back-packing is strenuous work.

Treading Lightly

Wilderness, by definition, means "untrammeled by man." To keep it that way, it's important to leave no trace of your passage. The National Outdoor Leadership School, a leading outdoor ethics training program, suggests the following:

- Plan ahead. Inform yourself about your backcountry destination. Keep group size small, avoid heavily traveled areas, use equipment and clothing in subdued colors, and package food in reusable containers or lock-top bags. Pack out everything you pack in.

- Watch where you walk. Travel single file on designated trails, and don't cut switchbacks. Keep to sand, rock, dry grasses, or snow if you travel cross-country. Use map and compass rather than leaving rock cairns, tree scars, and ribbons to mark your route.

- Choose the right campsite. Look for an established, compacted site not visible from the trail and at least 200 feet (70 adult steps) from lakes and streams. Hang food to avoid attracting wildlife.

- Properly dispose of what you can't pack out. Carry a small trowel and dig catholes six to eight inches deep for human waste. Re-cover with the soil plug. Pack out used toilet paper. Wash yourself and dishes with biodegradable soap at least 200 feet from water sources. Strain dishwater before disposal.

- Minimize or avoid campfires. Carry a lightweight stove for warming and cooking. If campfires are permitted, use established fire rings or fire pans. Don't build new ones: Fire scars rocks and overhangs, especially in the desert. Bring wood or use small sticks; never chop live trees. Even gathering dead and down wood removes wildlife habitat. Extinguish campfires completely and remove all unburned trash. Scatter the cool ashes away from camp.

- Respect your surroundings. Let nature's sounds prevail. Keep loud voices and noises to a minimum. It's illegal to remove plants, rocks, and artifacts from most public lands. Leave the natural and cultural heritage for others to enjoy. – *Nicky Leach*

Consider the terrain, the weather, and the season, and plan accordingly. Don't try to cover more ground than you can – wilderness travel is not a race. Build time into your plan to rest, linger, and appreciate the journey.

Hiring an experienced guide or outfitter is another way to enhance your experience. At their most basic, the services of a guide or outfitter might include trip planning, maps and trail information, equipment rental, and shuttle service to and from a trailhead or put-in point on a river. At the opposite extreme, many outfitters are equipped to script every inch of your trip in high style – toting your gear, setting up camp before you arrive, and capping each day with a sit-down dinner beneath the stars. Most of all, outfitters can share the knowledge they've acquired over years of travel in a particular locale. Going with an expert is a great way to learn about a place and acquire new skills – and, if you choose, sweeten the adventure with a touch of luxury.

High style or low, the most important thing of all is not to let the array of options intimidate you. A guided mule-pack trip in New Mexico or a weeklong trek up the Appalachian Trail? High-country fly-fishing in Wyoming or a raft trip down the roiling Colorado River? It's an embarrassment of riches. Let the trip begin the day you first imagine it.

A beginning kayaker can safely enjoy paddling across a lake like this one in Canada's Banff National Park (above).

Steep trails beginning at the rim of the Grand Canyon (left) lead hikers to the Colorado River thousands of feet below.

CHAPTER 2

Getting Equipped

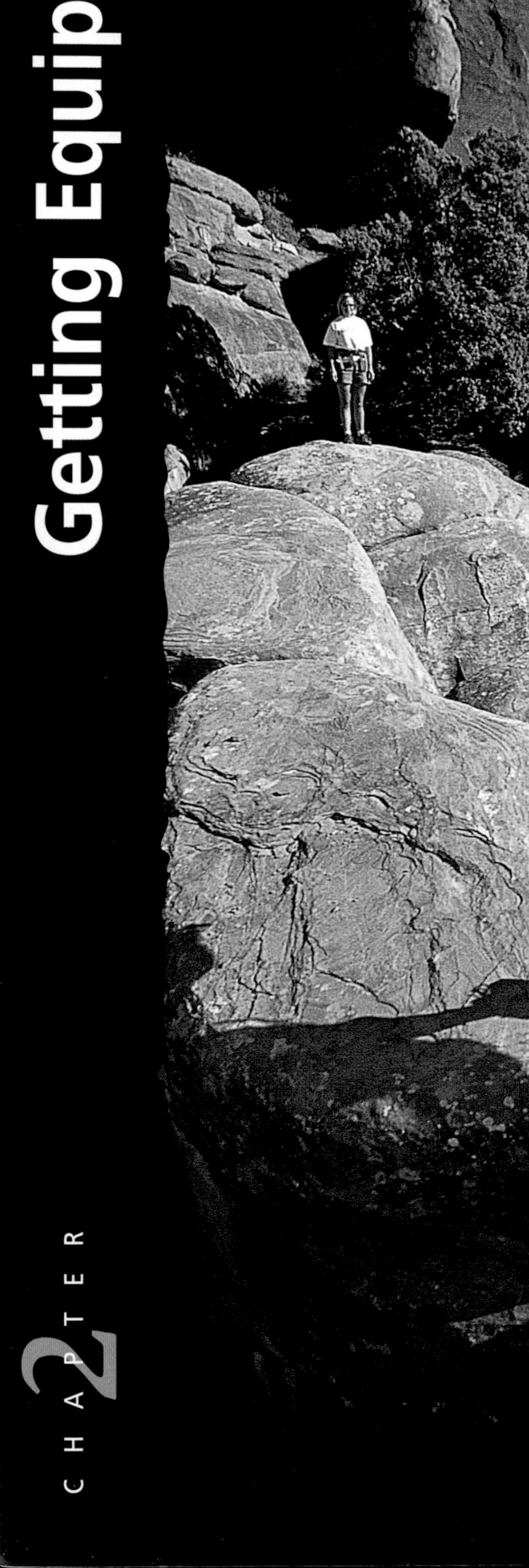

In the silence of night at just over 11,000 feet, shrouded in a puffy nest of insulating fibers, shielded by several artificial skins of tightly loomed, microscopically thin nylon, you hear the distant timpani of an approaching storm echoing off granite sentinels. Soon the booms turn to sharp pops as fat raindrops hit your tent's drum-tight rain fly, and the heavy clouds unzip and release their vertical rivers. If it gets just a few degrees colder, you think, the drops may turn to snow or hail the size of marbles. ◆ Does the storm delight you? Lull you back to sleep? After all, you are snug and warm inside a superb tent, stretched out in a sleeping bag with nary an uninsulated seam, gently lifted off a cold bed of glacial scree by a thin but comfortable pad that preserves your precious body heat. Or are you? ◆ Good equipment separates us from nature's harsh, sometimes life-threatening extremes. Nothing ruins a wilderness trip, shortens it, or plunges you into an emergency situation quite like inadequate or, worse yet, missing equipment, forgotten or left behind because you had no idea you would need it. Wilderness demands that you carry your house on your back. Or in your kayak or canoe. It laughs at your struggles if you bring too much. Or too little. Or if what you have is too weak and flimsy. ◆ Experienced backcountry travelers begin packing a few weeks in advance. They budget plenty of time to purchase, make, or pull items from storage, lay everything out, consider each piece of equipment, prepack, weigh the sum total, and then start deciding whether they really need an item or not. An early start allows you to

Ensuring an enjoyable trip starts when you pack your gear. Be sure to carry what you need to stay safe and comfortable.

A trekker with a well-fitted backpack scrambles unencumbered over sandstone boulders in southern Utah. A pack should not exceed one-fourth of a hiker's body weight.

research a destination's weather, terrain, and unusual hazards, as well as its delights. An area rich in wildlife, for example, may entice you to carry binoculars and a longer camera lens, two items that often don't make it into a backpack because of their weight.

Feet First

No one keeps statistics on blisters, but more wilderness trips are ruined by sore feet than by anything else. Blisters can appear in a matter of minutes and not necessarily within the first few miles of a trailhead. The days of breaking in heavy leather boots and at the same time toughening up feet by building layers of calluses have mercifully passed, replaced by the latest running-shoe technology applied to hiking-boot design.

For most purposes, look for lightweight, ankle-high boots with padded uppers made of a combination of leather and breathable synthetic fabrics. They should have high-traction soles that are moderately stiff but bend. Like good tennis or basketball shoes, these boots need little or no breaking in – ideal for today's hiker who seldom has adequate time to spend months day-hiking in advance of a long trip.

Boots touted as water-resistant or waterproof should still be breathable. They help keep feet dry in rain or light snow and over boggy terrain like tundra. Water-resistant boots offer little protection for crossing streams, so carry hiking sandals or old sneakers – or just take off your socks and wear your boots anyway.

Liner socks made of lightweight polypropylene wick moisture away from your feet. Over them, wear thick wool or polypro socks (some brands feature a combination of the two). Never wear cotton – it's a sure ticket to blisters, for the naturally rough fibers trap and hold moisture, and

An experienced backpacker (left) knows the importance of packing well before hitting the trail.

Boots (opposite, top) should be kept in a tent at night to avoid encountering unwanted guests in the morning.

A camper (opposite, bottom) enjoys glorious views in Canyonlands National Park.

Camping (below) at 14,256-foot Longs Peak in Colorado requires a sleeping bag rated to withstand freezing temperatures.

pinch tender skin. Wool and synthetic fibers also provide excellent insulation against cold, even when wet.

Think Layers

Layering has become the dominant theory in outdoor clothing for physically active people. Despite manufacturers' claims of inventing yet another awesomely miraculous (and awesomely expensive) does-it-best fabric, backcountry travelers must still rely on a layered combination of favored garments. Some can even be castoffs from everyday wear. It's hard to beat an old wool sweater for warmth and protection, especially when you're wet (though it takes forever to dry).

One layer you probably don't have already, even if you walk to work in Chicago in winter, is a lightweight but tough outer shell. This garment stops rain, snow, and wind, yet allows body moisture to escape as vapor through its fine weave and strategic vents before the moisture can condense and dampen the clothing close to your body. This shell should have a hood, adjustable wrist bands, plenty of storage pockets, and enough length to reach the midpoint of your buttocks. In extreme weather conditions, you'll want pants made of the same material. Unless you plan to remain immobile, rubber- or vinyl-coated ponchos and rain suits quickly become hothouses of condensation. Worse than discomfort is the danger of wet clothing and the ultimate risk of hypothermia.

Beneath your shell, wear a middle layer whose bulk traps and holds air near the skin. Wool, fleece pile, and quilted down are all popular, but synthetic fleeces have the inside track because of their light weight, insulating powers when wet, and ability to dry quickly. Some brands feature much-improved compressibility – a great asset when you try to stuff this garment in your pack.

The innermost layer has one vital job: to wick moisture away from the skin and send it on its way. Underwear shirts and leggings made of polypropylene and polyester do the job. Cotton and silk get damp too quickly and dry slowly.

Use the layering system as well on your head and

Camp Cooking

Serious chefs would probably have apoplexy if they saw what most backpackers eat: freeze-dried meals, most of them gloppy stews, straight from high-tech foil pouches. But something miraculous happens after a day of burning 4,000 calories in the high country. Even freeze-dried glop tastes pretty good.

Trekkers (left) at Caribou Glacier on Canada's Baffin Island dine inside the comfort of their tent. Creative meal planning, along with a selection of tasty condiments, is the best recipe for gourmet camp cuisine (bottom).

The weight of a backpack (opposite) should be carried by the hips, not by the shoulders.

The simplicity of freeze-dried meals is unassailable. Most are packaged in pouches that double as pots. Just add boiling water, stir, and wait for the ingredients to reconstitute. One downside is cost: freeze-dried foods are pricey and rarely feed as many people as they claim. Low-cost alternatives, such as dehydrated black beans, tomatoes, and soups, are available in bulk at health-food stores. Supermarkets also carry prepackaged, just-add-water meals and soups that can be doctored into a passable entree with the addition of a protein source like dry, granulated soy. Even if an outfitter is handling the cooking, bring a small selection of spices. Curry and chili seasonings can change just about any meal for the better. A couple of fresh carrots and a sack of crackers add a crunchy texture so lacking in the usual soupy fare.

Keep your energy up between meals by snacking on complex carbohydrates such as whole-grain cereals, energy bars, and trail mix. Candy bars and other sources of sugar offer a quick energy boost, but eat them sparingly and follow up with a meal in about two hours to prevent roller-coaster blood-sugar levels.

Because open fires are banned in most wilderness areas, you'll need a lightweight stove. Look for one that has a built-in nozzle-cleaning needle to keep the aperture free of carbon residue, and carry a small repair kit. Test-fire a few stoves before choosing one; the better models create a blowtorch flame. A windscreen is another necessity. Wilderness kitchens often come with wind, rain, and other challenges you never encounter when you're home on the range.

hands during harsh weather. You'll find many options at backpacking and especially ski equipment retailers.

Experiment with your layers as you hike. You may find yourself huffing over a high pass on a near-freezing, rainy day with your torso clad only in a polyester shirt protected by your outermost shell – and your legs still in shorts. The body is an incredible engine, and it loves staying safely cool, but not cold, when in use.

Sleep Warm

Many campers think down sleeping bags weren't invented until the mid-1900s. But writer and inveterate Sierra Nevada hiker Helen M. Gompertz reported in a 1901 *Sunset* magazine, "we shoulder our knapsacks and down-comforter rolls, thankful for the light weight of the latter."

A good bag is still an absolute necessity. Because weight and bulk are critical, bags have evolved into mummylike shapes of baffled fabric channels. The tapered shape also keeps insulation close to the body. The system of baffles prevents the filling – a few pounds of natural goose or duck down, or a synthetic – from shifting. Look for temperature ratings ("good down to 5°F," for instance) that match the expected weather extremes of your destination. You also want a bag that compresses into the smallest-possible "stuff sack." To help lower total backpack weight, you can choose a slightly lighter bag and sleep with more of your clothes on to stay warm.

Synthetic-fill bags keep you warm even if the fill gets wet, while soggy down is worthless as insulation. Synthetic fills are especially effective on canoe and kayak trips and in rainy country – though the careful camper always protects a sleeping bag from moisture with a good tent and a waterproof stuff sack.

A sleeping bag should be used atop an insulating layer because your body compresses the bag's insulation, rendering it ineffective against cold ground. In the old days, hikers gathered a huge pile of fresh-cut boughs or pine needles – something to trap warm air and provide comfort.

Today's wilderness travelers practice leave-no-trace techniques and disturb campsites as little as possible. Foam pads do the trick, especially the inexpensive closed-cell foam pads (these are light but bulky, and won't absorb water) and self-inflating pads. The latter have an inner layer of foam protected by an outer layer of heavy nylon cloth sealed with an air valve. They compress to a very tight roll but are heavier than simple foam. Test both types on a hard surface in the store before purchasing. No lightweight pad gives you true mattresslike comfort, but the self-inflating pads come close.

You may prefer sleeping under the stars, but tents are a godsend when the weather or the bugs turn ugly, and in some cases your life may depend on the protection of a good one. Lightweight tents – five to eight pounds – bear little resemblance to angular pup tents and other heavy canvas forebears. Today's best tents are made of ripstop nylon that can be tensioned with fiberglass or aluminum poles into organic, podlike shapes. These feats of engineering are mostly freestanding and can be set up easily after some practice – an essential drill before attempting to raise a tent on your first wet, windy night. Always stake a tent even if it's freestanding, or you may discover how easily it can become airborne, even with some of your gear inside.

Tents are usually rated by seasons. A three-season tent is engineered to withstand most North American conditions in spring, summer, and fall, and even in a light snowfall. Four-season tents are designed for winter camping. They are usually more expensive and several pounds heavier.

The best tents have a separate component called a rain fly. It covers the main tent like a second, waterproof skin and should extend to

within less than an inch of the ground. The air space between rain fly and main tent helps prevent condensation inside the living space. You should also be sure the tent is well vented at opposite ends. The seams on most tents must be treated by the buyer with a chemical sealer, a task best done outdoors and well before your first trip.

Load 'Em Up

A good backpack makes 30 to 50 pounds of gear feel like an extension of your body. Most backpackers carry a significant load even on a one-night trip, but you don't have to feel as if your collarbones are being chainsawed or your hip bones cut into stair steps. A rule of thumb: Don't carry a pack heavier than one-fourth of your body weight.

Choose a pack by walking around the store with a fully loaded model. Work with a knowledgeable sales representative who knows how to measure your back for a good fit. Then experiment by putting weight high, close to your back, and low, and make all necessary adjustments. Many stores offer equipment rentals, allowing you to try out a model on an actual trip or two.

Two basic styles of backpack dominate the market: internal frame and external frame. Internal frame packs look more like the rucksacks of old and position a load close to the body. They're excellent for helping you maintain good balance over uneven terrain, but they make your back hot and sweaty. External frame packs tower over your shoulders, getting the load up high while transferring the weight down to your hips. What they give up in overall balance they gain in air-conditioning for your back. Most packs are not waterproof, so you'll need a pack cover.

Backpackers are an eclectic lot. Even while cutting the handles off their toothbrushes to save weight, they contemplate bringing a small 10-ounce candle lantern, or a pack of cards, or a thick paperback bestseller, or a chunky Swiss Army knife because it "just might come in handy." Consider your destination carefully, gleaning information about necessary gear from guides, local experts, and park rangers. Will you need an ice ax for the north side of a high pass in early spring, even though guidebooks tell you the trail is a virtual cakewalk? Will bears be a problem, requiring you to hang your food or keep it in a bear-proof canister? Whatever you decide, the gear you bring plays a large role in making your trip a comfortable success or a stress-filled walk on the wild side.

A compass (top) and a map (left), and the ability to use them properly, are essential for backcountry travel.

Modern tents (opposite) are easy to carry and assemble into a variety of aerodynamic shapes.

CHAPTER 3

Survival Basics

A black, moisture-laden cloud builds quickly over the ragged stone surf of the White Mountains, then rushes toward you like a pirate ship spouting cannon fire. What began as a shirt-sleeve day turns into a hair-raising battle with lightning. Should you stay put or backtrack to a lower elevation? What body position should you assume, other than kneeling in terror and prayer? ◆ Or say your ankle suddenly wobbles on a desert trail, then swells into a balloon. You're hiking in late spring, but it's only mid-morning and the temperature is over 100°F. What do you do while a companion goes for help? Hack open a cactus the way you saw in the movies? Or sit quietly in what shade you can find and breathe through your nose? ◆ Backcountry emergencies bring on the biggest adrenaline rush you may ever experience. Your life may be in the balance. You need to be prepared and keep your wits about you. Michel de Montaigne wrote in the 16th century, "The thing I fear most is fear." Talk to rescue crews and you'll hear tales of the insidious ways that fear grips a lost or weary traveler, prompts a bad decision or unleashes sheer panic, and leads to tragedy – or, at the very least, an expensive helicopter flight back to town. ◆ Every step into the backcountry is an act of survival. Far from emergency services, piped water, shelter, and ready food sources, you rely solely on your skill and equipment. Problem solving is paramount, and education is your first line of defense. Since the brief advice offered here is only an introduction, consider enrolling in a wilderness survival-skills course. It will teach you how to find your way, build a basic shelter,

Whether it's bears, foul weather, or a washed-out trail, be prepared to take on wilderness hazards.

Deep water often has hidden currents and conceals dangerous terrain. It's much safer to cross where the water is shallow or find an alternative route.

and assemble a first-aid kit so you can treat that sprained ankle and hike out of the desert under your own power.

If your destination requires special skills such as using an ice ax and crampons, or new activities such as snow camping or paddling a sea kayak, you'll want to seek expert instruction before your trip. Some guided treks teach specialized skills before departure or en route the first day or two. Remember, the basics are readily learned but not easily mastered. To prevent injury, avoid taking unnecessary risks.

Armed with the following tools and strategies, you're better equipped than most to deal with some of the hazards peculiar to wilderness travel.

The Must-Haves

Carrying a selection of simple survival aids tips the odds dramatically in your favor. You should have these essential items along at all times in a small kit in your backpack or in a belt pack for day hikes from base camp. Some veterans won't even board a puddle jumper without their essentials in a belt pack and a warm jacket at the ready.

The essentials can be customized to suit any location and any climate:

- Warm item of clothing (with insulating qualities, such as a fleece pullover)
- Water and food (high-energy snacks)
- Way-finding aids (map and compass)
- Emergency shelter (survival blanket or trash bag)
- First-aid kit
- Fire-making supplies (waterproof matches and mini-candle)
- Signal devices (whistle and signal mirror)
- Edge tool (sharp pocket knife)
- Flashlight
- Rope (50 feet of strong cord)

Never underestimate your need for water. Over a long day of exercise, it's important to drink water often and in great quantity. Without water, dehydration soon sets in. But even when water is present in abundance, certain precautions must be taken. Microscopic *Giardia* and other waterborne organisms can cause severe intestinal cramps and diarrhea, starting about a week after ingestion. Small but efficient backpackers' water filters and pumps should be used to treat all water, no matter how apparently clear the source. Look for a pump with a prefilter that keeps sediment from clogging the main filter too quickly. Boiling water is also effective against *Giardia*.

Making Your Way

You can prevent getting lost by taking an active role in advance planning. Let someone know where you're going and when you're expected back. Secure all necessary permits with local authorities, and always sign in at trailhead registers.

Each morning while on the trail, review the day's route with your companions and stay in contact while hiking, even if someone wants to rest and catch up later. Every member of your party should have a map and compass and know how to use them.

If you do get lost, remaining calm is essential. Conserve water and energy, and listen carefully for the calls of your searching companions. Blow a whistle regularly (whistles can be sounded indefinitely, but vocal cords grow hoarse quickly). If you decide to bivouac for the night, leave a rock cairn or a bandanna flag in a nearby open space that can be seen by ground searchers. During the day, create something visible from the air: a smoky fire, a pattern stomped in a meadow, dark rocks arranged on a light-colored desert floor. Signal air searchers with the mirror from your essentials kit.

When you're forced to cross a river, go out of your way to find a safe, shallow section above any deep stretches or waterfalls. Even swift-moving water that is only knee-deep poses a hazard. One little-recognized danger is getting a foot stuck momentarily between rocks on the stream bottom, falling, and being held under while the force of the water pulls your body downstream.

Cross streams tripod style. Use a stout stick for a third point of balance, keep your back facing upstream, and move only one "leg" of the tripod at a time. Be sure to unbuckle the hip and sternum belts on your backpack so you can slip out quickly if you fall. Rigging the rope from your essentials kit across a stream can help provide support and balance. But never tie yourself to a rope – turn back instead.

Confronting the Elements

An unexpected plunge into a river, a drastic drop in air temperature and a soaking rain, or simply chilling down too much while resting in breezy shade after a hard, sweaty climb can all bring on hypothermia, a life-threatening drop in the body's core temperature. If you or one of your companions show symptoms, including uncontrollable shivering, apathy, incoherence, and diminished coordination, take immediate action.

A tool with a sharp edge (above) is among the essential items to carry on both extended treks and day hikes.

Water from all sources, even a seemingly pristine alpine lake, must be filtered before drinking (opposite).

Using a walking stick when fording streams (left) gives added support for moving through fast currents and over slick rocks. This hiker should have also unbuckled the hip strap of her backpack.

Get out of the wind, and build a fire (with caution in areas prone to forest fire). Remove the victim's wet clothing if you have a dry alternative, then provide a source of heat. Use warm rocks, warm bottles of water, and, best of all, body heat to warm the victim (two other people, if possible, inside a sandwich of two or three sleeping bags).

Learn as well to recognize the symptoms of oncoming heat exhaustion and its more serious cousin, heat stroke: loss of balance, fatigue, blurred speech. Find or make shade, using the rescue blanket and rope from your essentials kit; drink fluids; restore electrolytes (through a powdered sports drink mixed with water); dampen clothing (if water is abundant); and fan the victim. Because the body loses as much as two or more gallons of water a day in the desert, adequate water is essential along with an electrolyte-laced drink supplement to maintain vital salt and other mineral levels. Cramping and extreme fatigue are imminent if these elements aren't adequately replenished.

Intense sunlight at altitudes above about 3,000 feet, where you're also around many reflective surfaces such as rock, water, and snow, greatly magnifies your chance of ultraviolet poisoning – sunburn and other effects of overexposure. Sunblock lotions can give a false sense of security; be sure to apply them frequently and use a sun-protection factor (SPF) of 30 or 45. It's best to cover up most or all of your skin and wear a wide-brimmed hat with neck strap (so a gust of wind doesn't blow it away) and sunglasses that guard against ultraviolet and infrared rays. Don't forget to use plenty of sunblock on lips, neck, face, and ears, give your nose added protection with zinc or titanium oxide, and bring a big bandanna for your neck.

The growing popularity of short trips to high places, requiring a rapid rate of ascent, has increased incidents of altitude illness. Symptoms include headache, nausea, loss of appetite, and fatigue. In short, you feel lousy, not unlike being hung over. One in three wilderness travelers will experience some or all symptoms of acute mountain sickness when above 10,000 feet if not acclimatized properly by allowing a couple of days to reach altitude. Avoid overexertion, cold temperatures, alcohol, and sleeping pills – all of these can exacerbate the problem. If you're particularly uncomfortable, wait a day or two, or descend at least a thousand feet.

High-altitude pulmonary edema is much rarer but also much more serious and potentially fatal. It begins with marked fatigue, dry cough, and racing pulse, and progresses to phlegmy cough, bluish skin, pronounced shortness of breath, and sometimes coma or sudden death. High-altitude cerebral edema has similar symptoms. In each case, descent is the best cure, but slow ascent is the best prevention. Limit progress to about 1,000 feet per day when hiking and

A topographical map used with a compass (above) enables hikers to find their way in all kinds of terrain.

GPS receivers (right) are gaining in popularity but are not always reliable.

Hiking at high elevations (opposite) may cause nausea, headache, and other symptoms of mountain sickness if you're not accustomed to the altitude.

Wilderness Navigation

Your survival in the backcountry may depend upon how skilled you are in finding your route with a map and compass. Whether you're traveling on established routes or cross-country, consider taking a class or consulting a book on the subject.

Topographical or topo maps in different scales, available for the United States and Canada, depict the landscape through contour lines showing elevations above and below sea level. They also show a wealth of other information: man-made and natural features such as roads, trails, lakes, rivers, woods, marshland, and permanent snowfields. For backcountry travel, use maps scaled 1:24,000, meaning that one inch on the map equals 24,000 inches (2,000 feet) on land, or about two-and-a-half inches per mile.

A compass is used with a topo map for taking bearings, determining your location, and plotting a route. Maps depict true north, the direction of the North Pole, but compasses are aligned to magnetic north. For an accurate reading, you must correct for magnetic declination, using the information in the map margin or published declination charts for the area.

Other navigational devices include Global Positioning Satellite (GPS) receivers. These handheld gadgets rely on a network of 24 satellites that constantly broadcast position and timing information, which the receiver calculates into exact latitude and longitude. They run on batteries and must be kept warm to function; their reception may be blocked by heavy tree cover or topography. Use them in addition to, and *never* as a substitute for, map and compass.

Similar problems apply to cell phones. Touted as lifesavers, they are also criticized as interfering with the wilderness experience. Because their range is limited in remote areas, they may offer little assistance in an emergency. – *Nicky Leach*

climbing over 10,000 feet. A doctor can prescribe medication that may prevent high-altitude illnesses.

Lightning is especially common in areas prone to afternoon thunderstorms. Begin ascents to high altitude early enough in the morning so that you can be on your way down by the time clouds build. Strikes usually (but not always) offer some advance warning. To determine your distance from a nearby strike, count the seconds between the flash and the following boom or rumble: five seconds equals about a mile.

If you can't descend away from open ridges or other high, open terrain, sit – or better still, squat – on your pack or ground pad for insulation in a vertical fetal position to minimize your contact with the ground. Stay well away from tall objects such as isolated trees, as well as low depressions and shallow caves, for ground currents are as potentially dangerous as a direct strike by a bolt of lightning.

Critter Alerts

Most animals are reclusive and, unless surprised, shy away from contact with humans. Other creatures, such as mosquitoes, can be impossible to escape.

Mosquitoes can be kept at bay with thick or tightly woven clothing, head nets, and the judicious use of DEET-based repellents in the 75 to 95 percent concentration range (no more than 15 percent should be used on children).

Repellents are essential in areas of heavy infestation, such as Canada and Alaska. Lyme disease, carried by ticks, is a serious hazard in a growing number of North American areas. In addition to applying repellent, wear elastic-cuffed, long pants and a long-sleeved shirt. Stay on trails and out of underbrush. A tick can be removed with tweezers, but take care not to leave parts of it under the skin. When you return home, report the tick bite to your doctor.

A first-aid kit should include basic supplies such as bandages and antibiotic ointment for treating simple cuts and scrapes (above).

Head nets (right) offer useful protection against mosquitoes, blackflies, and other pesky insects.

Food supplies must be hung from a tree (opposite) or stored in canisters in areas inhabited by black and grizzly bears.

When in snake country, you can avoid getting bitten by hiking with increased awareness and remaining on trails. A walking stick is an effective early warning system – more for the snake than for you.

In areas inhabited by grizzly bears, be alert, stay clear of bears and their signs (tracks and scat), and consider announcing your passage with a bell attached to your backpack or walking stick. Ask local experts about the behavior of resident bears and what precautions work best. Pepper sprays are available to repel bears, but be certain they're designed for use on the bruins, not muggers.

If you encounter a bear, make yourself larger and more imposing by standing with your companions, raising your arms, and holding your jackets or walking sticks over your heads. If a bear charges, stand your ground. Such advances, though frightening, are often bluffs. If attacked, assume a fetal position on the ground – legs tucked, hands behind the head – and play dead. In such an emergency, you can hope only to put a stop to the bear's notion that you are a threat.

Grizzly and black bears in many regions have figured out that a sack of food hanging from a high tree limb means one thing: free lunch. New barrel-shaped plastic food canisters are impervious to bear attack, weigh two to three pounds, and can hold up to five days of trail food for two. Despite their added bulk and weight, they're a necessity in areas inhabited by bears. Set them out in the open, away from your campsite at night.

Food should never be kept in or near your tent. Remove all food and toiletries from your backpack at night and leave zippers open so animals won't need to chew their way inside. If a pesky bear enters camp, bang pots or throw rocks (enough to make the brute uncomfortable rather than injure it), but don't get too close to a bear that already has your food. In areas of extreme bear problems, never leave your pack unattended during the day.

Though very real, backcountry hazards can also be kept in perspective with the old saying, "You're probably safer out there than you are driving to work each morning." Adequate preparation, a collection of practical tools, and a confident attitude can turn emergencies into adventures with happy endings that you'll recount for years to come.

CHAPTER 4
Seeking Challenges

Part of the attraction of wilderness travel is the chance to test ourselves – to push the boundaries of our strength, stamina, and smarts to see what we are made of, away from the comforts and repetitious duties of the modern world. For many, just setting foot in a woodland is challenging enough. They owe no apologies; challenge is in the eyes of the beholder. But for others – those perhaps more experienced, or more physically fit, or just plain more restless – the outdoors is just the place to break a sweat. ◆ Something about a mountain cannot be ignored. Rising above the landscape, it seems the purest challenge to our will. As a group, technical climbers are almost fanatically devoted to their sport and speak in rapturous tones about the "holiness" of "going vertical." For many, the view from the top, however stunning, is almost beside the point. The pleasure is in the ascent itself and its demanding combination of mental and physical rigor – in the words of one veteran climber, "like playing chess and dancing a mid-air tango at the same time." ◆ True mountaineering – the climbing of mountains for sport – began in the late 1700s in the European Alps, and for most of the last two centuries, it was the exclusive province of the most intrepid daredevils. But in the last 30 years, innovations in techniques and equipment and a new emphasis on grace and athleticism have transformed the sport and brought even the most challenging climbs within the reach of healthy people willing to learn. Artificial indoor climbing walls allow the neophyte to practice in safety (or the more advanced climber to try out new techniques), and climbing schools around the country

Hiking's too tame? Try rock climbing, caving, river running, or other white-knuckle adventures.

A mountain biker tests the limits of his strength and endurance on a muddy ride through Montana's Flathead National Forest.

continue to introduce beginners to the sport and its variations. These are boom times for climbing. Even in the middle of Manhattan, climbers can be found bouldering (a version of low-altitude free climbing, using cushioned crash pads for safety) on Central Park's granite and limestone outcroppings.

Going Subsurface

At the opposite end of the geophysical spectrum, but no less challenging to master, lies the dark, chilly world below daylight's reach. Spelunking, or caving, as it is more commonly known, may not be for everyone (particularly the claustrophobic). But what the sport lacks in spaciousness it more than makes up for in physical challenge and eye-popping scenery – a trip to an otherworldly realm of stone and stillness, where vast underground ballrooms drip with stalactites and fantastic geological formations blaze in the light of the caver's headlamp.

Like climbers, cavers are a famously fanatical lot, more than willing to share the gospel of their sport, and joining a caving club, called a grotto, is usually the best

way to learn. Commercial caves ("show caves") developed for public visitation are another way to test the waters. Access to these caves is usually restricted to guided tours and requires no special training or equipment; visitors travel safe, well-lighted walkways, many of which are even wheelchair accessible. If this seems too tame or whets your appetite for more, some caving destinations, such as Mammoth Cave in Kentucky or Carlsbad Caverns in New Mexico, also offer "wild caving" tours, which take visitors away from developed areas for a more arduous and authentic introduction to the sport.

No less alluring is the world beneath the waves. Scuba is actually one of the easiest of adventure sports to learn and is neither prohibitively expensive (since most gear can be rented) nor particularly risky. If you're a competent swimmer, a series of lessons in a pool by a certified instructor can prepare you to dive with confidence down to 33 feet (the equivalent of one additional atmosphere of pressure). That's deep enough, since plenty of vivid undersea life hovers fairly close to the surface. Additional instruction can prepare you for night diving, wreck diving, and cave diving. Though most people associate scuba diving with coastal waters, there's plenty of diveable water inland, from the Great Lakes of the Upper Midwest to the reservoir systems of some of the nation's largest cities.

Need for Speed

The first mountain bikes were heavy, homemade contraptions, two-wheeled behemoths with reinforced road-bike frames, coaster brakes, fat tires, and no gears or suspension. Early

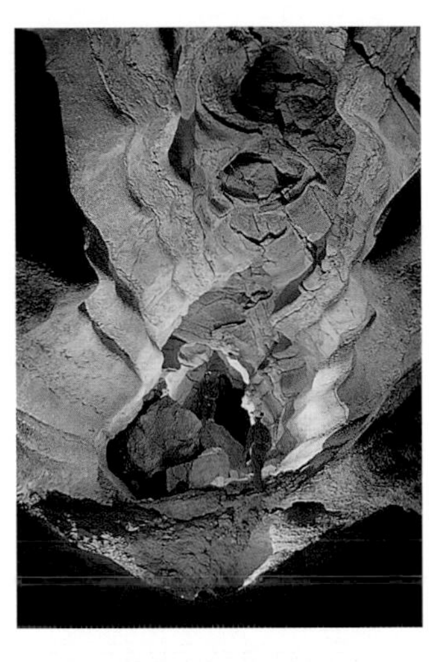

Cavers (above) explore a subterranean passage in Texas. Joining a caving club, known as a grotto, is the best way to learn caving skills.

A kayaker (opposite) threads through a stretch of whitewater. River running is a thrilling experience and is often the best way to enter wilderness areas.

Dogsledding (below) is both a sport and a means of backcountry travel. Adventurers on guided trips are often assigned their own team and are taught how to care for the dogs.

Snow Camping

Think of it as summer camping squared. To the uninitiated, camping in winter may sound like sheer craziness. But veteran snow campers tell a different tale. In the cold, they will tell you, everything about the wilderness is magnified – not only its discomforts but also its pleasures.

The backcountry in winter is a demanding place, and snow camping is correspondingly more gear intensive than its warm-weather counterpart. You'll need snowshoes or skis to get around, and the right sleeping bag and plenty of clothing to keep you warm and dry. The only food you'll find is what you pack in, and you'll need more of it – you'll burn twice as many calories as you would camping in summer. Sweating and breathing hard in the dry, cold air can dehydrate you rapidly as well. Unless you camp near an open water source, you'll need lots of extra fuel to melt snow for drinking water. Storms can blow in suddenly and last for days; be prepared to beat a retreat if the weather looks nasty. Days are shorter, and darkness can seem to descend in minutes, so always leave plenty of time to make camp.

As for shelter, seasoned snow campers maintain that sleeping in an igloo or snow cave is the zenith of the sport. But building one is a delicate and practiced art. Don't try to erect your first in the wild, and even if you've built a few in your backyard, bring a sturdy, four-season tent as a backup.

The reward for all this work? No mosquitoes or blackflies, and most of the bears are asleep for the season. And solitude – sweet, deep solitude – in abundance.

Winter camping (left) is within reach of travelers who like to snowshoe or cross-country ski and feel confident about their outdoor skills.

Mountaineers who want to enjoy their sport year-round take up ice climbing. One of the prime winter destinations is the Rocky Mountains (opposite).

A climber (below) uses a technique called rappelling to reach an otherwise inaccessible area of the Grand Canyon.

enthusiasts raced them down the steep hills of the San Francisco Bay Area, and the body counts were high. By the time racers reached the bottom, the oil in the coaster break drum had usually vaporized to pungent smoke; the trick was to finish the race before it was all gone.

A lot has changed in the two decades since then. Mountain bikes (and their streetwise counterparts, the hybrids) now account for the vast majority of bike sales in the United States, and mountain biking has become a staple of the outdoor diet. The appeal is obvious. If road bikes are the gracious elder statesmen of the two-wheeled world, mountain bikes are the bad-boy rogues – flashy, fast, and wild. The abundant public lands and open spaces of the inter-mountain West, especially the area around Moab, Utah, have made it ground zero for mountain biking in North America, but the sport has grown so quickly that extended mountain biking excursions (with or without vehicle support) can be arranged in just about any region of the country where riding is allowed. Be aware that in some places it isn't; mountain bikes, with their knobby tires, are hard on trails, and many parks have banned them. In any case, you should always limit your riding to bike-approved trails.

Depending on your point of view, mountain biking is either not as easy or just as treacherous as it looks. Achieving basic mastery of its techniques can take many, many hours, and even the most experienced riders dump their bikes from time

to time – and acknowledge that the bumps and scrapes are all part of the experience.

Pioneering Paddlers

The voyageurs – French fur trappers who paddled their canoes up the St. Lawrence and into the Upper Great Lakes in the 17th and 18th centuries – were the first Westerners to plumb the North American continent by water, following the routes used for centuries by Native Americans. Most of their routes have long since been domesticated for shipping, but the North American backcountry remains a place laced by thousands of miles of traversable waterways.

In fact, many of America's most remarkable places can be reached only by water. Sea kayaking along Alaska's rocky southern coast, rafting the canyons of the Colorado River, or canoeing the Boundary Waters region of northern Minnesota – each melds the pleasures of visiting a pristine wilderness with the satisfaction of getting yourself there by your own power. In the case of whitewater rafting and kayaking, the pleasure is doubled, as human brawn and skill combine with nature's might to produce a pulse-quickening ride.

Snow-Season Adventures

Winter provides as many, if not more, opportunities to challenge yourself and see a wholly different face of the

El Capitan (left) rises 3,000 feet above the floor of Yosemite Valley. Partway up the granite wall, a climber bivouacs for the night.

A mountaineer clears a crevasse (bottom) on Columbia Icefield near Mount Athabasca in British Columbia.

A climber (opposite) dangles from a rock face in Eldorado Canyon, Colorado. Confronting danger is an integral part of rock climbing.

wilderness. Otherwise impenetrable backcountry can be traversed on snow-shoes or cross-country skis, giving you access to a frozen world of stillness and solitude that few people witness. Ice climbing, a form of mountaineering that uses steel toe spikes (or crampons) and handheld axes to bite into the ice, gives expert climbers the chance to scale the peaks in the off-season (and make nonclimbers gasp).

Dogsledding, once limited to the Far North, now attracts new enthusiasts anywhere there's snow. Competitions are held as far south as New England and New York and throughout the Rocky Mountains, although Alaska, with its famed Iditarod, remains North America's uncontested capital of mushing culture. Skijoring, long practiced in Scandinavia but increasingly popular in the United States as well, is dogsledding without the sled; participants wearing cross-country skis are pulled by dog power, usually a single animal or a small team, in a headlong dash across the snow.

The larger question looms: why do any of it? Some would say that life is exciting – and treacherous – enough. Why up the ante by rappelling the face of a mountain waterfall, or plunging pell-mell down an abandoned logging road on 30 pounds of shuddering titanium, or squeezing through a lightless underground passage so tight you need to hold your breath to fit? Indeed, such activities are truly optional, and perhaps that's the point. The appeal lies in learning something new, or conquering a fear, or experiencing the pure, biological thrill of risk itself.

But for all who test themselves in the clarifying crucible of adventure, one motive is nearly always shared: the chance to rekindle some of the wildness within themselves and, at the end of the day, to speak this simple, delighted utterance: "I can't believe I did that."

SECTION TWO

Backcountry Destinations

Pick a passion: backpacking or canoeing, llama packing or mountain biking, exploring geological wonders or encountering wildlife. North America's backcountry, from the Arctic to the subtropics, invites you to realize your quest.

Gros Morne National Park
Newfoundland

There's something inescapably melancholy about being abandoned by a boat at a remote lakeshore, miles from parking lots and pay phones and supermarkets. ◆ Yet that's the best way to launch a four-day traverse of the **Long Range Mountains** at **Gros Morne National Park** in Newfoundland. You board a doughty tour boat at the mouth of **Western Brook Pond**, an achingly beautiful, landlocked fjord near the island's western coast. You gently jostle with camera-toting tourists for good railside position. The boat then casts off and arcs up a bend in the fjord as a towering cliff some 1,800 feet high – a seemingly solid wall from a distance – gradually slides apart to reveal a long, stunning lake. It's like a stage curtain parting before a glorious, natural show. ◆ The voyage itself isn't melancholy in the least. Admiring the granite cliffs scored with dikes of dark green igneous rock while swapping notes with other passengers heightens the anticipation. No, it's after disembarking, as you're crouched on the embankment, fussing with your backpack straps, and look up and see the boat heading away, that the flutter of doubt arises. It suddenly dawns on you: There's no changing your mind, no doubling back for forgotten sunglasses, no second thoughts. ◆ The boat glides out of sight, then minutes later eases out of earshot, the *chugga-chugga-chugga* replaced by the gentle chop of water on rocks, by the chatter of unidentifiable birds, by something possibly quite large crashing through the understory across the lake. Everything around you becomes more vivid and immediate, like the sky. As you shoulder your pack and eye the ascent ahead, you wonder: Did those clouds really have that damp

Breathtaking fjords and boreal wildlife await hikers in Canada's "Big Gloomy."

The lighthouse at Lobster Cove on the Gulf of St. Lawrence is a landmark for boats entering and departing Bonne Bay.

Preceding pages: A mountain biker uses a natural bridge to cross a canyon in Arizona.

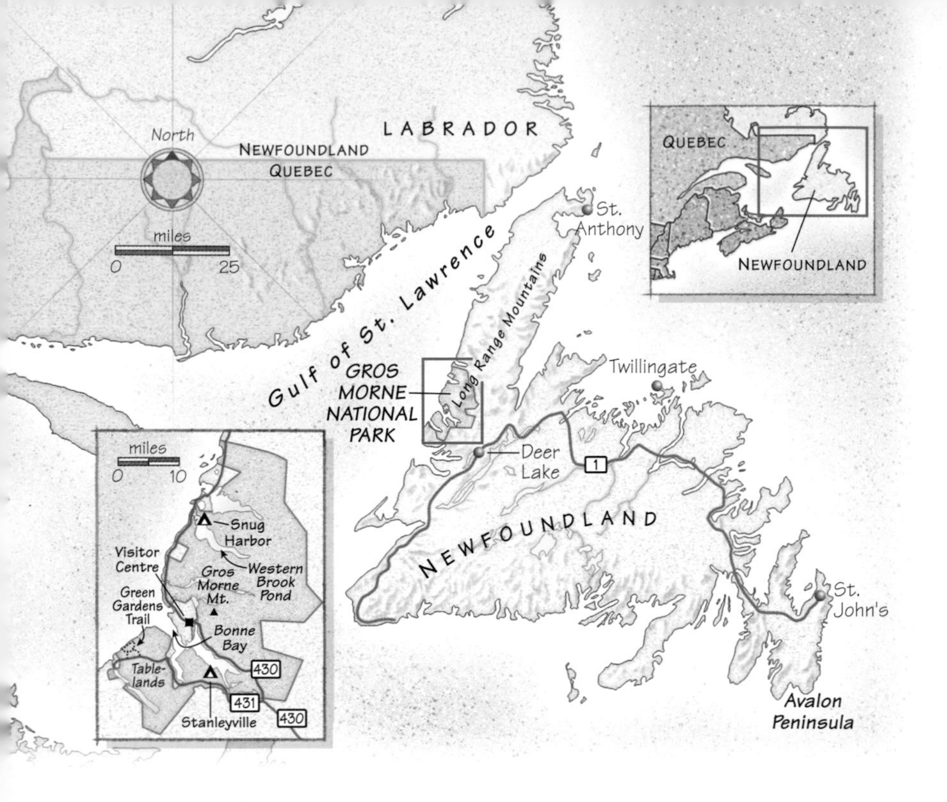

stubborn beauty that seems to waft through one's soul rather than fill one's heart. Even on days of brilliant sun, there's a spare hollowness to this raw landscape, which in places feels as primitive and unfinished as a construction site.

Above all, Gros Morne has far more natural drama than one would expect of the eastern seaboard. For lovers of solitude, the sprawling island of Newfoundland – about the same size as Cuba – may be the last best place in the East. This fact is all the more remarkable when you consider that Newfoundland was among the first places settled by Europeans. Vikings spent a brief time here a millennium ago, and some 500 years ago English, French, and Portuguese fishermen started drifting in to colonize these shores, attracted in large part by the bountiful cod.

Newfoundland remains surprisingly accessible, especially for those living in the

cottage-cheese look, all puckered with rain, when you left the parking lot?

Lure of the North

Gros Morne National Park is the Great North writ small. It doesn't have quite the epic sweep of the high Arctic, or its vicious extremes of weather. But the park boasts what amounts to the Great North's greatest hits. Crossing the blustery **Long Range**, you're likely to sight caribou, moose, or black bear ambling along the trail. On the high plateaus, rock ptarmigan flutter past, and you may spot an ungainly arctic hare, grayish in summer and weighing in at a beefy 12 pounds.

During the course of the trek, the terrain ranges from bog to boreal forest to twisted tuckamore with its stunted, wind-sculpted spruce and fir, similar to the krummholz found in the Alps. When the sun sets, it dips behind a shimmering **Gulf of St. Lawrence**, beyond which, just out of view over the horizon, lies Labrador.

Gros Morne translates as "Big Gloomy," which is somehow appropriate. On misty days when scud clouds drift eerily across the high rounded peaks, there's a profound mournfulness about the place, a sort of

eastern United States. From, say, New York, you can fly to **Deer Lake**, drive a rental car to **Western Brook Pond**, then board the boat for the 90-minute trip to the trailhead. Total elapsed time from the auditory chaos of New York to a silence as big as your imagination: about 12 hours.

One caveat: This timetable doesn't include a stop at the visitor information center at **Rocky Harbour**. And that's mandatory. The Long Range traverse is rightly considered serious business. At the center, you'll be required to view an 11-minute video about the trek, read a pamphlet about the park's black bears, and demonstrate that you know your way around with a map and compass. You'll plot out a preliminary course on a topo map with a park warden. And then, just in case, you'll be outfitted with a wilderness transmitter (about the size of a pager), which will help rescue teams track you down should you become disoriented and fail to appear 24 hours after your scheduled return.

Which very well might happen. Bear in mind that no established trail system crosses the Long Range. Instead, moose and caribou tracks lattice the uplands and constantly tempt hikers with primrose paths that lead only to thickets and heartbreak. You'll need to trust your map and your compass rather than your eyes. Even then, simple misfortune can befall you. One hiker became separated from his map owing to a thieving gust of wind, then got lost trying to backtrack out of the wilderness.

Moose (left), caribou, and black bear, along with smaller creatures such as arctic hare, inhabit the park.

The Long Range Mountains (below) reach 2,672 feet, the highest point on Newfoundland.

Mountain of an Island

Once you've made the ascent up from Western Brook Pond and left the prickly forest behind, you'll find the trek along the high plateau profoundly elemental. It's all sky and rock and water, with vegetation almost an afterthought. Gnomelike, gnarled trees stud the landscape, and you'll need to get down on your hands and knees to admire the flora, especially the delicate mosaic of mosses and alpine plants, including Labrador tea and mountain heather.

Among your discoveries as you cross the Long Range: the dampness of the uplands is unremitting. (Of course, you've remembered to pack old sneakers for sloshing through brooks.) You wade through icy streams

and work your way through sloppy marshes. You camp along isolated ponds and tentatively explore the spongy bogs.

And the dampness isn't limited to the ground. The plateau is frequently capped with dense clouds, thanks to moist winds blown across the Gulf of St. Lawrence and then forced upward over the mountains, where they condense. The range is riven with precipices and gorges, so it's unwise to travel when visibility is poor. Better to hunker down and wait for the clouds to lift, which may take a day or two.

The payoff comes on the final day, after ascending the park's highest peak, 2,644-foot **Gros Morne Mountain**. It's scrappy, rough, and surrounded by a moat of ankle-twisting scree, but let's assume you've surmounted those problems and timed your arrival to reach the summit on a crisp and clear summer day.

The views are something to behold – across the deep azure indent of **Bonne Bay** to the coppery **Tablelands** and to the broad waters of the expansive gulf beyond. Before you begin your descent, turn around and take a last over-the-shoulder look at the Long Range, where much of your traverse can be seen in a humbling instant.

Meadow and Coastal Retreats

Travelers lacking the experience or wherewithal to mount a four-day trek across trackless terrain have other options if they'd like to sample Gros Morne's wild backcountry. At Western Brook Pond, you'll find **Snug Harbor**, a lovely backcountry campsite amid impressive cliffs of the northern lakeshore; it's a relatively undemanding, two-and-a-half-hour hike from the trailhead. From the Lomond day-use area on the south shore of **Bonne Bay**, there's a pleasant, one-hour hike to the former lumber outpost of **Stanleyville**. You can camp here for the night, watch the lights twinkling down the bay, and snoop around gardens that still flower seven decades after the town was abandoned.

Backpackers are divided into two basic breeds: those who like to be up at dawn to rack up the miles and those content to idle a few days at a prime backcountry bivouac. For the latter, a much-recommended destination is the **Green Gardens Trail**, which follows the rocky coast along the park's southern section.

En route, you can detour past one of the world's more remarkable freaks of nature, called the **Tablelands** – a barren

Finding the Ice

If you can't get to the Arctic, let the Arctic come to you. Early each summer, a parade of icebergs floats down the Labrador Current past Newfoundland. This frozen flotilla brings up the tail end of a long journey that began a year or two earlier on the remote west coast of Greenland, where icebergs calve off a massive sheet of ice some 5,000 years old.

Of the 10,000 icebergs that depart from Greenland's shores each year, an average of just 500 make it as far south as Newfoundland. As always, averages can be deceiving: In 1988, only 187 icebergs made the journey. Six years later, 1,765 icebergs floated past.

What determines a good iceberg year? A number of variables, but a cold winter that produces a thick layer of sea ice is a boon. The sea freezes around the icebergs and insulates them from their primary enemy: lapping waves.

Among the best places to view icebergs are the northern and eastern coasts of Newfoundland, from **St. Anthony** on the tip of the **Great Northern Peninsula**, down through **Twillingate**, and on to the rocky coast of the **Avalon Peninsula**. May and June are the prime months for iceberg viewing, though some impressive specimens can linger into summer. You can often view them from the shore, but going on a tour boat allows an even closer examination.

Icebergs (above) take up to two years to reach Newfoundland from ice sheets in Greenland.

Wildflowers (opposite, top) fill seaside meadows in summer.

Stone arches (opposite, bottom) have been carved by the sea just north of the park.

A boardwalk (below) leads to Western Brook Pond, a landlocked fjord.

and rock-strewn hill that looms high above the road. It looks for all the world like an oddly rounded butte from the American Southwest. In fact, this happens to be a sizable slab of the Earth's mantle, which normally lies far beneath the crust. Around 570 million years ago, a chunk of the mantle was dislodged and driven up and over the crust when two continental plates collided. The rarely exposed rock has such a high content of magnesium, iron, and other heavy metals that few plants can survive on it, giving it a barren, desertlike landscape in sharp contrast to the adjacent hills.

The Green Gardens Trail, a demanding, 10-mile loop, begins in seemingly lifeless terrain as you weave from the parking lot through rust-colored hillocks. Then comes a plunging descent. Down and down you go, and the terrain grows more lush with every step. Soon you'll hear the restless ocean, then you emerge into a wondrous Oz-like tableau: an open coastal

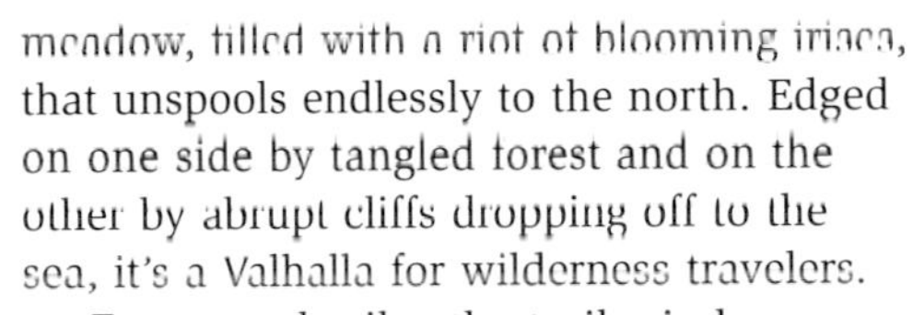

meadow, filled with a riot of blooming irises, that unspools endlessly to the north. Edged on one side by tangled forest and on the other by abrupt cliffs dropping off to the sea, it's a Valhalla for wilderness travelers.

For several miles the trail winds northward through these magical meadows before veering back up a ravine to circle back to the parking lot. Three backcountry campsites are spread widely along the trail, just far enough from the cliffs to be away from the ocean's spray. Days can be spent exploring the cobblestone beaches, scanning for whales, sighting pelagic birds, or – most exquisitely – indulging in the occasional nap on an isolated promontory.

During your coastal retreat, you may reach a conclusion. There's one thing more melancholy than watching a boat recede as you stand on a lonely shore. And that's to sit alone amid a field of blooming irises, without a crew of friends and family to share the sight.

TRAVEL TIPS

DETAILS

How to Get There

The Deer Lake airport is 19 miles from the park entrance at Wiltondale. Car rentals are available at the airport. Marine Atlantic operates a ferry service for passengers and automobiles between North Sydney, Nova Scotia, and Port-aux-Basques, Newfoundland, 180 miles from the park; call 800-341-7981 or 902-794-8109 for schedules and reservations. The boat on the park's Western Brook Pond operates from late May through September; call 709-458-2730 for information.

When to Go

Most backcountry visitors come to Gros Morne from late June through early September. High-elevation trails such as the Long Range Traverse often do not open until July 1 but can usually be hiked through late September. Daytime temperatures reach the mid-60s in July and August; lows are in the 50s. Expect cooler temperatures – 10 degrees or more with wind chill – at high elevations, as well as occasional rain. There is frost at night in the high country from mid-September, and snow by late September. Winter temperatures are below freezing. Most of the snow – 8 to 15 feet, with up to 20 feet at high elevations – accumulates from late December to early February.

What to Do

Hikers may explore the park on 136 miles of maintained trails as well as cross-country routes such as the Long Range and North Rim Traverses. Paddlers may kayak on the fjord lakes and along the coast, stopping at backcountry camping sites accessible by water. The cross-country ski season usually runs from mid-January until April, sometimes into May in years of heavy snowfall. Winter visitors camp in the park or stay at two backcountry ski huts.

Backcountry Permits

Camping sites are located along park trails. Backcountry travelers must register in advance and pay a fee to use the sites. A permit is required for hiking the Long Range, as is a 45-minute back-country briefing at the visitor center south of Rocky Harbour. Briefings are arranged by appointment; call 709-458-2417 for information.

Special Planning

Weather is unpredictable throughout the year; even in summer, backcountry travelers should carry reliable raingear, including jacket and pants. Waterproof gaiters are handy for keeping the lower legs dry when hiking off-trail in boggy areas. Campfires are allowed only on the beach at Green Gardens and Stanleyville; portable gas stoves must be used elsewhere in the backcountry. Visitors hiking cross-country are required to rent VHS transmitters used to pinpoint their location. Wind and tide conditions make kayaking at some coastal locations suitable only for experienced paddlers.

Car Camping

More than 250 sites in five campgrounds are available on a first-come, first-served basis. Reservations can be made for all campgrounds except Green Point; call 709-458-2417 for details.

INFORMATION

Gros Morne National Park

P.O. Box 130, Rocky Harbour, NF A0K 4N0; tel: 709-458-2417.

Newfoundland Department of Tourism, Culture, and Recreation

P.O. Box 8730, St. Johns, NF A1B 4K2; tel: 709-729-2830 or 800-563-6353.

LODGING

PRICE GUIDE – double occupancy

$ = up to $49 $$ = $50–$99

$$$ = $100–$149 $$$$ = $150+

Gros Morne Cabins

P.O. Box 151, Rocky Harbour, NF A0K 4N0; tel: 709-458-2020.

These are 22 log chalets over-looking the Gulf of St. Lawrence, each with one or two bedrooms, separate living areas, and fully equipped kitchens. $$–$$$

Ocean View Motel

Main Street, Rocky Harbour, NF A0K 4N0; tel: 709-458-2730.

The motel has 44 rooms, some with views. A restaurant is on the premises. $$

Spruce Grove Cottages

P.O. Box 214, Rocky Harbour, NF A0K 4NO; tel: 709-458-2212.

Each of Spruce Grove's three cottages has kitchen facilities. $$

Wildflowers Bed-and-Breakfast

Main Street North, Rocky Harbour, NF A0K 4N0; tel: 709-458-3000 or 888-811-7378.

Situated on three acres, this sixty-year-old home has six guest rooms, each with private bath, one with a balcony. $–$$

TOURS AND OUTFITTERS

Gros Morne Adventures

9 Clarke's Lane, Norris Point, NF A0K 3V0; tel: 709-458-2722 or 800-685-4624.

Guided treks include backpacking trips on the Long Range Traverse and sea kayaking the fjords of

Bonne Bay in the national park. From January to April, travelers may sign up for multiday backcountry skiing in the Long Range Mountains; at night they stay in the park's two huts or in nearby lodges. The outfitter also leads backpacking and paddling trips in areas outside the national park.

Long Range Adventures

General Delivery, Sops Arm, NF A0K 5K0; tel: 709-482-2223.

Trips from three to five days take backcountry travelers hiking in the Long Range. Visitors may also arrange guided fishing trips, as well as snowmobile tours in winter.

Northland Discovery Tours

P.O. Box 728, St. Anthony, NF A0K 4S0; tel: 709-454-3092.

Visitors board a boat at the St. Anthony harbor and head into the Atlantic Ocean to view the Labrador current's icebergs, spot migrating humpback, fin, and minke whales, and observe seabirds and bald eagles. Onboard guides discuss the area's ecology and history. Northland also offers daylong and extended trips specializing in hiking, fishing, wildlife watching, and wildlife photography.

Onward Tours

P.O. Box 969, Deer Lake, NF A0K 2E0; tel: 709-686-5333.

Backcountry travelers are taught how to drive and care for their own dogsled teams before taking off for the Long Range, where moose and caribou are common sightings. On multiday trips, nights are spent snow-camping or staying in small towns. The outfitter provides all winter-camping gear, including snowshoes for day-hiking. Onward also arranges mountain-biking treks up to two weeks long and multiday sea-kayaking trips in White Bay on the eastern side of the island.

Excursions

Cape Breton Highlands National Park

Ingonish Beach, Ingonish, Nova Scotia B0C 1L0; tel: 902-285-2691.

Stretching across the northern end of Cape Breton Island in Nova Scotia, this 235,000-acre park looks west onto the Gulf of St. Lawrence and east onto the Atlantic Ocean. Trails lead backpackers from sea-level beaches to the 1,500-foot-high Breton Highlands, with views of the surrounding waters, passing whales, and soaring bald eagles. Inland lakes host moose and other boreal creatures, and the park's forests display vibrant colors in late September and early October.

Forillon National Park

122 de Gaspé Boulevard, Gaspé, PQ G4X 1A9; tel: 418-368-5505.

The Appalachian Mountains – and, with them, the International Appalachian Trail – end at this national park in Quebec, where Cap Gaspé juts into the Gulf of St. Lawrence. Backpackers may hike and camp along the 27-mile section that crosses the park and ends with a spectacular view from Cap Gaspé. Wildlife such as black bears and moose inhabit this rugged area. Sea kayakers navigating the coastal waters can observe marine mammals and get close-up views of the abundant seabird colonies.

Fundy National Park

P.O. Box 40, Alma, NB E0A 1B0; tel: 506-887-6000.

Seven linked trails enable backpackers to circle this park on the New Brunswick coast. The 62-mile loop runs near the shore, along lakes and waterfalls, and through Acadian forests of birch, spruce, and maple. A half-dozen trails, some steep and challenging, are open to mountain bikers. One cross-country ski route has a cabin for overnight stays. Visitors will not want to miss seeing the incoming tide at the Bay of Fundy – the highest in the world, reaching nearly 70 feet at the bay's head.

White Mountain National Forest

New Hampshire

CHAPTER 6

You're sitting on a granite outcropping encrusted with lichens high above **Franconia Notch**, watching the sun sink over a distant ridge. Cars snake along the valley floor in the gloaming far below, brake lights flaring up as one car comes suddenly upon another in a balky conga line down the valley. You watch as the parking lot near the bike path slowly empties out as one car, then another, arcs onto the road. The whole automotive kabuki is performed in an eerie, unnatural silence, the disconnected soundtrack provided by the persistent *quork-quork-quork* of a raven soaring overhead and the dying wind catching in the stunted firs on the mountain flanks below. ◆ A blazing planet slowly punctures the deepening azure sky overhead, and you realize it's time to go. You stand and turn your back to the valley, and amble off toward that fractured mound of rock near your tent. The sound of an owl drifts up through the clear evening air, and you realize you might as well be a thousand miles from the nearest soul. ◆ That's the thing about New Hampshire's **White Mountains**. You can be so close to civilization and its discontents, yet so very, very far away. With the region's unpredictable weather and tortured topography, it's not all that hard to disappear intentionally into the cracks, finding your own private wilderness amid boreal forest and windswept peaks. ◆ That may come as a surprise. At 775,000 acres, White Mountain National Forest is one of the smaller national forests. It's also one of the most accessible. Nearly 50 million people live within an easy day's drive – and in a region where untrammeled terrain is becoming ever more elusive. Alarming fact: Some seven million

Wild mountains lie within easy reach of New England's crowded cities and suburbs.

A footbridge, 160 feet in length, leads hikers across the Pemigewasset River and into the Pemigewasset Wilderness, one of five wilderness areas in the White Mountains.

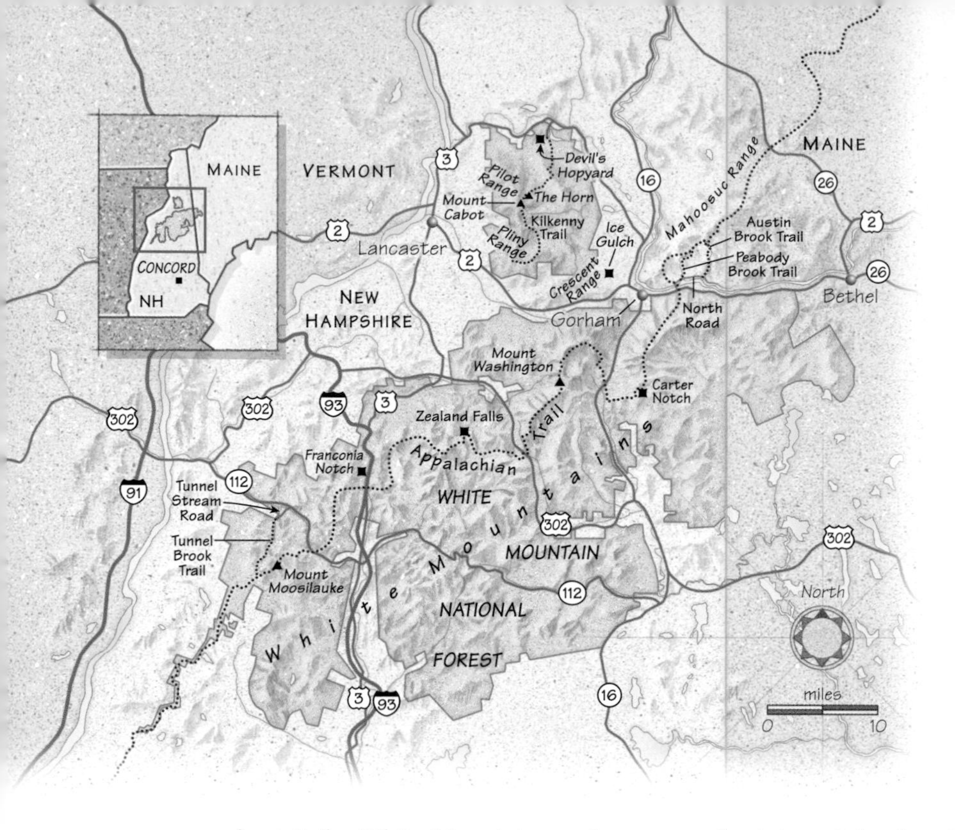

head to the forest's fringe in summer or just about anywhere in winter.

Minor Peaks, Major Rewards

Because the national forest's southern edge bustles with a fair amount of hubbub, the best bet is to head for the other three points of the compass, edging out to the margins of the forest. The trails are fewer and often harder to follow, and the terrain can be more physically demanding and less forgiving of simple mistakes. But these are the places to go if you want to find real peace and quiet.

Far to the northeast, along the Maine–New Hampshire border, is the **Mahoosuc Range**, which is traversed by the **Appalachian Trail**. Through-hikers heading from Georgia to Maine often report that this is the most grueling stretch of the entire trek, with thigh-burning ascents and knee-jarring descents that refuse to cut hikers any slack. What's more, frequent blowdowns and decaying log bridges through swampy terrain require a bit of persistence and creative problem-solving at times.

The payoff? Backpackers can explore upland ponds and craggy notches, and share early mornings with black bears, beavers, and the occasional moose. You'll get more than a taste of the boreal forest in this region. The flinty, dusky landscape bristles with spruce and fir – the only contrast provided by the curiously smooth glacial erratics left scattered about the forest like oversized marbles.

Potential hikes range from the full 30-mile traverse of the Mahoosucs from Route 2 (east of Gorham) to Route 26 (northwest of Bethel, Maine). Or you can take smaller bites by

people visit the White Mountains each year, and the number is expected to rise.

About 15 percent of the forest is federally designated wilderness, where humans only pass through, and all mechanical devices, including mountain bikes, are banned. Striking out for these official wilderness areas – five of them are scattered about – isn't necessarily a guarantee of solitude, but it's not usually difficult to slip away from the crowds. Try these two strategies:

Biking (right) is permitted on trails throughout much of the forest but is prohibited in designated wilderness areas.

The great spangled fritillary (opposite, top) lives in meadows and deciduous woodlands.

Mount Washington (opposite, bottom), the highest point in the Northeast, rises above the hotel named after it.

looping in on one of several connector trails. **Peabody Brook Trail** and **Austin Brook Trail**, both off North Road in Shelburne, demand sacrifice but reward you with waterfalls and three jewel-like ponds that are stunning in their stillness.

Northwest of Gorham are three minor ranges, **Crescent**, **Pilot**, and **Pliny**, collectively known as the **Killkenny** region. This is one of the least-visited areas of the national forest, and despite the occasional evidence of logging, the attractions are many. The most distinctive peak in the region – visible from clearings and along stream banks – is called the **Horn**, a distinctive, pyramidal peak. The **Kilkenny Ridge Trail** is the premier route, offering access not only to the summit of the Horn (3,905 feet) with its sweeping views in every direction, but also to 4,170-foot **Mount Cabot**, where you can survey the region while you sun on ledges just below the summit. Other reasons to hoist a pack here include the **Ice Gulch** in the **Crescent Range**, with its erratics dramatically strewn about, and a rugged gorge called **Devil's Hopyard**.

On the western edge of the White Mountains lies **Mount Moosilauke**, which once boasted a handsome, 19th-century hotel on its summit. That's long gone, as is the well-maintained carriage road that once serviced it. But the mountain, the most westerly of the major White Mountain peaks, remains admirably imposing and features breathtaking views both east and west from its knobby crown.

The 4,802-foot peak is ascended by several trails and is traversed by the Appalachian Trail. There's no longer a shelter near the summit, but the views alone make the ascent worthwhile. Backcountry explorers will find solitude and peaceful campsites in the surrounding region. One route worthy of note is **Tunnel Brook Trail**, which traverses the deeply indented valley between Moosilauke and Mount Clough. Among

the highlights here is a series of scenic beaver ponds along the brook, which varies year to year depending on the industriousness of the residents.

New England's Arctic

Mount Washington is the region's Mount Olympus – broody, tempestuous, and dominant, often swaddled in clouds or blanketed with snow. In fact, the summit of this 6,288-foot massif won't fit anyone's definition of wilderness. In the warmer weather, you can ascend via chauffeur-driven van or drive your own car up the old carriage road. You can ride the cog railroad to the top, have lunch at the cafeteria, then catch the train back to the base.

But it's rather easy to avoid the crowds – just ascend during the off-season. In the blustery winter months, venturing to Mount Washington's summit feels like making a trip to the Arctic. As early as 1839, Henry David Thoreau calculated that every 400 feet gained in elevation up the mountain was equivalent to traveling 70 miles north. Thirty years later, C. H. Hitchcock determined that the summit ecology corresponded with Labrador and Greenland. "It is an arctic island in the temperate zone," he wrote. Encased in a bulky cocoon of insulated clothing, you can find an unrivaled sense of remoteness in the harsh conditions. At the summit, you feel a closer kinship with Baffin Island than with Boston.

While a self-guided trip to the summit should be attempted

Heavy Weather

It's a peculiar boast, but one you'll hear often in the White Mountains: Mount Washington has the worst weather in the world outside the polar regions.

Worst is subjective, but by any measure, the mountaintop isn't an especially alluring place. A few figures: The temperature dips below zero some 65 days each year. The highest temperature ever recorded was 72°F, and that was in August. The summit is shrouded in fog about 60 percent of the year.

Then there's the wind. The good news: In summer, winds rarely top 150 miles per hour. The bad news: The rest of the year they do, and even in summer, 100-mile-per-hour winds aren't uncommon. Indeed, the highest wind speed ever recorded on land – 231 miles per hour – was measured atop Mount Washington in 1934.

At 6,288 feet, Mount Washington is less than half of the height of many Rocky Mountain peaks. Why is it so blustery and grim?

Blame it on compression. Major air masses tend to follow a track through northern New England from the west or northwest. Surface topography offers little resistance until the wind comes to Mount Washington. As the wind is channeled upward over this lone mountain and over the formidable wall of the Presidential Range, it's also compressed from above. The tropopause, a temperature inversion that serves as a sort of invisible ceiling, prevents the moving air mass from rising up as a whole and flowing smoothly over the peak. Like a river forced to pass through a narrow gorge, the current gets faster and more turbulent.

More than 100 lives have been lost on Mount Washington over the years, about one in three because of the harsh weather. "A bad day in January or February on Mount Washington," noted mountaineer and filmmaker David Breashears has said, "is as fierce as any day you'll encounter on Mount Everest."

The wind atop Mount Washington often reaches or exceeds 100 miles per hour, even in summer (left).

A winter trekker (opposite, top) battles formidable gusts while setting up camp.

The Ellis River (opposite, below) tumbles through a rocky chute. Hikers in the Whites will encounter beautiful streams and waterfalls along with wildlife such as moose, black bear, and beaver.

only by experienced mountaineers, anyone in reasonably good shape can sign up for a guided ascent offered daily throughout the winter, weather permitting. You'll be equipped with crampons and ice ax, and trained in self-arrest techniques before topping timberline and confronting the more ferocious elements. Arriving at the top in the face of fearsome winds, all but alone with the humming of the cables and the rime ice, is an experience like no other.

Those of lesser constitution or confidence can still experience howling winter atop Mount Washington. The weather observatory, which is occupied year-round, hosts overnight workshops focusing on weather and other natural history topics. A small number of guests are brought to the summit via snowcat and housed in observatory bunkrooms. You'll learn about the routines of the weather observers and make brief forays around the blustery summit.

Winter brings a stillness to many of the protected valleys and lowlands of the White Mountains. The snow is often as perfect as in one's imagination: deep, fluffy, and muffling, producing a powerful silence. Winter camping is an option for those so prepared. So is overnighting at one of the two cabins maintained by the Appalachian Mountain Club, where trekkers sleep in bunk beds and gather in the evening around woodstoves. Kitchens with utensils and gas stoves lighten the load on the trek in. At **Zealand Falls** hut, you can arrive via cross-country skis; if the snow is cooperative, you can start the day with fresh telemark tracks down the adjacent frozen cascades. The **Carter Notch** hut is a bit more rugged and remote, and travelers coming in via the Appalachian Trail should have crampons in the event of glazing – a not-uncommon event.

Whether you travel here in winter or summer, and whether you strike for mountains or valleys, always keep one thing in mind. Like the lynx or pine marten, wilderness is wily and wary in the White Mountains. It's out there – you just need to stalk it quietly and persistently. Finding it yields great rewards.

TRAVEL TIPS

DETAILS

How to Get There

The closest airport is in Manchester, New Hampshire, a three-hour drive from the Pinkham Notch Visitor Center in Gorham. The visitor center is a four-hour drive from Logan International in Boston. Rental cars are available at both airports.

When to Go

The national forest is popular year-round, but most visitors come in summer and early fall. The weather can be harsh and changeable, with rain, snow, and fog possible at any time. Mountain and valley temperatures can vary from 12° to 20°F. In summer, temperatures range from the 60s at low elevations to the 40s at Mount Washington. By late fall, temperatures at low elevations are near freezing and those at the summit have dipped below freezing.

What to Do

More than 1,200 miles of hiking trails, including portions of the Appalachian Trail, are open to backpackers. Visitors also canoe and kayak the waterways, and anglers fish the brooks, rivers, and ponds. Bicycles are permitted on main roads and backroads but not on trails in wilderness areas. Winter travelers come to ski and snowshoe, as well as go to the summit of Mount Washington. Backcountry users may stay in one of more than 40 lean-tos and at various sites with tent platforms; call 603-528-8721 for locations.

Backcountry Permits

Visitors staying overnight in the backcountry need a parking pass to leave their cars unattended. Passes may be obtained from ranger stations and local vendors; call 603-528-8721 for further information.

Special Planning

Throughout the year, backcountry travelers should be prepared for unpredictable weather by carrying dependable raingear and extra layers of clothing. The national forest also advises visitors to use portable gas stoves rather than build campfires. To avoid attracting wildlife, food should be hung 10 feet above the ground and five feet out on a tree limb, or stored in a bear-resistant canister. Insect repellent is handy during black-fly season, from late spring to early summer. Winter travelers need to bring skis or snowshoes and, if traveling above treeline, ice axes and crampons. They should contact the Androscoggin Ranger District (603-466-2713) or the Pinkham Notch Visitor Center (603-466-2721) for updates on avalanche and ice-fall conditions.

Car Camping

The national forest's 20 campgrounds have more than 800 campsites. Most sites are available on a first-come, first-served basis. Some may be reserved; call 877-444-6777 for details.

INFORMATION

White Mountain National Forest

719 Main Street, P.O. Box 638, Laconia, NH 03247; tel: 603-528-8721.

Five ranger stations are located throughout the national forest. Four are in New Hampshire: Ammonoosuc in Bethlehem (603-869-2626), Androscoggin in Gorham (603-466-2713), Pemigewasset in Plymouth (603-536-1310), and Saco in Conway (603-447-5448). The fifth, Evans Notch (207-824-2134), is in Bethel, Maine.

Appalachian Mountain Club

Pinkham Notch Visitor Center, Route 16, P.O. Box 298, Gorham, NH 03581; tel: 603-466-2721.

Backcountry travelers may stop at Pinkham Notch for information on trail conditions and weather. The center carries maps and guidebooks on the White Mountains.

Mount Washington Observatory

P.O. Box 2310, North Conway, NH 03860; tel: 603-356-8345.

Mount Washington Valley Chamber of Commerce

2617 Village Square, P.O. Box 2300, North Conway, NH 03860; tel: 800-367-3364 or 603-356-3171.

LODGING

PRICE GUIDE – double occupancy

$ = up to $49	$$ = $50–$99
$$$ = $100–$149	$$$$ = $150+

Appalachian Mountain Club

Pinkham Notch Visitor Center, Route 16, P.O. Box 298, Gorham, NH 03581; tel: 603-466-2721.

AMC operates a lodge at Pinkham Notch. Breakfast and dinner are included in the rate. The club's Crawford Notch Hostel has two bunkhouses, each of which sleeps 12. Guests bring their own food and prepare it in a communal kitchen. Backcountry travelers can stay at eight huts in the White Mountains, reached by hiking routes that range from relatively easy to rugged. $–$$

Wilderness Cabins

P.O. Box 1289, Conway, NH 03818; tel: 603-356-8899.

Five cabins set in the woods have separate living and sleeping areas, fully equipped kitchens, and private baths. Four sleep up to six guests; one sleeps 10. $$

Will's Inn

P.O. Box 533, Glen, NH 03838; tel: 603-383-6757 or 800-233-6780.

Set on the banks of the Saco River, this inn has 21 rooms, some with kitchenettes. Also on the property are three cottages, an apartment, and a house, all of which have fully equipped kitchens. $$–$$$$

TOURS AND OUTFITTERS

Appalachian Mountain Club

Pinkham Notch Visitor Center, Route 16, P.O. Box 298, Gorham, NH 03581; tel: 603-466-2727.

The AMC organizes workshops and guided trips: backpacking excursions; treks that teach outdoor skills; kayaking and canoeing trips; courses in first aid; and workshops on winter camping, weather, and skiing.

Bartlett Backcountry Adventures

P.O. Box 93, Bartlett, NH 03581; tel: 603-374-0866.

This outfitter arranges customized climbing and backpacking trips for all ability levels, and teaches backcountry and mountaineering skills. Winter activities include skiing, snow camping, and ice climbing.

Eastern Mountain Sports Climbing School

P.O. Box 514, North Conway, NH 03860; tel: 800-310-4504 or 603-356-5433.

Guided ascents of Mount Washington are offered in winter; some trips include an overnight stay at the Mount Washington Observatory. Winter visitors may also arrange ice-climbing trips and mountaineering instruction. The school specializes in rock-climbing and hiking trips from spring through fall.

Mountain Quest

99 Powers Street, Suite 172, Milford, NH 03055; tel: 603-673-2833.

This outfitter leads small groups on backpacking trips in the White Mountains. Also offered is a two-day adventure that begins with a 14-mile float down the Pemigewasset River. Participants spend the night at a remote base camp and the next day explore the national forest on foot.

Excursions

Allagash Wilderness Waterway

Bureau of Parks and Recreation, Maine Department of Conservation, State House Station 22, Augusta, ME 04333; tel: 207-287-3821.

Paddling trips on this river and lake corridor begin in Champlain Lake and continue nearly 100 miles to the village of Allagash at the Canadian border. Best enjoyed from late summer through early fall, canoeing through the remote Maine woods offers opportunities to see black bears, bald eagles, and osprey. Backcountry travelers may spend a week or more covering the entire route, camping along the way, or they may plan shorter overnight excursions.

Baxter State Park

64 Balsam Drive, Millinocket, ME 04462; tel: 207-723-5140.

Seekers of wilderness are drawn to this rugged, remote park whose 202,000-plus acres include Mount Katahdin, the highest point in Maine, and a portion of the Appalachian Trail. More than 170 miles of trails lead around ponds inhabited by moose and loons, alpine tundra dotted with wildflowers, and numerous peaks over 3,000 feet. Mountain bikers may travel the park's challenging gravel perimeter road, overnighting in campsites along the way. Winter campers, cross country skiers, and snowshoers are guaranteed to find ample snow and solitude.

Green Mountain National Forest

231 North Main Street, Rutland, VT 05701; tel: 802-747-6700.

This 350,000-acre national forest is a New England sampler of hardwood forests, bogs, streams, waterfalls, and some of the highest mountains in the state – plus year-round opportunities for backcountry adventures. The Appalachian Trail passes through parts of the forest, including some of its six wilderness areas. Mountain biking is allowed on designated trails and gravel roads. Paddlers come to canoe the Class II and III rapids of the White River. Various footpaths and back roads make ideal routes for cross-country skiers.

Adirondack Park

New York

Sunlight pours into the forest as you clamber over the last few rocks to the summit of **Mount Jo**. Everywhere you turn, a collage of green and blue rolls toward the horizon. Up above, **Mounts Marcy** and **Algonquin**, New York's tallest peaks, stand shoulder to shoulder. Like thousands of hikers who have stood at this very spot, you stare into the distance, awestruck by the enormity of the landscape that unfurls before you. ◆ Sprawling across some six million acres, Adirondack Park is a very big place – so big, in fact, that you could fit better-known parks such as Yellowstone, Yosemite, Grand Canyon, and Olympic into its boundaries and still have plenty of room to spare. If you feel the need to hike or paddle through the woods for a few days in search of what local author Sue Halpern calls "confrontation of the self by the self," solitude's true vocation, then Adirondack Park may be just the sort of place you're looking for. ◆ A strange combination of history and legislation makes Adirondack an anomaly among parks, harmoniously blending state land with private property. Equally odd is that, with the exception of summer weekends, Adirondack is seldom overrun with tourists – all the more remarkable considering that Manhattan is a mere 200 miles away. Perhaps it's because Adirondack is a state park, without all the hoopla a national park attracts. More likely, the sheer immensity of the region simply swallows people up. ◆ The Adirondack Mountains have always been a place apart. Even the Algonquin and Iroquois tribes found conditions here too harsh for permanent settlement, making only fishing and hunting forays into what they called a "howling

Hikers, climbers, and canoeists seek adventure in the "howling wilderness" of upstate New York.

A solitary maple leaf, reddened by autumn and dappled by rain, rests on a bed of club moss and leaf litter.

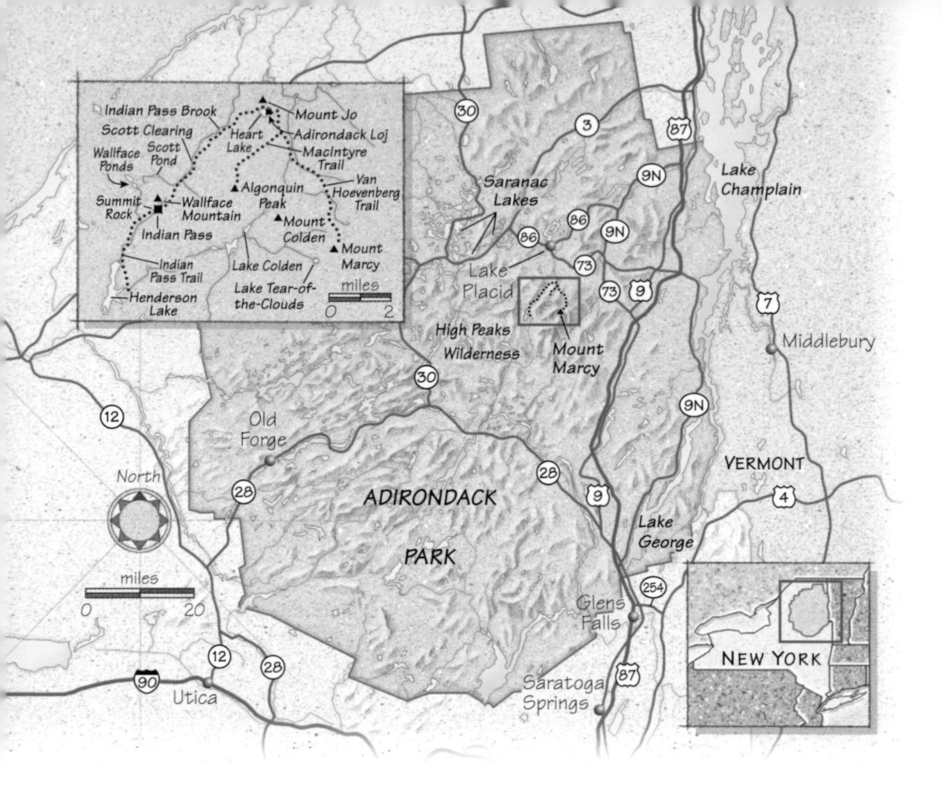

wilderness." The first European to encounter the Adirondacks was explorer Samuel de Champlain, who in 1609 stumbled across the lake that now bears his name. By 1820, vast tracts of land had been sold for a pittance to lumber companies. When the state finally decided to protect 2.6 million acres of land in the 1890s, making them "forever wild," much of the mature forests that covered these hills had been razed and hunters had eradicated many native species, including gray wolves, moose, cougars, lynx, beavers, bald eagles, and wolverines.

The return of wildlife in the last few decades is a testament to the park's success. Only the wolf, wolverine, and cougar remain absent, though there is some talk of reintroducing them. Moose have wandered in from Canada and Vermont, as have coyotes. Even beaver have rebounded. Just as important, the land devastated by rapacious cut-and-run logging has undergone a magnificent rebirth. Today, Adirondack Park is a vast green carpet of forested hills, wetlands, spruce bogs, and tangled hardwood thickets. Landscapes range from brooding coniferous caps on the ridges to sunny blueberry flats, from dense fir forests to alder swamps.

Retreating glaciers long ago carved out a mountain range of awesome beauty. Many of the 2,800 lakes and ponds shimmer in the park's hilly southwest quadrant, while wetlands dominate the northwest section. The east is bordered by two long, deep lakes, Champlain and George. And on the northeast fringes, the state's tallest summits, the High Peaks, soar skyward.

Base Camp

To savor this wilderness, you can canoe up to 120 miles of waterways or hit more than 2,000 miles of hiking trails. Choices for backpackers can be overwhelming, but most trekkers opt for the **High Peaks** region.

Whether you want to climb a tall peak, take a relaxing stroll up a short summit, or hike through a narrow rock chute, this area offers a great diversity of trails. Routes branch off in every direction, so you can plot any number of courses, and you're nearly guaranteed to find a place where you have the woods and mountains all to yourself.

Beavers (left) emerge from their log-and-mud dams to feed on bark.

Winter delivers two to six feet of snow, ideal conditions for snowshoeing (opposite) and cross-country skiing.

Trekkers can set up a base camp (below), then wander through the park on foot or by canoe.

Route 73, the gateway to the High Peaks, is a serpentine road bordered on both sides by cascading creeks where anglers are often seen fly fishing in waders, water up to their knees. Cars line the route, parked near the ubiquitous yellow-and-brown trailhead signs that indicate your arrival at hiking nirvana.

Many hikers choose to spend their first night at the **Adirondack Loj**, a rustic retreat built by the Adirondack Mountain Club on the shores of **Heart Lake**. If you don't feel like roughing it just yet, Adirondack Loj offers bunkbeds and meals. Otherwise, there are 37 campsites and 16 lean-tos nestled in the woods or on the beach. Since the Loj is a mecca for hikers, it's an excellent place to meet other back packers and discuss the various trails. It's not uncommon to run into "46ers" here, climbers who have bagged all 46 mountains

over 4,000 feet in the Adirondacks.

After your arrival, throw on your boots and take the hour-long climb behind the Loj to the summit of Mount Jo. For such little effort, the rewards are great. The views from Jo are an excellent introduction to the fertile terrain you'll soon be delving into. Afterward, take a quick dip in Heart Lake, rent a canoe, or simply lie back in your tent and enjoy the chorus of trilling frogs.

Heading for the Summit

In the morning, hoist your belongings onto your back and hit the red-marked **Indian Pass Trail**. This dramatic, 8.3-mile, one-way trek covers a variety of terrain before snaking through a narrow chute, where cliffs soar about 1,000 feet on either side. The trail has a vertical rise of only 674 feet, but walking on the rugged rock as it bisects the High Peaks will certainly make you sweat.

The trail starts north of the Loj and heads south along the shores of Heart Lake. In less than 15 minutes, you enter a second-growth forest of cedar and birch draped across rolling hills. The next mile and a half are a treat – an easy stroll on a hard-packed trail shaded by enormous spruce and balsams. In summer, the trail is crowded with wildflowers, ferns, and clintonia's blueberries. Near the **Rocky Falls** lean-to, take a short detour along **Indian Pass Brook** to view a small waterfall as it drops into a deep bedrock pool.

The Adirondacks by Canoe

"The Adirondacks, that Venice of the woods, whose highways are rivers, whose paths are streams, and whose carriages are boats." So wrote the Reverend William H. H. Murray, who in his 1869 volume, *Adventures in the Wilderness; or, Camp-Life in the Adirondacks*, extolled the therapeutic value of backcountry travel. The book went through 10 printings in three months as enthusiasts known as "Murray's Fools" flocked to the Adirondacks for boating tours through the mountains.

With about 2,800 ponds and lakes, 1,500 miles of rivers, and 30,000 miles of brooks and streams, the Adirondacks remain one of North America's premier flatwater paddling destinations. Trails connecting the waterways allow paddlers to choose from any number of routes but require portaging, or carrying, your canoe and other gear from one to the other.

One fine jaunt is a four-day, figure-eight loop in the **St. Regis Canoe Area** that traverses eight ponds and the **Upper** and **Middle Saranac Lakes**. Creeks, inundated with beaver dams and lily pads, connect the placid waters of the ponds. Mountains towering over 2,500 feet surround the lakes. Despite occasional strong winds and challenging currents, the trip is ideal for the advanced beginner or intermediate paddler. A more challenging journey is a 90-mile paddle from **Old Forge** in the southwest corner of the park to the **Saranac Lakes**.

Canoes (top and left) are an ideal mode of travel in the backcountry. They are quiet, won't spook wildlife, and allow trekkers to pack enough supplies for extended trips.

Forty-six mountains in the Adirondacks are higher than 4,000 feet, beckoning hikers to ascend a summit and appreciate the view (opposite, top).

Hemlock varnish shelf (opposite, bottom), a type of mushroom, grows on a fallen tree.

Easy walking continues as you cross several streams and view small ledges on the left. About four miles from the Loj, the ledges start to enclose the pass. You reach **Scott's Clearing**, a meadow filled with raspberries and white birch. Just beyond, a blue marked trail, recommended for more experienced backpackers, leads to **Wallface** and **Scott Ponds**. Both are good swimming holes for a cool dip before continuing on your way. Small beaver dams, if not the animals themselves, can often be seen here.

Returning to the trail, you'll notice how narrow the valley has become and the proximity of the sheer cliff walls to the east. This is where the Indian Pass Trail really gets exciting. After walking by a yellow-marked trail that heads east to Lake Colden, you climb rapidly on a faint footpath that meanders over boulders and moss-covered ledges. You'll need to use your hands and a hanging ladder to climb the steepest parts. The jagged rock walls rising sharply to the left are humbling.

At the end of the ravine, Wallface and its sheer cliffs loom on the right, and on hot summer days, mist rises from nearby caverns. The trail weaves through large lichen-encrusted boulders, but your eyes will be focused on the columns and hanging ledges of Wallface. Within 10 minutes, you'll be dwarfed by those same cliffs as they rise 1,000 feet above you. Many locals agree that this is the wildest and most spectacular spot in the Adirondacks. A half-hour descent leads to **Summit Rock**, a huge boulder at the southern edge of **Indian Pass**. The vista overlooks the pass as it fades into Henderson Lake and the mountain of the same name behind it.

It's a precipitous climb down several

The Ausable River (left) pours through a sandstone chasm.

The Oswegatchie River (opposite) is one of the thousands of lakes and waterways that are found in the park.

ladders back to the valley floor. You'll cross a stream and soon leave Wallface and its naked rock behind as you re-enter the forest. Just over one mile through woods and bogs, you'll come upon the Wallface lean-to. Close to several rambling streams and underneath yet another ledge, this is a peaceful place to spend the evening. Roll out your sleeping bag, and listen to white-throated sparrows whistle from balsam thickets. In the late hours, you may hear owls hooting across Henderson Lake, lulling you into the deepest night's sleep you've had in some time.

In the morning, rise to a cacophony of birds sounding the alarm. If you came with a buddy and left a second car at the southern terminus, you can simply continue on the Indian Pass Trail through the woods for another two to three miles and drive back to the Loj. If not, retrace your steps and rest up for the next day.

View from the Top

It would be foolish to venture to the High Peaks region without bagging a high peak. At 5,334 feet, Mount Marcy is the tallest in the state. Unfortunately, since it is *numero uno,* Marcy's trails can often be crowded in the summer months. A good alternative is 5,114-foot **Mount Algonquin**, New York's second-highest peak. Algonquin's summit offers the finest views in the High Peaks, without the typical standing-room-only crowds.

Give yourself about six hours for the eight-mile round-trip. Starting from the Loj, you'll follow the blue-marked **Van Hoevenberg Trail** for the first mile, then switch to the yellow-dotted **MacIntyre Trail** for the beginning of your ascent.

As you follow the gradual switchbacks, paper birch yields to copses of balsam and spruce. At the three-mile mark, the trail becomes very steep and rocky, laboring about a thousand vertical feet in a mile. Rest assured that you'll be atop the summit in an hour or so, gaping at exquisite views. To the north, on a clear day, you'll have no trouble spotting Whiteface Mountain and its Olympic ski jump. Just west of Whiteface are the cliffs of Wallface. To the southeast is Mount Colden, with a slide of boulders running down the summit; due east of Colden is Mount Marcy.

The view alone is worth the climb, but after a sojourn in the Adirondacks, you'll have discovered other benefits: your body will be a little tougher, your mind clearer, your soul nourished by vast and wild spaces.

TRAVEL TIPS

DETAILS

How to Get There

Adirondack Regional Airport, nine miles from Saranac Lake, is just west of the park's High Peaks region. The closest major airport is in Burlington, Vermont. After renting cars, travelers take a short ferry ride across Lake Champlain and then drive one hour to the High Peaks. There are also airports in Albany, south of the park, and Utica, to the southwest, both of which have automobile rentals.

When to Go

Most visitors come to the Adirondacks in summer, especially on weekends, and in early October, when fall colors are at their height. During peak season, the park is less crowded on weekdays. The backcountry receives the fewest visitors in winter. Daytime temperatures in June, July, and August range from 60°F to 90°F. Nights are in the low 40s or 50s, with frost appearing at high elevations. Temperatures drop below freezing beginning in mid-October and do not start to rise until mid-spring. Precipitation averages 40 inches per year. Snowfall ranges from two to six feet, depending on elevation.

What to Do

More than 2,000 miles of trails are open to hikers and backpackers. Paddlers can take canoes, as well as kayaks, on 2,800 ponds and lakes, 1,500 miles of rivers, and 30,000 miles of streams. Fishing is permitted on the park's waterways. Mountain bikers are allowed on designated trails and roads, but not on trails in state wilderness areas. In winter, footpaths are used by cross-country skiers and snowshoers.

Backcountry Permits

Permits are not required for visitors staying in the same location for up to three days. A permit, obtained in advance, is needed for stays of over three days and for groups of 10 or more regardless of length of stay. Permits are obtained from forest rangers in the applicable areas; for ranger locations, call Public Lands Information Services at 518-897-1200.

Special Planning

Backpackers may stay in the park's 200 Adirondack lean-tos, which are available on a first-come, first-served basis. Hikers are advised to pack a tent in case they encounter a filled lean-to and must camp at another site. Hikers should use portable gas stoves rather than build campfires. Even in summer and especially if traveling by canoe or kayak, visitors should be prepared for unpredictable weather by carrying dependable raingear and extra clothing. Food must be hung in a tree at least 12 feet above the ground and five feet away from the trunk, or stored in a bear-resistant canister. The park recommends that backcountry travelers sign in at trail registers and have in their possession the 24-hour number for search and rescue (518-891-0235).

Car Camping

Forty-four state-run campgrounds are scattered throughout the park. For locations and reservations, call 518-457-2500.

INFORMATION

Public Lands Information Services

New York State Department of Environmental Conservation, P.O. Box 296, Route 86, Ray Brook, NY 12977; tel: 518-897-1200.

Adirondack Mountain Club

814 Goggins Road, Lake George, NY 12845; tel: 518-668-4447.

The club provides free hiking information and carries guidebooks and trail maps (see Resource Directory).

Adirondack Regional Tourism Council

P.O. Box 2149, Plattsburgh, NY 12901; tel: 518-846-8016.

LODGING

PRICE GUIDE – double occupancy

$ = up to $49	$$ = $50–$99
$$$ = $100–$149	$$$$ = $150+

Adirondack Loj

P.O. Box 867, Lake Placid, NY 12946; tel: 518-523-3441.

Guests stay in bunkhouse accommodations. Breakfast is served, and dinner can be arranged. Also on this property owned by the Adirondack Mountain Club are 37 campsites and 16 lean-tos overlooking Heart Lake. $–$$$

Moose Country Cabins

2909 Route 28, P.O. Box 368, Old Forge, NY 13420; tel: 315-369-6447.

Twelve cabins each sleep six to twelve guests. Some are equipped with kitchens; others have only refrigerators. $$–$$$

Mount Van Hoevenberg Bed-and-Breakfast

HCR 01, Box 37, Route 73, Lake Placid, NY 12946; tel: 518-523-9572.

Eight one-room cabins each have kitchen facilities. Two have sleeping lofts, and the largest sleeps four guests. An old farmhouse on the property serves as a bed-and-breakfast with three guest rooms. $$–$$$$

TOURS AND OUTFITTERS

Bear Cub Adventure Tours

30 Bear Cub Road, Lake Placid, NY 12946; tel: 518-523-4339.

Guides take visitors into the backcountry on foot, by canoe or kayak, on mountain bike, or on cross-country skis for short trips or extended treks. Assisted climbs, whitewater kayaking, and telemark instruction are also offered.

Fort Noble Adirondack Adventures

P.O. Box 75, Cold Brook, NY 13324; tel: 315-826-3771.

Backcountry travelers may arrange extended backpacking and canoeing trips as well as one-day hikes and paddles. For some trips, visitors and their canoes are transported on the Adirondack Scenic Railway. Guides also offer instruction in snow camping, orienteering, and other wilderness skills.

High Peaks Cyclery and Mountain Adventures

331 Main Street, Lake Placid, NY 12946; tel: 518-523-3764.

One-day trips introduce visitors to canoeing, kayaking, mountain biking, cross-country skiing, and ice climbing; multiday trips may follow. For overnight treks, travelers can combine activities, such as backpacking and cycling.

McDonnell's Adirondack Challenges

R.R. #1, Box 262, Lake Clear, NY 12945; tel: 518-891-1176.

Travelers choose among numerous activities – backpacking, canoeing, fishing, cross-country skiing, snowshoeing, and winter camping – when they sign up for trips. Treks are customized to suit participants' interests and ability.

St. Regis Canoe Outfitters

P.O. Box 318, Lake Clear, NY 12945; tel: 518-891-1838 or 888-775-2925.

Guided canoe and kayak trips into the St. Regis Wilderness Canoe Area and nearby waters range in length and cater to paddlers of varying abilities. Guides remain with the paddlers for the entire time or for a day or two of orientation. St. Regis also rents equipment and helps plan itineraries.

Excursions

Algonquin Provincial Park

P.O. Box 219, Whitney, ON K0J 2M0; tel: 613-637-2828.

Within this Canadian park west of Ottawa are an astounding two million acres protecting vast stands of deciduous and boreal forests, as well as northern bogs and marshes. Nearly a thousand miles of canoe routes allow paddlers to explore the backcountry lakes and waterways, stay at remote campsites, and see wildlife including loons, beavers, muskrat, and moose. Loop trips on the park's three backpacking trails take hikers to ridges with commanding views. Snow camping, dogsledding, and cross-country skiing are popular winter activities.

Allegheny River Islands Wilderness

Allegheny National Forest, U.S. 6, Sheffield, PA 16347; tel: 814-968-3232.

Paddlers with limited experience will enjoy floating 85 miles of the slow-moving Allegheny River in northwestern Pennsylvania designated as wild and scenic. Interspersed along the waterway are seven small forested islands, each a small oasis of wilderness. The largest is 96-acre Crull's Island; the smallest is 10-acre No-Name. Kayakers and canoeists may stop to hike the islands, observe the wildlife, and spend the night.

Finger Lakes National Forest

5218 State Route 414, Hector, NY 14841; tel: 607-546-4470.

This modestly sized forest straddles the ridge between Seneca and Cayuga Lakes in upstate New York. Backpackers using the 25 miles of interconnecting trails – including 12-mile Interlocken National Recreation Trail – crest ridges with views of the surrounding forest and pastureland, and can make camp in shelters along the routes. Some of the acreage supports blueberries and other crops, which visitors may harvest. Fall brings a spectacular display of maple and dogwood foliage. In winter, the trails become paths for cross-country skiers.

Monongahela National Forest
West Virginia

These highlands mantled in the hemisphere's lushest forests are an ecological meeting place, with a name as melodic as water music: Monongahela. Here, in the middle of the ancient Appalachian chain, the spine of eastern America is lifted so high that a little bit of Canada makes its way into Dixie. Northern trees such as aromatic balsam fir and sugar maple meet their southern kin, the magnolias and hollies. ◆ Here, the massive **Allegheny Front** stands across the path of clouds streaming in from the Great Lakes and Canada. The clouds rise and cool as they cross the front, dumping rain and snow on the western ridges. Cherry and maple are lords of the woods on these moisture-rich slopes. In the rain shadow across the crest thrive plants that require less water such as oak, cedar, and even cactus. ◆ Everywhere you turn, a surprise is in view. Wind-scoured barrens pocked with huckleberry bogs give way to hardwood glades so remote and quiet you can almost hear the fiddleheads unfurling. Alpine meadows are latticed with beaver ponds. The ancient forces that crafted such a land still lend it an untamed aspect. Jagged, knife-edged ridges of quartzite soar 1,000 feet high. Cliffs of sandstone fall away to distant vistas of innumerable ridges. ◆ West Virginia's **Monongahela National Forest** is just shy of a million acres, thrown like a rumpled quilt along the alpine border with Virginia. Five major rivers spring to life in the Monongahela, spilling water through woodlands that cloak the highest reaches of a state whose average altitude is 1,500 feet greater than any other in the East. The forest covers a vast territory: from tip to tip, it spans nearly a full

Hold tight to your bike grips or ski poles. You'll be awed by the southern Appalachians' natural wonders.

Two climbers scale the South Peak of Seneca Rocks, a 900-foot-high sandstone formation and one of the Monongahela's landmarks.

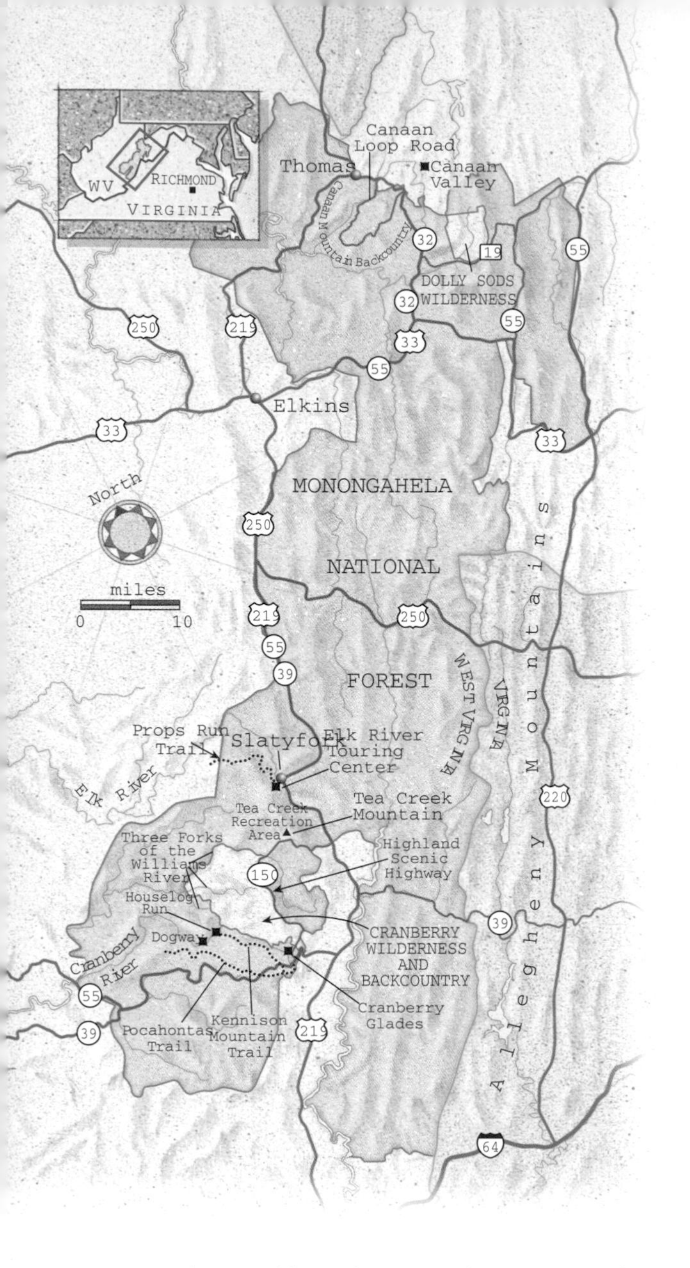

degree of latitude. Its northernmost reaches are but 70 miles from Pittsburgh; from its southern toe, Roanoke is only 50 miles distant.

The first logged-over lands purchased for the Monongahela were bought back in 1915. It took impressive vision to see how 1,400 square miles of clear-cut mountain might one day attract solitude seekers, but nature's healing hand has worked wonders. Today the national forest encompasses five designated wilderness areas, several well-known botanical preserves, and 700 miles of hiking trails. Horseback riders and off-road-vehicle enthusiasts flock to the Monongahela, but there is still land aplenty to get lost in, with woods so deep it seems that the sun sets between you and the nearest road. Hiking is a favorite activity, but the forest has recently established a reputation for two surprising backcountry sports: mountain biking and cross-country skiing. Choose your season and your method of locomotion. The Monongahela can fit the bill whether you're looking for a quick backcountry overnighter or a weeklong journey through the wilderness.

Mountain-Biking Mecca

With its hiking paths, old logging roads, serpentine narrow-gauge railroad grades, and gentle riverside rails-to-trails routes, the Monongahela's trail diversity has made the national forest one of the nation's premier backcountry destinations for mountain biking. Fat tires are allowed throughout the forest, with the exception of the federally designated wilderness areas. Since camping is virtually unrestricted, there's an unlimited opportunity to load up panniers for long routes through the mountains or more pastoral trips along rivers and valleys.

Bike-packers who want to sample both rugged trails and easygoing touring head for the southern end of the national forest. Paths such as the **Kennison Mountain Trail** and **Pocahontas Trail** meander through birch and spruce forests, then edge along the fringes of the **Cranberry Glades** wetlands, where warblers and a variety of carnivorous plants thrive. At times, soaring views into forested river

canyons fall away from ridgetop fern gardens, and overturned logs hint at the presence of foraging black bears. It's a cold ford across the **Cranberry River**, but nearby trail shelters at **Houselog Run** and **Dogway** make good places to dry waterlogged socks. The shelters are also convenient campsites for bikers who would rather not pedal a tent up and down the spine of West Virginia.

The ride along the Cranberry River is a pleasant spin through the heart of the 80-square-mile **Cranberry Wilderness and Backcountry**. The river is loaded with trout, and the woods teem with bobcat, deer, and wild turkey. It's an easy hop over to the **Three Forks of the Williams River** for a ride into the **Tea Creek Recreation Area**, with a mountain-biking trail network that is one of the best in the country.

Tea Creek is a hodgepodge of rugged, single-track trails and long-forgotten railroad grades that spill like waterfalls from 4,485-foot **Tea Creek Mountain**. You pick your way through mixed forests of yellow birch and hemlock, skirting lush green beaver bogs and hopscotching over rocks. Views of four river valleys give plenty of excuses for rest stops as you climb toward the peaks over the **Elk River.**

You'll want to make the free fall down **Props Run** the last trail of the trip. Regarded as one of the top downhill trails in the country, Props Run starts out in a cool stand of spruce trees. Breathe deeply, because the bottom of the world is about to drop out. The trail falls from 4,500 feet to 2,700 feet in fewer than five miles. For the first few, the trail is little more than a roughshod track down a rocky creekbed. Hang on tight as your bike skids over slick roots and loose cobbles, rattling your noggin.

Negotiating Props Run is like trying to ride an avalanche: your brakes clench as you will the front wheel over fallen logs, patches of moss, and a hodgepodge of

Mountain bikers (top and right) can map out routes on more than 500 miles of trails and nearly 1,000 miles of back roads.

Anglers fish for trout and bass in the Monongahela's streams (opposite), some of which support native brook trout.

rocks and boulders. The trail eventually moves away from the streambed and onto an old railroad grade, but the adrenaline meter is still buried in the red. This is a narrow-gauge logging track, snaking down rough mountain flanks and littered with logs. It's a technically demanding trail, for sure, but there's a big payoff at the bottom: the **Elk River Touring Center**, where the bike shop will straighten out your wheels, and you can load up on the Monongahela's finest dining – after a shower.

Snow Country

There are ways to experience this West Virginian wilderness that are more serene than riding herd on a mountain bike and dueling with granite and gravity. That broad Allegheny Front squaring off with cold Canadian weather systems turns the mountains into a self-contained polar region; parts of the national forest average nearly 130 inches of snowfall a year. The rugged slopes, with their rocky soils and hundreds of streams and seeps, are difficult to negotiate on skinny skis. But the Monongahela's high-elevation plateaus trap snow in boggy glades and conifer forests carpeted with pine needles, perfect for cross-country skiers. Coupled with railroad grades and more than 200 miles of unplowed roads, the trail system offers plenty of opportunity for both beginning skiers and hard-core telemarkers.

The **Canaan Mountain Backcountry** is at the top of the list for overnight ski touring. Here, a high-elevation plateau rises above the valley floor, dissected by mossy streams and crowning a 13,500-acre, semi-primitive recreation area. As the last of the Wisconsin glaciers retreated from North America some 10,000 to 12,000 years ago, the crown of the Canaan Mountain region provided a place for alpine vegetation to "retreat" and thrive. It's now cloaked in dense forests, with sprawling red spruce stands and sphagnum bogs that look like a little piece of arctic

Hiking the Sods

If the notion of West Virginia backcountry brings to mind cathedral forests, the Monongahela's **Dolly Sods Wilderness** will have you thinking you've been dropped onto another continent.

This 10,215-acre area is a checkerboard of sphagnum bogs, boulder flats, and windswept plains. Gale-blasted red spruce trees grow branches only on the downwind sides of their trunks. Spectacular vistas from enormous rock promontories are too numerous to count. Such exotic environs make Dolly Sods a popular place. Still, trails are not marked and are minimally maintained, and weather extremes discourage the timid. To get to the good stuff, you'll have to ford creeks, scramble over boulder gardens, and slog through boot-sucking heath bogs.

The blueberry bushes of the Dolly Sods (above) turn brilliant scarlet in autumn.

Cross-country skiers (opposite, top) can explore the national forest on extended trips, either camping in the backcountry or staying in trail shelters or backwoods cabins.

Table Rock (opposite, bottom) overlooks vast stands of Appalachian hardwood forest.

This crazy country takes its name from a family of 19th-century German immigrants named Dahle, who grazed sheep on open grassy areas they called "sods." At the turn of the century, those meadows were hemmed in by one of the East's most magnificent spruce and hemlock forests, with centuries-old trees growing 12 feet in diameter. Once those woods were discovered by northern timber barons, their days were numbered. As the trees were removed, the deep organic soils dried out. Burning cinders from logging equipment sparked massive fires, laying bare the rocky core of the sods.

Congress ensured in 1975 that chainsaws and timber skidders would never again scar the Dolly Sods Wilderness, leaving the land to backpackers, berry pickers, and a healthy population of black bears. Thirty miles of trails score the windy, open Dolly Sods, including part of the proposed route for the coast-to-coast **American Discovery Trail**. In late spring, rhododendrons and wild azaleas turn the evergreen shrub gardens into impressionistic bursts of color. Come in late June and early July, and you can feast on blueberries and huckleberries. Winter is a time for solitude and extreme weather skills. No matter the season, the Dahles' sods are fertile, if rocky, grounds for wilderness adventure.

muskeg lost among Dixie's highlands.

Strap on skis and you can spend days in these southern-fried North Woods. Canaan Mountain is a wild jumble of vegetation types. Nearly 2,500 acres of red spruce mantle the slopes, edged with open, oak-hickory woods and capped with highland marshes. Skirting the mountain's base is the 18-mile **Canaan Loop Road**, passable with a four-wheel-drive vehicle in summer, but a blissful, unplowed cross-country ski trail when covered with snow. The Canaan massif is wedged between two state parks, with miles of trails stitching them together and three trail shelters.

It's thrilling country. As you glide through whisper-quiet woods, each turn in the trail opens up into another snapshot of solitude. The prints of wild turkey and grouse crosshatch a white blanket underfoot. Each evergreen is as perfect as a Christmas tree, green as dark emeralds and laden with snow. Climbing to a ridgeline, you break out of the woods into high alpine meadows with an otherworldly panorama: from atop the Allegheny Front you look down into enormous **Canaan Valley**, 13 miles long and three miles wide, and blanketed with alder thickets and the largest freshwater wetland in the southern Appalachians.

TRAVEL TIPS

DETAILS

How to Get There

Airports are located in Roanoke, Virginia, 50 miles from the southern boundary of the national forest, and in Pittsburgh, Pennsylvania, 70 miles from the northern boundary. Rental cars are available at both airports.

When to Go

The national forest is enjoyable throughout the year, especially in spring, summer, and fall. Summer days are in the 70s and 80s, sometimes in the 90s; nights are in the 50s and 60s. Daytime temperatures in spring and fall are in the 50s and 60s; nights are in the 40s. In winter, temperatures range from the 20s and 30s down to the teens at night. High elevations receive several feet of snow.

What to Do

The national forest has 700 miles of hiking trails, plus numerous rivers suitable for fishing and for float trips by canoe or kayak. Mountain bikers are permitted to use designated trails outside the wilderness areas. Backcountry travelers may also take horse and llama pack trips. Those looking for more challenging activities rock-climb and explore caves. Winter visitors can travel by cross-country skis and snowshoes on trails and backroads.

Special Planning

The weather is unpredictable throughout the year; even in summer, frost can occur at high elevations. Extra layers of clothing and dependable raingear are essential backpack items. Particularly in spring, backcountry travelers should take extra caution when fording or camping near streams, which may rise suddenly during rainstorms. Visitors are advised to use portable gas stoves rather than build campfires. The trails in some wilderness areas are not marked or blazed; hikers and bikers should carry trail maps and compasses.

Backcountry Permits

Permits are not required for overnight stays in the national forest. For wilderness areas, there is a voluntary registration system; backcountry users sign in at trailhead kiosks or at the visitor centers.

Car Camping

The national forest's 18 campgrounds have more than 500 sites. Some campsites may be reserved in advance; call 877-444-6777 for more information.

INFORMATION

Monongahela National Forest

Headquarters, 200 Sycamore Street, Elkins, WV 26241; tel: 304-636-1800.

Cranberry Mountain Nature Center

P.O. Box 110, Richwood, WV 26261; tel: 304-653-4826.

Seneca Rocks Discovery Center

P.O. Box 13, Seneca Rocks, WV 26884; tel: 304-567-2827.

Pocahontas County Tourism Commission

P.O. Box 275, Marlinton, WV 24954; tel: 800-336-7009.

Potomac Highland Travel Office

P.O. Box 151, Petersburg, WV 26855; tel: 304-257-9315.

LODGING

PRICE GUIDE – double occupancy

$ = up to $49 | $$ = $50–$99
$$$ = $100–$149 | $$$$ = $150+

Elk Mountain Outfitters

P.O. Box 8, Slatyfork, WV 26291; tel: 304-572-3000.

Guests stay in two apartments above this outdoor outfitter. Both have two bedrooms and full kitchens. $$–$$$

Elk River Touring Center

HC 69, Box 7, Slatyfork, WV 26291; tel: 304-572-3771.

The center has 10 bed-and-breakfast rooms – five in the Inn and five in the Farmhouse – and three cabins, each of which has a kitchen. A restaurant is on the premises. $$–$$$$

Greenbrier River Cabins

HC 64, Box 544, Seebert, WV 24946; tel: 304-653-4646.

These two- or three-bedroom cabins sleep two to 10 guests. Each has an equipped kitchen and a fireplace or woodstove. From the cabin decks, guests can see the Greenbrier River and the Greenbrier River Trail, which is open to hikers, bicyclists, and horseback riders. $$$

Riverside Log Cabins and Motel

HC 59, Box 39, Seneca Rocks, WV 26884; tel: 304-257-4442 or 304-257-1705.

Guests stay in 10 standard motel rooms or in 40 cabins with fully equipped kitchens. $–$$$

TOURS AND OUTFITTERS

BIKEWVA

Camp Monongahela, P.O. Box 280, Durbin, WV 26264; tel: 888-245-3982.

Mountain bikers go on four-day, three-night self-guided trips in the national forest, staying each night at a rustic cabin. The route begins in the Slatyfork or Snowshoe area and ends in Canaan Valley or Seneca Rocks. Cyclists choose among various routes that suit their abilities and interests. The fully equipped cabins have woodstoves, and the outfitter provides all meals.

Eagle's Nest Outfitters

P.O. Box 731, Petersburg, WV 26847; tel: 304-257-2393.

This outfitter's canoe trips range from placid floats down the South Branch of the Potomac to whitewater adventures through Lower Smoke Hole Canyon. Paddlers can take one-day trips or longer excursions that allow for camping along the way. Eagle's Nest also offers multiday fishing trips and can provide shuttle services for backcountry travelers with their own canoes.

Elk Mountain Outfitters

P.O. Box 8, Slatyfork, WV 26291; tel: 304-572-3000.

Backcountry travelers may sign up for guided fly-fishing trips and for advanced instruction beforehand. Elk Mountain also rents mountain bikes and ski equipment and can provide up-to-date information on trail conditions.

Elk River Touring Center

HC 69, Box 7, Slatyfork, WV 26291; tel. 304-572-3771.

The center offers multiday trips for mountain bikers. Nights are spent at inns and bed-and-breakfasts, or camping en route. Cyclists new to mountain biking may arrange for tours that begin with technical instruction. There are also women's clinics and trips combining mountain biking and river rafting. The center rents mountain bikes as well as cross country skis, and provides shuttle services.

New River Llama Treks

P.O. Box 697, Edmond, WV 25837; tel: 304-574-2524.

Llamas carry the gear of hikers going to a backcountry lodge that becomes the base for exploring the Cranberry Mountain area. The outfitter also offers multiday trips into the Cranberry Backcountry and Cranberry Wilderness to fish, watch wildlife, raft and kayak, rock-climb, birdwatch, and descend into caves.

Excursions

Assateague Island National Seashore

7206 National Seashore Lane, Berlin, MD 21811; tel: 410-641-1441.

The northern half of this 37-mile-long barrier island is in Maryland; the southern portion, in Virginia, is protected as the Chincoteague National Wildlife Refuge. The Maryland side is of the greatest interest to backcountry travelers, who can set out on foot or by kayak or canoe and make camp at designated sites along the white-sand beach and dunes. In addition to shorebirds and other avian residents, visitors will see the famous "wild" horses, pony-sized equines brought to the island in the 1600s.

Daniel Boone National Forest

1700 Bypass Road, Winchester, KY 40391; tel: 606-745-3100.

Narrow valleys, steep forested ridges, and sandstone cliffs up to 200 feet tall, formed some 70 million years ago, draw backpackers and horseback riders to this national forest and its 500-plus miles of trails. Paddlers float the rivers on canoes and kayaks, and climbers test their skills at the Red River Gorge, part of the Clifty Wilderness. Trails outside the wilderness areas are open to mountain bikers.

Shenandoah National Park

3655 U.S. 211 East, Luray, VA 22835; tel: 540-999-3500.

More than 400 miles of trails wind through this narrow national park spread along 80 miles of the Blue Ridge Mountains at the eastern boundary of the Appalachian Range. Nearly half of the 196,000 acres are designated wilderness, and the Appalachian Trail runs through the park for more than 90 miles. Backpackers can plan itineraries that take them through dense forests with cascading streams or along crests offering classic Blue Ridge views. Spring wildflowers and fall foliage are popular seasonal attractions.

Great Smoky Mountains National Park

Tennessee–North Carolina

CHAPTER 9

Ecologists call it the Great Forest and tell us it once stretched nearly unbroken from Maine to Georgia, from the Atlantic to the Mississippi. A resourceful squirrel, they say, could scamper from tree to tree, from coastline to heartland, without ever touching the ground. ◆ It was a dark, tangled, gorgeous forest, as splendid as it was sprawling. Tulip trees towered 175 feet tall; white pines loomed over 200 feet. American chestnuts, sycamores, maples, hemlocks, and white oaks grew to over 25 feet in circumference, as wide as a circle formed by five adults with outstretched arms. Sunlight was devoured by a multilayered green canopy and reached the ground only in dapples and tints, like light through a stained-glass window. ◆ Between the 18th and 20th centuries, the Great Forest was sheared by the lumberman's ax and turned under by the farmer's plow. Only a few scattered islands were spared, either by the good fortune of inaccessibility or by the efforts of conservationists. A handful of these islands lie within the boundaries of **Great Smoky Mountains National Park**, where more old-growth hardwood forest is protected than anywhere else in the East ◆ Of the 800-square-mile area encompassed by the national park, more than 95 percent is forested and 20 to 25 percent (more than 100,000 acres) is old-growth. North America's temperate deciduous forest reaches its zenith in the Smokies, where 100 species of native trees find a home, more than in all of northern Europe. Many tree species grow to record size in the Smokies, and plants that are mere shrubs elsewhere attain tree status in the park. The best way to enjoy the park's magnificent

Wander among the giants of the East's most extensive old-growth hardwood forest.

The lush valley of Cades Cove is the starting point for trails that lead through old-growth forests to "balds" filled with wildflowers.

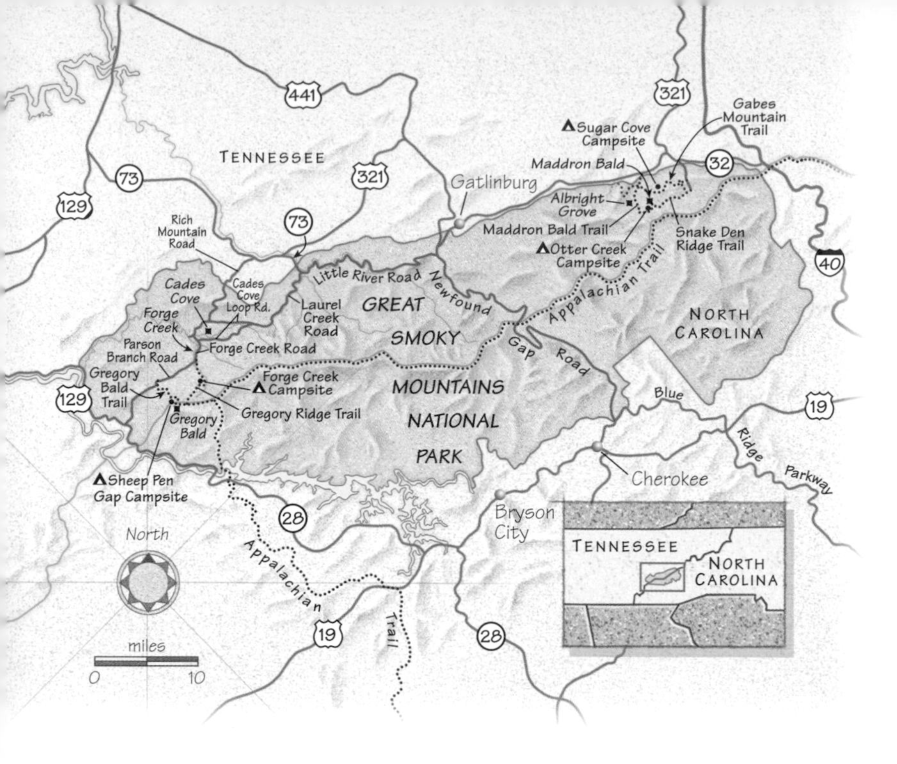

Once you acquire a taste for eastern old-growth, you begin to savor its nuances. There are some large trees, but not all are giants. Variety is as important as size. While second-growth forest is characterized by even-aged trees (since most started life at the same time, after the last clear-cut), old-growth consists of saplings as well as whoppers and everything in between. This blending of ages, along with species diversity, creates the layered canopy that scientists claim shelters a greater population of migratory songbirds than other woodlands. Hike this route in spring or early summer and you'll be amazed by the cacophony of singers – vireos, winter wrens, black-throated blue warblers, veeries, ovenbirds, wood thrushes, and pileated woodpeckers.

forests is on foot. No fewer than 150 different hiking trails crisscross the Smokies, totaling 800 miles of maintained pathways. Of America's national parks, only Yellowstone and Yosemite claim more.

Old-Growth Sanctuary

Two loop hikes offer exceptional opportunities for exploring eastern old-growth and provide grand vistas from mile-high mountaintops. The Gregory Bald route begins in **Cades Cove**, a fertile, wildlife-rich valley flanked on all sides by verdant mountains. The 14-mile loop combines **Gregory Ridge Trail** and **Gregory Bald Trail** with an easy walk back to your car down unpaved **Parson Branch Road.**

The Gregory Ridge Trail climbs gradually at first, shaded by an evergreen jungle of rosebay rhododendron and mountain laurel and accompanied by a fresh mountain stream. After only a half mile, you encounter the first virgin forest, including stately tulip trees, members of the magnolia family, stretching 10 stories tall.

Big dead trees, both vertical and horizontal, are another clue you've entered old-growth. Dead logs are a smorgasbord for insects, mushrooms, and myriad microorganisms, and offer housing for everything from salamanders to bears. Old-growth forest also has a more open quality than second-growth, airy enough for riders on horseback to pick their way through without undo difficulty.

Night on a Bald

Forge Creek Campsite, tucked into a pocket of old-growth, is a delightful place to catch your breath or spend the night. The site's namesake stream murmurs pleasantly nearby, and the camp is large enough to afford some privacy. Beyond, the climb stiffens but the old-growth continues. In April, some 30 species of colorful wildflowers bloom along this path, so keep your field guide handy. Count on seeing spring-beauty, trout-lily, white trillium, yellow trillium, foamflower, hepatica, Dutchman's breeches, and fringed phacelia.

An even greater floral phenomenon lies ahead. The flame azalea on **Gregory Bald** has attracted botanists from around the world. In mid-June, when the wild shrubs reach full bloom, they decorate the bald with colors from cream to orange, yellow to red. Abundant blueberries ripen in midsummer, attracting savvy hikers and voracious black bears.

Balds like Gregory are grassy meadows that occur along only a few of the higher peaks in the southern Appalachian Mountains. Their origins are still unexplained, but for hikers they offer terrific views and the chance to emerge from the shadow land of the Great Forest into the warm southern sun. **Sheep Pen Gap Campsite**, located just a stroll from the bald, is one of the park's best-situated overnight stops. Campers may be awakened at night to the grunts of wild boars, large but harmless beasts inadvertently introduced from Eurasia. The bald is one of their favorite spots to root for acorns and wildflowers with their rigid snouts.

On the descent to **Parson Branch Road**, you pass through an interesting variety of forest zones. Note how the makeup of the woods also changes as you swing from a sunny, south-facing slope to a cool, northern exposure. The beech and birch forests similar to New England's give way to pines, scarlet oak, and mountain laurel. Near the trailhead, hemlock groves cloak misty ravines, and rich cove hardwood forests thrive where soils have washed down from the peaks to sheltered slopes and hollows.

Black bears (left, upper) in the park number 1,600; most shy away from human contact.

Red foxes (left, lower) inhabit the high elevations and are most active after dark.

Solitude awaits winter visitors, who can hike as well as cross-country ski and snowshoe (bottom).

The exposed roots (opposite) of a long-lived sycamore have been battered by the overflow of nearby Little River.

Meeting the Giants

Combining three trails, **Maddron Bald, Snake Den Ridge**, and **Gabes Mountain**, makes a 19-mile loop hike that circumnavigates the

park's premier virgin forest. Start on Maddron Bald Trail and head for **Albright Grove**, home to the park's most impressive stand of old-growth forest and record-sized trees. After about three miles of steady cardiovascular conditioning, the appearance of big hemlocks, maples, and Fraser magnolia trees signals your approach to the grove. Some of the trees within a stone's throw of the trail are the largest specimens of their kind in North America.

Pull up a log and pause for a moment to enjoy the openness and grandeur of this green cathedral. Local New Agers identify the grove as one of the region's "power spots," and it does indeed possess a certain magic. If you remain still, you may glimpse deer browsing, chipmunks rifling through the leaves, or a box turtle lumbering toward the next blackberry bush. Look up into the big trees and notice how the limbs themselves harbor miniature gardens – ferns, mosses, rhododendron shrubs, even small hemlock trees can live upon other trees. Such epiphytic behavior is widespread only in very wet places like the Amazon rain forest and the higher elevations of the Great Smoky Mountains.

This particular remnant of the Great Forest was named for Horace Albright, second director of the National Park Service and champion of the creation of a national park in the Smokies. Albright's efforts, and those of hundreds of other politicians, businesspeople, and private citizens, came none too soon as Albright Grove had already been purchased by a lumber company and had to be condemned by the state of Tennessee to be spared.

From Albright Grove, you climb to **Otter Creek Campsite** where, at 4,500 feet, you can count on cool sleeping weather

Record Trees

An organization called American Forests keeps the official list of the biggest trees in the United States. This *Guinness Book of Records* for tree lovers is organized by species and ranks specimens on a point scale based on each tree's circumference, height, and average crown spread. Most submissions are made by ardent big-tree hunters who spend considerable portions of their lives scouring every place from wilderness areas to city parks and searching out new monarchs of the forest.

The 1998-99 list includes 21 national champion or co-champion trees in Great Smoky Mountains National Park. That's more record trees than in any other national park or national forest in the United States. In fact, according to a report published by the U.S. Park Service, several trees currently residing in the Smokies are the largest of their kind ever recorded anywhere.

Park giants include a red maple 23 feet in circumference and 141 feet tall, an eastern hemlock nearly 17 feet around and 165 feet tall, a northern red oak 21 feet in circumference and 134 feet tall, and a red spruce 12 feet in circumference and 146 feet tall. Other notable arbors are a 565-year-old blackgum and a white pine measured at 175 feet tall.

Why so many big trees in the Smokies? Plenty of rain is one reason, though equally important are a long growing season, variety of habitats, biological diversity, and national park protection.

A trekker (above) checks the route of a Great Smokies loop hike.

An eastern hemlock (left) on the Maddron Bald Trail measures 14 feet in circumference.

A rhododendron (opposite, top) is encased in ice after a cold snap.

Backpackers (opposite, bottom) in the Cades Cove area encounter the remains of log cabins and outbuildings from the late 19th and early 20th centuries.

even during the steamy months of July and August. Seeing a river otter is a possibility, but these creatures generally prefer larger streams at the lower elevations. Bears are more likely visitors. Although Smoky Mountain black bears are powerful enough to shatter a car window with one swipe of a paw, they have a remarkably clean record in terms of inflicting serious injuries on people. One theory purports that the boldest bears were eliminated from the gene pool during a century of relentless hunting prior to park establishment. According to this theory, the meek have inherited the mountains.

Above the campsite, you hike skyward a mile and gain memorable views from **Maddron Bald**, a heath (rather than grassy) bald, mobbed with shrubby vegetation like Catawba rhododendron, pinxter bush, sand myrtle, and galax. In June, these species blossom as a mass of pink flowers visible from distant mountains. Continue along the Appalachian spine to **Snake Den Ridge Trail**, where you descend from the Christmas-tree-scented evergreen forest of the high country to the massive cove hardwoods of the valleys. **Sugar Cove Campsite**, the next stop, is set along the wonderfully narrow **Gabes Mountain Trail**. It is surrounded by ancient forest and in spring is adorned with an amazing array of wildflowers. Waking here at dawn, with warblers singing, a rocky stream chuckling, and the scent of flowers on the breeze, offers pleasures not often experienced in the modern world.

Each of the park's picture-postcard seasons has its own virtues. In winter, the absence of leaves on the deciduous trees has the effect of a raised curtain. Revealed are scenic views from every trail. Spring wildflowers peak in mid-April, though May has its own parade of flowering trees and shrubs. From mid-June to mid-September, the Smokies are hot, humid, and hazy, enhancing the pleasures of full immersion in bouldery streams and hikes in the Canadian zone spruce-fir forest. In autumn, the woodlands outdo themselves with a visual feast of colorful foliage. It is truly one of the greatest shows on earth, and only one of the miracles the Great Forest has to offer.

TRAVEL TIPS

DETAILS

How to Get There

The nearest major airports are in Knoxville, Tennessee, 50 miles from the park, and Asheville, North Carolina, about 60 miles away. Car rentals are available at both. From June to October, the city of Gatlinburg operates a daily trolley shuttle to popular park sites; call 423-436-3897 for information.

When to Go

The park receives the most visitors in midsummer and in October. Lowest visitation occurs in November through February and in early spring. Summer is warm and humid, with temperatures ranging from the low 60s to the high 80s. Rain, occurring mostly as afternoon thunderstorms, averages five to six inches in June, July, and August. In late spring and early fall, days are in the low 70s, nights in the 40s and low 50s. Temperatures are up to 10 degrees cooler and precipitation is greater at high elevations. Winter can surprise visitors with sunny days in the mid-60s, but in the high country, temperatures can fall below zero. Snowfall ranges from a dusting at low elevations to several feet at high elevations.

What to Do

The park has more than 800 miles of trails for hiking and backpacking. Bicycles are permitted only on the Gatlinburg, Oconaluftee River, and lower Deep Creek Trails and may be used on park roads. Fishing is allowed throughout the park. From mid-March to November, horses are available for hire, and five drive-in horse camps give access to backcountry horse trails. Winter visitors come to cross-country ski and snowshoe the high country, including the Clingmans Dome area.

Backcountry Permits

A permit is required for overnight travel and may be obtained at campgrounds, visitor centers, and ranger stations. Backcountry camping is allowed only at designated sites and shelters, which must be reserved in advance. For information, call 423-436-1231; visitors should have their itineraries planned before calling.

Special Planning

Visitors should be prepared for changeable weather, especially in early spring. Though daytime temperatures can reach the 70s, snow can fall on any day, especially at high elevations. Because open fires are prohibited at most sites, visitors should bring portable gas stoves. Most backcountry campsites are equipped with cable systems for hanging food. Otherwise, food and trash should be suspended at least 10 feet off the ground and five feet from the nearest limb or branch, or should be kept in a bear-resistant canister. Bears are less visible from mid-November through March, when they retreat to their winter dens.

Car Camping

The park has more than 1,000 campsites at 10 campgrounds. Seven are open on a first-come, first-served basis. Three are on a reservation system from May 15 to October 31; reservations may be made three months in advance by calling 800-365-2267.

INFORMATION

Great Smoky Mountains National Park

107 Park Headquarters Road, Gatlinburg, TN 37738; tel: 423-436-1200.

Great Smoky Mountains Natural History Association

115 Park Headquarters Road, Gatlinburg, TN 37738; tel: 423-436-0120.

The association publishes field guides, hiking guides, and other publications about the park (see Resource Directory). Also available are trail maps and topo maps.

Gatlinburg Department of Tourism

234 Airport Road, Gatlinburg, TN 37738; tel: 423-430-4148.

LODGING

PRICE GUIDE – double occupancy

$ = up to $49	$$ = $50–$99
$$$ = $100–$149	$$$$ = $150+

Folkestone Inn

101 Folkestone Road, Bryson City, NC 28713; tel: 828-488-2730.

This 1920s farmhouse has 10 guest rooms, each with private bath, some with a private balcony and mountain vista. A large library is stocked with books and maps containing information about area excursions. $$

Fryemont Inn

P.O. Box 459, Bryson City, NC 28713; tel: 800-845-4879 or 828-488-2159.

The Fryemont has 37 guest rooms; a two-bedroom cabin with kitchen and living room; and seven cottage suites with kitchenettes and living rooms. $$–$$$

Hippensteal Inn

P.O. Box 707, Gatlinburg, TN 37738; tel: 800-527-8110 or 423-436-5761.

Set on 23 scenic acres, this stone-and-wood inn has rooms with gas fireplaces, private baths, and views of the Smokies. $$$

LeConte Lodge

250 Apple Valley Road, Sevierville, TN 37862; tel: 423-429-5704.

Five hiking trails lead to this cluster of rustic cabins, perched near the summit of the park's

6,593-foot Mount LeConte. The cabins, built in 1926, are supplied with kerosene lamps, heaters, sheets, and wool blankets. Meals are included in the price and served in the lodge. $$

TOURS AND OUTFITTERS

English Mountain Llama Treks

738 English Mountain Road, Newport, TN 37821; tel: 800-653-9984 or 423-623-5274.

Llamas carry travelers' gear on day or overnight pack trips. Provided are hearty meals, snacks, beverages, camping equipment, and fold-up tables and chairs. Excursions can be tailored to different levels of experience and fitness.

Great Smoky Mountains Institute at Tremont

9275 Tremont Road, Townsend, TN 37882; tel: 423-448-6709.

This year-round environmental education center offers guided backpacking and day-hiking trips. It also conducts workshops, available to people of all ages, on the park's wildlife, geology, and history. Room and board are provided for participants in multiday workshops.

Smoky Mountain Adventures

11460 Highway 19, Bryson City, NC 28713; tel: 888-259-5106 or 704-488-2020.

Outdoor programs include two- and three-night pack trips and fly-fishing excursions in the park; all are fully outfitted. Destinations range from remote backcountry sites to easily reached spots on Fontana Lake.

A Walk in the Woods

4413 Scenic Drive East, Gatlinburg, TN 37738; tel: 423-436-8283.

Guides take national park visitors on a variety of trips, from short hikes to extended backpack treks, and can supply all necessary equipment. This outfitter also helps hikers plan itineraries based on their interests. Shuttle services can also be arranged.

Excursions

Cohutta Wilderness

Cohutta Ranger District, Chattahoochee National Forest, 401 Old Ellijay Road, Chatsworth, GA 30705; tel: 706-695-6736.

Spring, with its wildflowers and other flowering plants, and fall, when the leaves of hardwood trees change color, are the best times to visit this 34,000-acre wilderness. Backpackers can follow trails along streams filled with brown and rainbow trout. One waterway, the Consasauga River, flows through the wilderness for 15 miles and is regarded as the most pristine stream in the state. Some trails allow horse packers.

Congaree Swamp National Monument

200 Caroline Sims Road, Hopkins, SC 29061; tel: 803-776-4396.

Protected within this 22,200-acre International Biosphere Reserve is the last sizable area of southern bottomland hardwood forest found in the United States – a forest that once covered more than one million acres in South Carolina alone. Within it are nearly 90 species of trees, including old-growth bald cypress and other giants, and a rich array of wildlife from nocturnal species such as opossums and bats to all eight species of southeastern woodpeckers. Parts of the monument are accessible on trails, but because the swamp is frequently flooded, the best way to see it is by canoe or kayak, camping along the way.

Pisgah National Forest

1001 Pisgah Highway, Pisgah Forest, NC 28768; tel: 828-877-3350.

Containing nearly 500,000 acres and hundreds of miles of trails, this national forest offers plenty of territory for back-country travelers to explore, including three wilderness areas. The Joyce Kilmer–Slickrock Wilderness, overlapping the North Carolina–Tennessee border, has 60 miles of trails through forests with century-old trees. Shining Rock, named for the quartz found in upland areas, and Linville Gorge, an adjoining wilderness area, have rugged terrain and stunning river gorges, plus geological formations that draw rock climbers of all abilities.

Ten Thousand Islands

Florida

Standing at the dock, the ranger stares across the reddish brown water. Nary a ripple mars the surface, save for the occasional undulating rings caused by the lightning-quick dart of a great blue heron's bill in pursuit of a fish. ◆ It is a hot, humid, late-spring morning under a startling blue sky in Everglades City, a gateway to the **Ten Thousand Islands**, the 200,000-acre archipelago of myriad verdant bumps along Florida's southwest coast from Cape Romano south to Lostman's Key. Although there are only hundreds rather than thousands of islands as the name implies, the Ten Thousand Islands is an astonishing labyrinth of virgin mangrove islands, sinuous rivers, narrow passes, deep channels, backwater lakes, and small bays. ◆ Eager to catch the tidal currents that will make their eight-mile trip to the first campsite easier, the ranger hurries her friend. They must first stop at the Gulf Coast Visitor Center, where overnight paddlers and boaters arrange for camping permits for the Ten Thousand Islands, part of **Everglades National Park** and the **Wilderness Waterway**, the park's 99-mile canoe trail that follows Florida's crenulate coastline from Everglades City to Flamingo. ◆ The two women study their route on the charts, then flip through a book describing the campsites. Their cheery banter segues into a discussion of the weather, which can be a problem in summer. By early afternoon, towering cumulus and cumulonimbus clouds can bring dangerous wind, lightning, and even waterspouts. Weather also affects the tidal currents, and because awareness of the tides is essential, paddlers must carry a tide table. The women

Choose your craft – canoe or kayak – and paddle through a subtropical realm shaped by the rhythms of the tides.

Canoes and kayaks are easy to steer through the labyrinth of waterways in the Everglades and bring visitors close to indigenous fauna and flora.

The strangler fig (right) earns its name by releasing a seed that attaches to another tree and ultimately grows to engulf its host.

Alligators (below) sometimes exceed 14 feet in length; they are among the largest creatures in the Everglades.

Platform campsites (opposite) called chickees are scattered throughout the islands.

know too well the stories of canoeists and kayakers who exhausted themselves trying to paddle against strong head winds and tidal currents and others who stranded themselves during ebb tide in shallow water.

Tides Govern All

Indeed, for thousands of years, everything in the Ten Thousand Islands has been inextricably linked to the tides. Together, the Ten Thousand Islands and the Big Cypress Swamp, a million-acre interior wetlands on the archipelago's northern edge, form the **Big Cypress Watershed**. As the tides rise and fall in this estuarine wilderness, the fresh water of the swamp and intercoastal rivers commingles with the salt water of the Gulf of Mexico. The interchange, combined with the region's subtropical location, produces an intertidal zone that supports an extraordinary variety of wildlife, all of which has adapted to the water's perennial flux.

When the tide rises, most of the action is underwater and out of sight. Bottle-nosed dolphins, mullet, sea trout, and sharks enter the channels that snake between the islands to feed on smaller fish brought in on the current and those that inhabit the sea-grass beds that serve as nurseries. West Indian manatees swim in to graze on aquatic vegetation and mangrove leaves. At low tide, the estuary visibly and audibly springs to life. The receding water exposes the abundant marine life amid the tangled mangrove roots, shimmering tidal pools, sharp oyster bars, gritty sandbanks, and crunchy, gushy mudflats.

A feeding frenzy takes place during the few hours before the water rises again. Sand crabs filter algae and detritus from the sand, then spit out the sand as balls littering the beach. Coffee-bean snails climb down the red mangrove prop roots to feed on the fragments. In search of stranded horseshoe

crabs, raccoons crawl through the tangled prop roots, looking like children on a jungle gym. Roseate spoonbills, egrets, herons, and other wading birds feed on the exposed mudflats. Plovers, sanderlings, and willets probe the shoreline for tiny crustaceans, and American oystercatchers pry open oysters with their chisel-like orange bills.

Even the sounds change. Clearly audible is the *snap, snap, snap* of snapping shrimp using their one enlarged claw to stun small fish and defend their territory. Loud, too, are the thousands of tiny fiddler-crab claws picking away at the mud's surface below the mangroves.

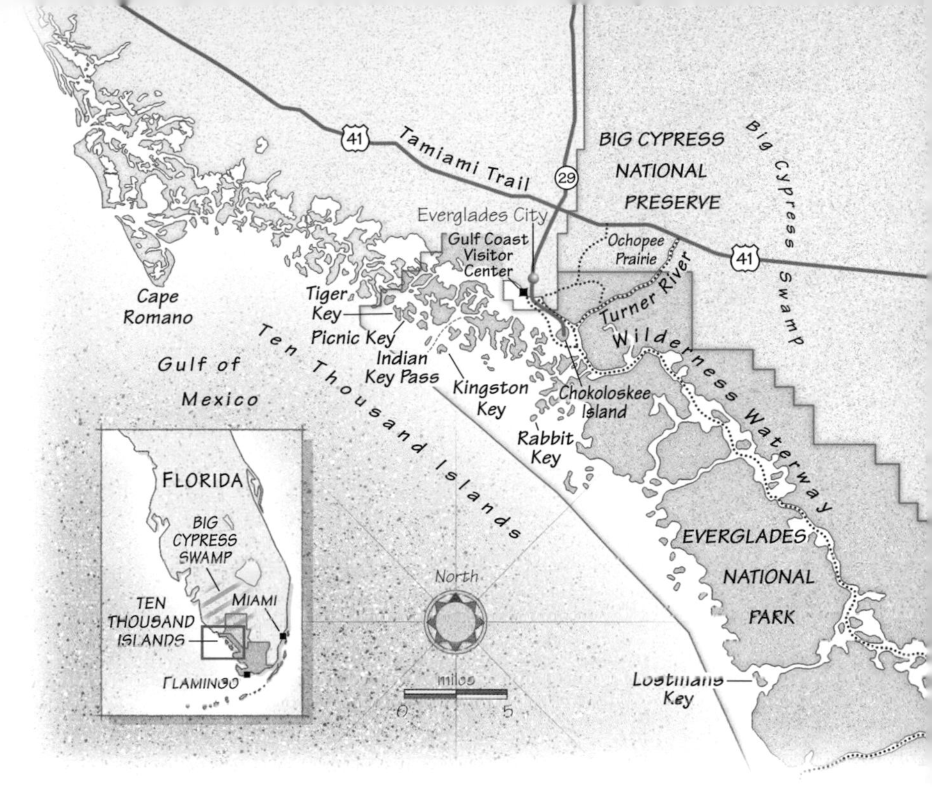

Island Hopping

Slathered with sunscreen and insect repellent, the two women head out to explore a roughly 30-mile route that runs through coastal islands, mainland mangroves, and cypress swamps fingered with rivers and creeks. Canoes, kayaks, and shallow-draft boats are the best means of navigating the Ten Thousand Islands, where, with the exception of the channels and passes, the water is less than three feet deep.

They head south through **Indian Key Pass** and cut northwest through the swift, narrow mangrove pass nicknamed "Le Mans," then cross Gaskin Bay to a choice of beach campsites at **Tiger Key**, which has nice breezes on its western side, and **Picnic Key**, where the twisted gray trunks of buttonwoods uprooted by storms clutter the beach as artfully sculpted driftwood. Sea oats, beach morning glory, and sea purslane grow above the tide line on the crescent-shaped, white quartz sand beaches. There are frequently tracks in the sand made by female loggerhead turtles that come ashore to lay eggs. Raccoons dig up the nests and eat the eggs, leaving behind discarded eggshells that look like crushed Ping-Pong balls.

Most of the small islands are covered with mangroves. Buttonwoods and other hardwoods line up behind the mangroves on the larger islands. Some islands started out as shell mounds, inadvertently built by Native Americans discarding oyster and clam shells.

The second day's route recrosses Indian Key Pass, where a gray dorsal fin slices through the water 30 feet away, then disappears. A few seconds later, a pod of

dolphins swims alongside. The women continue southeast two miles to the chickee camp, an elevated wooden platform overlooking **Kingston Key**, an excellent birding spot. The third day's trip is five and a half miles to the beach camp at **Rabbit Key**. It's tempting to camp on the sandbar on the north side, but those who do will find themselves wet at high tide. The site on the east side has a narrow beach with low, vegetation-covered dunes.

On day four, the route continues six miles northwest past **Chokoloskee Island**, then 10 miles up **Turner River**, one of South Florida's best canoe trails. Paddlers can choose to overnight at a waterfront campground on Chokoloskee Island, then continue upriver the next day.

Subtropical Wonderland

Plants of the Big Cypress and adjoining Everglades watershed are lush and diverse, with more than 3,500 species, many endemic. As the water transitions from saltwater to brackish to freshwater, the vegetation dramatically changes. The broad waterway, flanked by mangroves, crosses the border into **Big Cypress National Preserve**, then opens onto the **Ochopee Prairie**. This wide, flat coastal prairie of grasses and rushes, punctuated by an occasional lone mangrove, is an important feeding ground for wading birds, which number in the hundreds in winter.

The prairie gives way to dense thickets of mangroves interspersed with open ponds and tidal creeks. The trail passes through mangroves so tightly entangled overhead that they form a tunnel, and paddles become useless. The women pull themselves through by grabbing onto the mangroves' prop and drop roots. Hundreds of tillandsias and other epiphytes grow on the mangrove branches. In an open pond between mangrove tunnels, a startled limpkin flies onto a pond apple tree and cautiously watches the approaching canoe.

Above the intertidal zone, the landscape gradually changes to cypress and mixed swamp forest. Whirligig bugs skate across the clear, tea-colored fresh water, where tall, feathery cypress trees surrounded by cypress knees have anchored themselves for hundreds of years. Cabbage palms peek out in between. The limbs of pond apples sag under the weight of heavy green fruits, and the slender leaves of wispy willows shake in the slightest breeze. The warm air is heavy with the sound of buzzing clouds of mosquitoes and the deep, bass snorting of pig frogs.

What look like small branches on the surface are often baby alligators. Their black backs are striped with yellow bands, making them easy prey for great egrets as well as otters, raccoons, and even bass, especially when water levels are low.

The river narrows as it courses through tall blades of sharp-edged southern wild rice. Clumps of pinkish white apple snail eggs the size of BBs cling to the blades near the water's surface. When the snails crawl up to deposit eggs, they are vulnerable to being snatched by the outstretched talons of a swooping snail kite, an endangered bird of prey named for its limited diet.

The paddlers enter a shallow cove to examine orchids and look at the tillandsias on a pond apple tree. Their canoe drifts to a thicket of grass and spooks a large alligator. They are surprised to see the 14-foot reptile coming toward them. As they back away, the splashing paddles agitate the gator, and it dives under the 14-foot craft. The water is so shallow that the gator's ridged hide brushes the bottom of the canoe. It seems to take forever for the alligator's mass to pass under them. Once clear, it thrashes, then frantically swims away.

The women sigh in relief. But their ease is short-lived. Not more than 200 yards ahead, the waterway is too shallow to paddle through, and they must get out of the canoe and pull it. Every log looks like an alligator. They nervously keep a watchful eye. Fortunately, the pull-out is less than a mile away.

Botanical Aliens

Not even a science-fiction writer could have imagined such an alienlike plant. It "walks" across water, breathes through exposed roots, drinks salt water, and creates land out of the void. But nature had a broad imagination, saw a niche, and filled it with mangroves.

Red, black, and white mangroves share the ability to live with their roots bathed in seawater. As they absorb water, they are able to prevent salt from entering their roots. Combining this talent with unique reproduction methods has enabled the various species to adapt to an otherwise hostile environment.

The prop roots of red mangroves (above) form a rich habitat for snails, shrimp, and large fish like tarpon.

Channels (opposite, top) are sometimes so narrow that paddlers must pull themselves along using mangrove roots.

A green heron (opposite, bottom) preens in between sorties to spear fish and crustaceans.

A red mangrove begins when a propagule – a pendulous, 10-inch, torpedo-shaped seedling – falls into the sea and floats to a mudflat, shoal, or sandbar, then takes root. Within a year, it grows three feet and produces arching aerial prop roots. The roots trap and stabilize waterborne sediment and create a complex microhabitat. When the leaves drop, they too become trapped and decompose into highly organic detritus, providing food for worms, snails, and shrimp, which in turn are fed upon by young marine animals higher up the food chain, such as lobsters, snook, and tarpon.

The layer of sediment and detritus thickens into a rich, salty mud, an ideal environment for black mangroves, which send up pneumatophores – erect, fingerlike, air-breathing rootlets that stick up out of the water. Behind the black mangroves grow white mangroves. Black and white mangroves absorb the salt in the water and excrete it through their leaves. As their leaves fall, the sediment becomes thicker and drier, creating land where buttonwoods and other hardwoods can grow.

TRAVEL TIPS

DETAILS

How to Get There

Miami International is about 90 miles from Everglades City and the park's Gulf Coast Visitor Center, entry point for the Ten Thousand Islands. Car rentals are available at the airport.

When to Go

Mid-November through late April offers the most comfortable weather for visiting the area. Daytime temperatures during this period average in the 70s and 80s. The rainy season, May through November, is hot and humid, with frequent thunderstorms and temperatures in the 80s and 90s.

What to Do

Visitors can explore, via canoe or kayak, the Ten Thousand Islands and the 99-mile Wilderness Waterway, which is also used by motorboats. Paddlers stay at chickees (wooden platforms with roofs), elevated ground sites, and beach sites. Backcountry travelers doing one-way trips between Everglades City and Flamingo may arrange for private shuttle services.

Backcountry Travel

Permits are required for overnight stays in Everglades National Park and may be purchased at ranger stations and visitor centers no more than 24 hours in advance of a trip. For specific locations, call 305-242-7700.

Special Planning

Visitors paddling their own craft may contact park rangers for assistance in planning an itinerary and to request a "Backcountry Trip Planner." Gear should include a PFD (personal flotation device) for each passenger, compass, navigational charts, and tide table, plus one gallon of water per person per day. For backcountry campsites where fires are prohibited, a portable gas stove should be used. Sunscreen, insect repellent, and long-sleeved shirts and pants are advised. During the warmer months, visitors may want to wear head nets as protection from insects.

Car Camping

Three campgrounds in Everglades National Park have 362 sites, available on a first-come, first-served basis from May through October and by reservation from November through April. To make a reservation, call 800-365-2267.

INFORMATION

Ten Thousand Islands

Everglades National Park, 40001 State Road 9336, Homestead, FL 33034; tel: 305-242-7700.

Big Cypress National Preserve

HCR61, Box 110, Ochopee, FL 33943; tel: 941-695-4111.

Florida Parks and Monuments Association

10 Parachute Key, Box 51, Homestead, FL 33034; tel: 305-247-1216.

The association carries nautical charts and guidebooks (see Resource Directory).

LODGING

PRICE GUIDE – double occupancy

$ = up to $49 $$ = $50–$99

$$$ = $100–$149 $$$$ = $150+

Best Western Gateway to the Keys

411 South Krome Avenue, Florida City, FL 33034; tel: 305-246-5100 or 888-981-5100.

This motel has 114 guest rooms, including large rooms and mini-suites that have a refrigerator and microwave. A pool and spa are on the premises. $$–$$$

Everglades City Motel

P.O. Box 361, Everglades City, FL 34139; tel: 941-695-4224 or 800-695-4224.

Open year-round, this motel has 19 rooms, six of which have kitchenettes. $$

Flamingo Lodge

1 Flamingo Lodge Highway, Flamingo, FL 33034; tel: 800-600-3813 or 941-695-3101.

This resort at the southern tip of the park has 103 motel rooms and 24 duplex cottages. Each cottage has a full kitchen, two double beds, a sitting room, and a private bath. The lodge also has a restaurant and offers canoe and bicycle rentals. $$–$$$

Ivey House

107 Camellia Street, Everglades City, FL 34139; tel: 941-695-3299 or 860-739-0791.

A former boardinghouse for men working on the Tamiami Trail in the 1920s, this bed-and-breakfast has 11 guest rooms, most with shared bath. Free bicycles and a laundry are also available. $-$$$.

On the Banks of the Everglades

P.O. Box 570, Everglades City, FL 34139; tel: 888-431-1977 or 941-695-3151.

This bed-and-breakfast occupies the 1920s building originally used by the Bank of the Everglades. Guests have their choice of several accommodations: various rooms with shared or private baths; a large room, with a separate entrance, for families; and a suite with bedroom, living room, dining room, kitchen, and private bath. $$–$$$

TOURS AND OUTFITTERS

American Heritage Outdoor Adventures

P.O. Box 599, Everglades City, FL

34139; tel: 941-695-4150.

Visitors who want an overview of the history and wildlife of the Ten Thousand Islands can take half-day or all-day boat tours. American Heritage also provides guiding services for anglers.

Everglades National Park Boat Tours

P.O. Box 119, Everglades City, FL 34139; tel: 800-445-7724 or 941-695-2591.

Park Boat Tours, located on the first floor of the Gulf Coast Visitor Center, rents canoes and other equipment to visitors traveling on their own in the Ten Thousand Islands. The company also offers short boat trips through the area, narrated by park-trained naturalists.

Everglades Private Airboat Trips

P.O. Box 382, Everglades City, FL 34139; tel: 800-368-0065.

Airboat tours take passengers through a private, 2,000-acre preserve of hardwood hammocks, mangroves, and sawgrass inhabited by alligators and, in winter, hundreds of birds.

North American Canoe Tours

P.O. Box 5038, Everglades City, FL 34139; tel: 941-695-4666 or 860-739-0791 in the off-season.

Guides take backcountry travelers into the Ten Thousand Islands on overnight trips. The company also rents canoes, kayaks, and skiffs with motors, as well as camping equipment. Backcountry travelers may arrange for shuttle services from Everglades City and Flamingo and for water taxi services to remote campsites.

St. Regis Canoe Outfitters

P.O. Box 318, Lake Clear, NY 12945; tel: 518-891-1838 or 888-775-2925.

From January through March, St. Regis offers guided multiday paddling trips by canoe and kayak. Along the way, visitors camp at various sites in the Ten Thousand Islands. Other St. Regis-led paddles go to nearby river destinations.

Excursions

Canaveral National Seashore

308 Julia Street, Titusville, FL 33943; tel: 407-267-1110.

This 24-mile barrier island protects the longest strip of undeveloped shoreline on Florida's eastern coast. Visitors can camp at backcountry sites as well as canoe the seashore's waters. The more than 57,000 acres of beach and wetlands support some 300 species of birds, making the seashore a prime destination for wildlife-watching.

Cumberland Island National Seashore

P.O. Box 806, St. Marys, GA 31558; tel: 912-882-4336.

Visitors to this 16-mile-long barrier island with its ribbon of white-sand beaches and dunes arrive by ferry from mainland Georgia, then trek five to 10 miles to assigned campsites. Though small, the island has a variety of habitats that may be explored on trails from base camp. Wading birds and raccoons feed on the crabs and other creatures in the saltwater marshes. Forests of live oaks host songbirds, white-tailed deer, and armadillos. Hikers may even hear and see alligators in the freshwater lakes.

Okefenokee Wilderness

Okefenokee National Wildlife Refuge, P.O. Box 338, Folkston, GA 31537; tel: 912-496-3331.

Okefenokee is doubly protected – as a wilderness area and a wildlife refuge. Nearly all of the refuge is classified as wilderness, where visitors can follow canoe routes and stop at designated campsites to stay overnight. Other than a chance to relish the peaceful paddling, the main attraction here is the wildlife. Bird life is abundant, from wood storks, roseate spoonbills, and other waders to songbirds and woodpeckers found in the upland forests. Alligators and black bears are common sightings.

Ouachita National Forest

Arkansas–Oklahoma

Unless you're an early riser, the spring music of the **Ouachita Mountains** starts well before you open your eyes in the morning. As daylight suffuses your tent, an ovenbird is already singing its loud *tea-cher, tea-cher,* while a chickadee calls its name from a nearby pine. In the distance, a wild turkey cock lets loose an exuberant gobble, hoping to make itself irresistible to the opposite sex with its crazy laughter. ◆ Later, as you're sipping a warm cup of tea, the chatter of a fox squirrel erupts from a hickory, and a red-eyed vireo, hidden high in an oak, begins the warbling song it will repeat incessantly throughout the day. You may hear the murmur of running water in the distance, for rocky creeks splash in nearly every valley in the Ouachitas. What you won't hear, unless you want to, is the sound of other people. If there's one thing this rugged land offers, it's plenty of opportunity to be alone with nature's music. ◆ For those who love the Ouachita Mountains, it's just as well that these uplands in west-central Arkansas and eastern Oklahoma aren't terribly well known. The backcountry encompasses hundreds of miles of trails for hiking or biking and, here and there, the chance to stand on a ridge and look out over a landscape of trees and sky and little else. ◆ While the Ozark Mountains, the Ouachitas' northern neighbors, have become a popular tourist destination, many people aren't even sure how to pronounce *Ouachita*. (A Frenchified version of an Indian word, it's *WASH-ih-taw* in the local lingo.) And though the two areas are often lumped together, the Ozark and Ouachita Mountains are as different, geologically speaking, as

In the South's largest national forest, you'll hike through creek-laced woodlands and gain views of mysterious "rock glaciers."

Anglers fish sections of the Little Missouri River for trout, bass, and sunfish. During the spring and after heavy rains, the river offers exciting whitewater for kayakers.

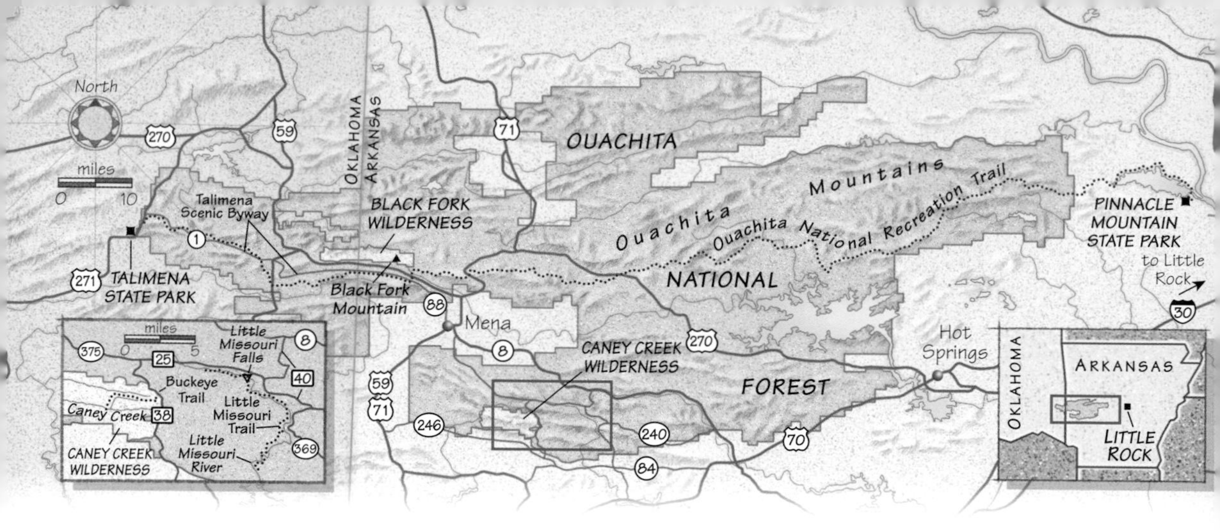

apple pie and orange marmalade. The Ozarks were uplifted as a broad plateau and then deeply etched by rivers; the Ouachitas were created when a continental collision 300 million years ago squeezed rock into long, parallel, east-west ridges separated by broad valleys.

Sheltering Forests

Centered on one of these Ouachita valleys about 15 miles southeast of the small town of Mena, Arkansas, the **Caney Creek Wilderness** ranks high with hikers for both beauty and ecological interest. One of six wilderness areas administered by the **Ouachita National Forest** (at 1.8 million acres, the largest national forest in the South), this 14,460-acre tract serves as an excellent introduction to the region's ecology and adventure possibilities.

The nine-mile trail that bisects the heavily wooded Caney Creek area makes a moderately strenuous day hike if a shuttle from the other end can be arranged, but that's hardly the best way to experience it. Better by far is to enter the wilderness from the east and stroll along the creekside ridges, taking time to enjoy the sights and sounds on the way. Head up one of the streams that enters Caney Creek from both north and south, and you may come across a perfect spot for lunch beside a picturesque waterfall. Find your own campsite wherever you like, and backtrack to the trailhead the next day for an easy but rewarding overnight trip. For variety, make a loop on your return by heading north on the intersecting **Buckeye Trail**, then walking south a mile along Forest Road 38 to the trailhead.

The sandstone that underlies much of the Ouachitas encourages the growth of shortleaf pine, which dominates the land in

many areas. But throughout the forest, hardwoods add variety to the flora, among them oaks, hickories, basswoods, and umbrella magnolias with their two-foot-long leaves. Especially notable in moister areas, such as along Caney Creek, are imposing specimens of American beech, with smooth, gray bark and triangular nuts that provide a tasty treat in fall, if you can find any that haven't been harvested by squirrels and birds. In June and July, hikers are always happy to come across low-bush huckleberry, a common shrub in the Ouachitas whose dark blue berries are as delicious as they are attractive. Wildflowers range from early bloomers such as bloodroot and toothwort, emerging through the carpet of dead leaves in February and March, to the asters of late summer and fall.

The Ouachitas boast a healthy population of black bears, but it's a lucky hiker who sees one of these shy animals. Evidence of their presence may come in the form of claw marks on a tree that's been used as a scratching post. The odds are slim, too, that you'll spot one of the resident bobcats, more common than bears but even more elusive. In summer, though, it's not at all unlikely that you'll stumble upon a flock of young turkeys being shepherded by a hen.

The Park that Got Away

Every season in the Ouachitas has its attractions. Some visitors prefer fall, when the hardwoods are changing colors, and oaks, maples, and hickories span the spectrum from yellow to red-orange. Many backpackers love hiking in Arkansas's mild winters, when ticks, chiggers, and mosquitoes have

Fire pink, spiderwort, and Indian blanket (opposite, left to right) are among the many blooms that carpet meadows, creeksides, and forest floors in the Ouachitas. The long wildflower season lasts from just before spring through fall.

The Ouachita River flows into Lake Ouachita (right) in west-central Arkansas. Its 48,000 acres, surrounded by national forest and state parklands, are ideal for fishing and boating.

The View from the Top

For a quick and easy visit to the top of the Ouachitas, take time before or after your backcountry excursion to explore the **Talimena Scenic Byway**, a spectacular route that winds along ridgetops for 54 miles between Mena, Arkansas, and Talihina, Oklahoma. The byway offers a splendid overview of these venerable highlands, running as it does along 2,681-foot Rich Mountain, the loftiest point in the Ouachitas.

Aside from its beauty, the byway serves as a primer in local geology. In places along the roadside, twisted and folded strata of sandstone and shale graphically demonstrate the awesome power of the tectonic forces that pushed up the Ouachitas. You'll see the results in the tree-covered, east-west ridges that roll away on both sides of the road. Overlooks provide especially good vistas of **Black Fork Mountain**, just across Big Creek Valley to the north, with its curious, boulder-strewn expanses, or "rock glaciers."

The cooler, moister north slope of Rich Mountain harbors colorful wildflowers and a notable array of trees and shrubs, including beech, black walnut, sugar maple, umbrella magnolia, pawpaw, Carolina silverbell, and Ohio buckeye. A variety of birds nests on the mountain, and hidden among the leaf litter live two amphibian species endemic to the Ouachitas, the Rich Mountain and Ouachita red-backed salamanders. For a closer look, take advantage of the byway's easy access to the Ouachita National Recreation Trail, which parallels the road for several miles atop Rich Mountain.

The Talimena Scenic Byway (above) winds through the Ouachita Mountains (below), one of the highest ranges between the Rockies and the Appalachians.

White-tailed deer (opposite, top) are common throughout the national forest.

The sun-dappled banks of the Little Missouri River (opposite, bottom) make scenic campsites. Jagged bluffs flank portions of the river.

disappeared and bare trees reveal ridgetop vistas hidden the rest of the year. Spring is the most popular time: birds are in full song, wildflowers are at their peak, and temperatures are pleasingly moderate.

For most people, summer is the least favorite season. It's hot and dry, birdsong is virtually silent, and the bugs are out in force. Nonetheless, even this time of year has attractions, foremost of which is finding a swimming hole in one of the innumerable rocky creeks and jumping in for a cool dip. Caney Creek has lots of such pools, but with a little searching off the back roads you can easily find your own private "spa."

Swimming, wading, and just enjoying the view are all popular pastimes at **Little Missouri Falls**, a spot that ranks with Arkansas's most beautiful natural areas. Off Forest Road 25 just a few miles northeast of Caney Creek, the Little Missouri River drops over tall rock ledges, creating a magnificent series of cascades during periods of high water in spring. The 15-mile **Little Missouri Trail** runs along the river both upstream and downstream from the falls, providing backpacking opportunities and allowing escape to more solitary swimming holes.

There's a fascinating bit of political history connected with Little Missouri Falls. In 1929, legislation to create a 163,000-acre Ouachita National Park passed both houses of Congress, but President Calvin Coolidge refused to sign the bill. Rumor had it that he was influenced by western congressmen, who didn't want an eastern park competing with theirs, and the Forest Service, which didn't want to give up any land. The falls would have been the centerpiece of the park, which was also opposed by some National Park Service personnel. They said the area wasn't sufficiently "superlative" – but look around and see for yourself.

Mountaintop Overnighter

The ultimate Ouachita challenge is the **Ouachita National Recreation Trail**, which runs more than 230 taxing miles from **Talimena State Park** in Oklahoma to **Pinnacle Mountain State Park** near Little Rock, Arkansas. Realistically, though, few have the time (a minimum of three to four weeks) or can arrange the logistics for such an adventure. Most backcountry travelers tackle segments of the trail, accessible at dozens of road crossings and recreation areas.

One short trip takes you on a side route off the Ouachita National Recreation Trail, just northwest of Mena, to one of the most fascinating spots in the Ouachitas. The center of 13,579-acre **Black Fork Wilderness** is 2,403-foot **Black Fork Mountain**, which has a six-mile (one-way) trail up its eastern flank. Expanses of jumbled boulders known as "rock glaciers" dot the south side of Black Fork; their geological origin is still being debated. At the top of the mountain, hikers find a bizarre forest of mature white oaks, trees more than a century old but only about 20 feet tall, stunted by a combination of poor soil and winter wind and ice. Plan to camp on the mountain so you'll have plenty of time to explore and enjoy the views. Here, as elsewhere in this lonely corner of the Ouachitas, the loudest sound you're likely to hear is the wind through the trees.

TRAVEL TIPS

DETAILS

How to Get There

Commercial airlines serve Fort Smith, Arkansas, 85 miles from the ranger district office in Mena, and Little Rock, 120 miles away. Rental cars are available at both airports.

When to Go

Most visitors prefer to come in spring, when temperatures range from the low 50s and mid-60s to the 70s. April and May have the heaviest monthly rainfall, averaging five inches. Summer is hot and dry, with daytime temperatures in the upper 80s and mid-90s, even into the 100s. Temperatures are moderate in fall, with days in the 60s and 70s and nights in the 40s and 50s. Fall color peaks in October and November. Winter is an enjoyable time to visit; insects and snakes have retreated, snow is rare, and daytime temperatures can be in the 50s.

What to Do

Backcountry users can hike more than 700 miles of trails, including some 200 miles on the Ouachita National Recreation Trail. Mountain biking and horseback riding are permitted on designated trails, and equestrian routes have campsites for both riders and their horses. Mountain bikes are not allowed in the national forest's six wilderness areas. Many rivers are open to paddlers in canoes, kayaks, or rafts. The streams and lakes also draw anglers.

Backcountry Permits

Permits are not required for backcountry travel. The U.S. Forest Service requests that visitors travel in small groups to minimize impact on the wilderness.

Special Planning

Thunderstorms are common in spring and fall and can occur at any time of day. Backcountry travelers should carry dependable raingear and tents. Backpackers should also bring portable gas stoves for use in areas where campfires are not allowed. Summer visitors will find insect repellent helpful.

Car Camping

Campgrounds are located throughout Ouachita National Forest, in both Arkansas and Oklahoma. Contact the forest supervisor or individual ranger districts for detailed information.

INFORMATION

Ouachita National Forest
Forest Supervisor, P.O. Box 1270, 100 Reserve Street, Hot Springs, AR 71902; tel: 501-321-5202.

Caddo Ranger District
P.O. Box 369, Glenwood, AR 71943; tel: 501-356-4186.

Choctaw Ranger District
HC 64, Box 3467, Heavener, OK 74937; tel: 918-653-2991.

Mena Ranger District
1603 Highway 71 North, Mena, AR 71953; tel: 501-394-2382.

Ozark Interpretive Association
P.O. Box 1279, Mountain View, AR 72560; tel: 870-757-2211.

The association carries trail and nature guides covering the Ouachita Mountains (see Resource Directory) as well as maps for various wilderness areas in the national forest.

Arkansas Department of Parks and Tourism
One Capitol Mall, Little Rock, AR 72201; tel: 501-682-7777.

On request, the department sends out "The Arkansas Floater's Kit," an invaluable package of information including maps, lists of outfitters, and descriptions of streams, many of which are in the national forest. Also available is the "Arkansas Camper's & Hiker's Guide."

LODGING

PRICE GUIDE – double occupancy

$ = up to $49	$$ = $50–$99
$$$ = $100–$149	$$$$ = $150+

Arrowhead Cabins and Canoes
69 Arrowhead Drive, Caddo Gap, AR 71935; tel: 800-538-6578 or 870-356-2944.

Seven one- and two-bedroom cabins with kitchens are situated on the Caddo River and surrounded by national forest. A bunkhouse on the property accommodates groups. Guests and visitors may rent canoes. $$

MacMorgan Ranch Outfitters
P.O. Box 1216, Polk Country Road #47, Mena, AR 71953; tel: 501-394-6443.

Guests stay in cabins that sleep four and have kitchens. Campers may rent tents or pitch their own near the ranch's 200-acre mountain lake. Visitors can canoe and kayak on the lake and arrange for paddling instruction. $$-$$$

Ouachita River Haven Resort
122 Ouachita River Haven Road, Pencil Bluff, AR 71965; tel: 870-326-4941.

Four cabins with kitchens have views of the Ouachita River. Campers can pitch their tents at the resort's campgrounds. Canoes and kayaks are available for short- and long-term rental. $$–$$$

River View Cabins and Canoes
18 Stoney Point Road, Oden, AR 71961; tel: 888-547-1146 or 870-326-4630.

Set on 117 acres within the national forest, the River View's eight cedar-and-pine cabins overlook the Ouachita River. The cabins sleep two to nine guests and have kitchens and hot tubs. Guests may rent canoes and take guided horseback rides. $$$–$$$$

TOURS AND OUTFITTERS

Caddo River Canoe Rental, Inc.

713 North Main, Amity, AR 71921; tel: 800-665-2791 or 870-342-5684.

Paddlers on the Caddo River are taken upstream for a 16-mile float to De Gray Lake. Canoes and all other necessary equipment, as well as shuttle services, are provided.

MacMorgan Ranch Outfitters

P.O. Box 1216, Polk Country Road #47, Mena, AR 71953; tel: 501-394-6443.

Guided pack trips take visitors on horseback into the national forest. The outfitter provides all camping gear and meals.

Ouachita Mountain Outdoor Center

P.O. Box 65, Pencil Bluff, AR 71965; tel: 870-326-5517 or 800-748-3718.

The center rents canoes, kayaks, rafts, and other paddling equipment. It also provides shuttle service for paddlers and for hikers using national forest trails, including the Ouachita National Recreation Trail.

Two Spirits Ltd. Canoe Adventures

1167 Pucket Bend Road, Mount Ida, AR 71957; tel: 800-841-3632 or 870-867-5028.

Backcountry travelers float the Ouachita River and spend one or two nights at the outfitter's campground, where all equipment and meals are provided. Avid canoers may arrange trips up to 20 miles. Trips can combine canoeing with hiking the Ouachita National Recreation Trail or biking on the Womble Trail, both of which are near the campground. Two Spirits also offers shuttle services.

Excursions

Buffalo National River

402 North Walnut, Suite 136, Harrison, AR 72601; tel: 870-741-5443.

Beginning in the Ozark Mountains of northwestern Arkansas, the Buffalo River flows 150 miles, dropping almost 2,000 feet through scenic mountains, sandstone bluffs, and box canyons. Paddlers can stop to camp and explore such treasures as the Upper Buffalo Wilderness, with its caves, waterfalls, and abundant wildlife, including black bears, white-tailed deer, beavers, and bobcats. Farther downstream lies 175-foot Hemmed-In Hollow, the highest waterfall in the region, and an array of irresistible swimming holes.

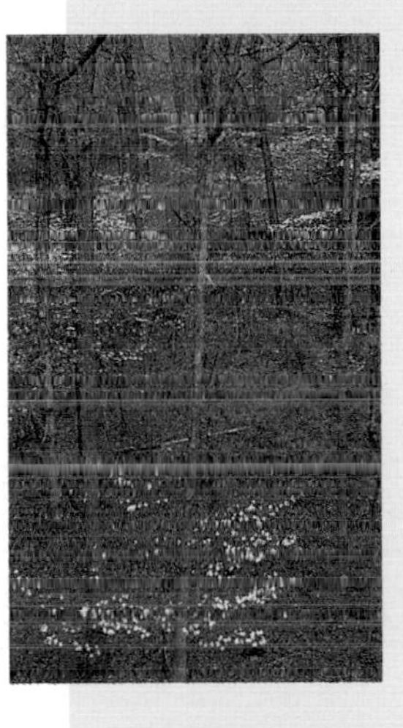

Mark Twain National Forest

401 Fairgrounds Road, Rolla, MO 65401; tel: 573-364-4621.

Hundreds of miles of trails, including 225 miles of the Ozark Trail, entice backpackers to Missouri's only national forest, most of which lies in the Ozark Plateau of deep winding valleys and gently rolling plains. In this part of southern Missouri, backcountry travelers pass through a varied landscape of tall-grass prairies, northern hardwood forests, and woodlands with southern coastal vegetation. The Eleven Point Scenic River is an ideal waterway for canoeing. Seven wilderness areas are scattered throughout the national forest.

Ozark National Scenic Riverways

P.O. Box 490, Van Buren, MO 63965; tel: 573-323-4236.

Seven major springs and dozens of smaller ones feed the Current and Jacks Ford Rivers, 134 miles of which are protected in this 80,790-acre park. Floating the rivers by canoe or kayak, camping en route, is the best way to appreciate the broadleaf forests, steep-sided hollows, and diverse wildlife. On land, travelers can investigate caves, except those closed to protect habitat for endangered Indiana and gray bats, or view the 19 sites deemed of archaeological and historical significance – evidence that Paleo-Indians lived in this area 12,000 years ago.

Isle Royale National Park

Michigan

If you were to view North America from the stratosphere, you might imagine that Lake Superior looks somewhat like the head of a wolf. The eye of the beast is **Isle Royale**. ◆ Though part of Michigan, whose lakeshore is about 50 miles south, the island is actually much closer to Ontario, Canada. The international boundary swerves around the park thanks largely to the diplomatic efforts of Benjamin Franklin, who believed the island held deposits of copper. He was right. Ancient Indians made tools and jewelry of the copper they found here, removing more than 250 tons of the metal over the course of a thousand years. Centuries later, in the mid-1800s, several attempts were made at industrial mining, but they never turned much of a profit. In the interim, the island was visited by Ojibway Indians who harvested the sap of maple trees, French traders known as voyageurs who paddled the area's waterways, and fishermen who set up scattered camps along the lakeshore. Several resorts were built in the early 1900s to service a modest tourist trade, but only one, Rock Harbor Lodge, still stands. ◆ Throughout it all, the island has simply shrugged off these minor interventions, and today it remains nearly as untrammeled and wild as it was several centuries ago. There are no roads, few buildings, and no permanent human residents. Its forests are traversed only by hikers, its lakes parted only by the wakes of kayaks and canoes. Wolves prowl rugged heights in search of moose; red fox hunt small birds and rodents; beavers construct dams and lodges;

Campers thrill to the sound of howling wolves on a wild island in Lake Superior.

Backcountry travelers can bring their own canoes and kayaks to Isle Royale or rent boats at Rock Harbor and explore the shoreline and inland lakes.

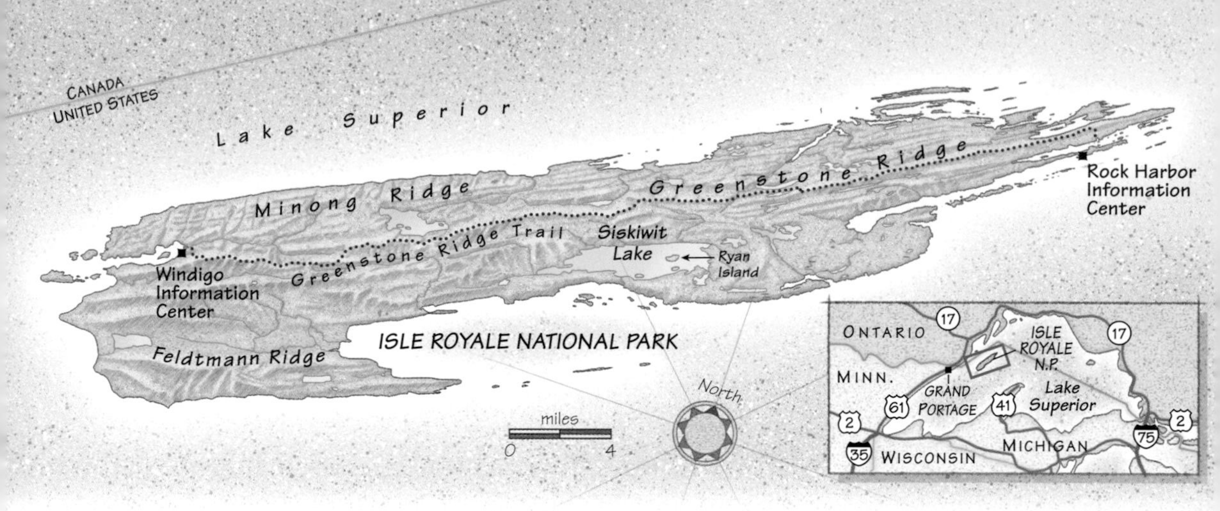

colonies of gulls screech on the guano-stained rocks that rise from the world's largest lake.

Volcano's Spawn, Glacier's Orphan

Oriented northeast to southwest, Isle Royale and the 200 small islands around it are the spawn of volcanoes that spewed lava across the Earth's surface starting about a billion years ago. The region that is now the Lake Superior basin was then near the head of the Mid-Continent Rift, a giant split in the Earth's crust from which magma gushed to the surface. As the reservoir of molten rock emptied, the land above it sank inward, forming what would later become the basin of Lake Superior.

Wind and water shaped this part of the continent for millions of years after the volcanic upheaval, and only in relatively recent time – geologically speaking – did the final cataclysmic chapter in the island's birth begin. A series of glacial epochs, beginning 2.3 million years ago, alternately crushed, scoured, and washed the region. But it was the last glacial age, ending only 10,000 years ago, that actually created Isle Royale.

The settling of the basin begun by the earlier volcanic eruptions increased under the weight of the glaciers. When the ice retreated, however, the land, now free of its frozen burden, rose up. Hikers will surely note that the island's spine runs northeast to southwest – the sharp edges, or cliffs, facing the northwest, the slopes facing southeast. Melting glaciers gradually filled the basin with water and orphaned high spots like Isle Royale from the mainland.

Hikers' Challenge

Boaters troll the shorelines seeking the big lake's abundant trout. Sailors and scuba divers visit, finding their own delights, and canoeists and sea kayakers ply the inshore waters and interior lakes. Yet only by hiking can one truly come to know this primitive island. While some visitors arrive in boats of their own, most reach the island via one of the four ferryboats that depart from either Michigan or Minnesota.

Almost the entire island is officially designated as wilderness. Practically speaking, this means that you have to travel under your own steam, either by hiking or by paddling. Most visitors who explore the interior do so under the weight of a backpack.

The hiking is arduous. The 45-mile-long, nine-mile-wide island is ribbed by three parallel ridges. **Greenstone Ridge**, named after one of the lava flows, dominates Isle Royale and runs roughly down the island's center, while the nearby, slightly lower **Minong Ridge** follows the island's precipitous north shore. **Feldtman Ridge**, found only on the wider, southern third of the island, is not as formidable as the other two, but it offers one of the park's finest vistas.

The ridges rise 600 or 700 feet above scattered lakes, and because the trails can't always follow the crests of the ridges, hikers are often forced to make considerable up-and-down traverses. Combined with the fact that most of the trails are on hard granite or ancient beach cobbles, knees tend to twist and feet take a pounding. But if the ridges sometimes test hikers, the troughs in between make cross-country travel impossible, for the valleys are filled with bogs and marshes, and the forest is cross-hatched with deadfalls.

Nonetheless, observant trekkers will soon discover why this primeval tract of north woods is so appealing. Several loops of hiking trails give backpackers a range of options. Campsites are found primarily along the lakeshore or on the banks of interior lakes for both scenery and a source of water.

Island Flora and Fauna

At intervals along the ridges, hikers can expect to stand

A young backpacker (above) leaves the trail to pick blueberries.

Backpackers (left) hike Greenstone Ridge, the island's most prominent geological feature, named for one of the lava flows that shaped the terrain.

Anglers (opposite) fish Lake Superior for trout, salmon, northern pike, and walleye.

in awe as the forest gives way to startling vistas. Canada's Sibley Peninsula and Minnesota's shore glint green on the northern horizon. The majesty of Lake Superior–whose waters around the park are so crystalline that you can see the bottom clearly some 20 feet below – sweeps to the end of sight in almost all directions.

Backpackers will also hike past or camp near some of the island's pristine 38 named lakes and an even greater number of ponds, places to observe moose, loons, and beavers. **Siskiwit Lake**, where the native lake trout swim, is the island's largest freshwater lake and is itself seven miles long and nearly 150 feet deep. Siskiwit's **Ryan Island** has the distinction of being the largest island in the largest lake in the largest island in the largest lake in the world. A few short but lovely rivers, home to the delicately beautiful brook trout, run largely in the troughs between the ridges.

The woods are a study in northern forest and island ecology. The first European explorers thought the island to be impenetrable, since the fir and cedar grew shoulder to shoulder along the shore, making entry difficult. A major fire in 1936 and the intense browsing of moose altered the forest, but the cool, damp shoreline still favors conifers; birch and aspen grow in the thin soil found on dry, exposed ridges. A spectacular climax forest, bisected by the **Greenstone Ridge Trail**, lies on the lush western fifth of the island, filled with stately sugar maples and yellow birch and forming a dense canopy above hikers.

Some plant and animal species common on the mainland aren't found here. While

Of Moose and Wolves

Woodland caribou once roamed Isle Royale, but moose are now the only ungulates found here, having arrived in 1912 by swimming the 15 miles from Canada or by coming across the ice.

Finding suitable habitat, the moose flourished, nearly denuding the island by 1930, when they numbered perhaps 3,000. Having destroyed their forage base, they began to die off, then bounced back, reaching a population of nearly 1,000 by 1940. The cold, hard winter of 1948–49 allowed an ice bridge to form to the Minnesota–Ontario shore, across which came the gray wolf. By 1960, some 20 wolves were thought to be on the island, and since that time, every suitable portion of Isle Royale has been colonized by packs.

The relationship of wolves and moose, predator and prey, has been intensely studied for nearly half a century. Among the discoveries is that the amount of prey determines the number of wolves and that the populations of both swing wildly.

Wolves peaked at 50 in 1980, but within two years, all but 14 were killed by canine parvovirus, perhaps brought to the island by a dog on a visiting yacht (dogs are illegal in the park) or by a wolf that crossed on a more recent ice bridge (mainland wolves have developed a resistance to the disease). In 1993, only 11 wolves survived, but five years later, the population numbered 24. Nearly half of the wolves died during the following winter. Biologists speculate that since only 500 of the 2,400 moose survived the difficult winter, the shortage of prey or another outbreak of canine parvovirus led to the recent wolf decline.

The moose population is now at about 700 and growing, and there is hope that the wolf population will follow suit.

The island's wolves (left) and moose (below) maintain a delicate predator-prey relationship.

A paddler (opposite, top) carries a canoe over one of the island's 16 portages.

Campsites for paddlers, like this one at Pickerel Cove (opposite, bottom), are interspersed throughout the island.

white-tailed deer and black bears join moose and wolves on the mainland, only the latter two are found on the island, and both are relatively recent immigrants. Ruffed grouse, porcupine, several varieties of mice, and other species, like the lynx, are also absent. And few large pines, so characteristic of the mainland's forests, can be found here, owing to the island's exposure and poor soil.

But what is found here is enough. Moose are common, seen even along hiking trails, and wolves, though rarely observed, can occasionally be heard howling at night. Red fox are common and can even be pests near campsites as they look for handouts. Loons nest both in quiet Lake Superior bays and on inland lakes, and at dusk and dawn they fill the air with their haunting yodel.

Hikers can also find the pits dug by ancient Indian miners in search of copper. Commercial fishing camps, now abandoned, are scattered in back bays, their net racks empty, but looking as if the families who once worked them might return at any moment. And when emerging from the dark forest onto an open, windswept ridge, hikers are rewarded with uncommon vistas of a land that looks much as it has for thousands of years.

TRAVEL TIPS

DETAILS

How to Get There

Isle Royale can be reached via three ferry routes: Grand Portage, Minnesota, to the Windigo Visitor Center at the western end of the island (22 miles/two to three hours); Copper Harbor, Michigan, to Rock Harbor at the island's eastern end (56 miles/four-and-one-half hours); and Houghton, Michigan, to Rock Harbor (73 miles/six hours). Ferries also circle the island, stopping at Windigo, Rock Harbor, and other areas. A 30-minute seaplane flight takes passengers from Houghton, Michigan, to Rock Harbor or Windigo. Full transporation services are available from mid-June until Labor Day; services are reduced in spring and fall. The closest major airport is in Duluth, Minnesota; cars can be rented at the airport.

When to Go

Most backcountry visitors come from mid-July through late August. Visitation is lowest in April and May and in September and October. The park is closed from November 1 through April 15. Summer temperatures range from lows in the mid-40s to highs in the mid-60s and 70s. Monthly summer rainfall averages two to three-and-a-half inches. Spring and fall days are in the mid-50s; lows are in the mid-30s and low 40s. Snow can fall as late as May and as early as September.

What to Do

Nearly all of Isle Royale is federally designated wilderness, where backpackers may hike 165 miles of trails or forge cross-country routes. The park's inland lakes are ideal for canoeing and kayaking; canoe routes and portages are found on the northeast half of the island. Paddlers can also ply the offshore waters. Fishing is allowed on interior lakes and Lake Superior.

Backcountry Permits

Permits are required for all overnight stays. Groups of seven or more must make advance reservations. Backcountry travelers camp in Adirondack-style shelters or at designated sites, available on a first-come, first-served basis. Off-trail camping is arranged when visitors obtain a permit upon arrival at Rock Harbor or Windigo. Permits are also required for boaters staying overnight at anchor, at docks, or in campgrounds.

Special Planning

Backpackers and paddlers should carry extra clothing as protection against hypothermia, which can occur at any time of year, especially near Lake Superior, with its cold water and air temperatures. Paddlers are advised that fog and waves, even on inland lakes, can quickly create dangerous conditions. Mosquitoes, black flies, and other insects peak in June or July, when use of repellent and head nets is recommended. Campfires are not allowed at every campground; backcountry travelers should bring portable gas stoves.

INFORMATION

Isle Royale National Park

800 East Lakeshore Drive, Houghton, MI 49931; tel: 906-482-0984.

Isle Royale Natural History Association

800 East Lakeshore Drive, Houghton, MI 49931; tel: 800-678-6925 or 906-482-7860.

The association carries books on Isle Royale's natural history and guides to the island's trails and water routes (see Resource Directory) as well as topo maps.

Grand Portage–Isle Royale Transportation Line

1507 North First Street, Superior, WI 54880; tel: 715-392-2100.

Isle Royale Line

P.O. Box 24, Copper Harbor, MI 49918; tel: 906-289-4437.

Isle Royale Seaplane Service

P.O. Box 366, Houghton, MI 49931; tel: 906-482-8850 (late May to late September) or 715-526-5103 (October to mid-May).

Houghton Chamber of Commerce

P.O. Box 366, Houghton, MI 49931; tel: 906-482-5240 or 800-338-7982.

LODGING

PRICE GUIDE – double occupancy

$ = up to $49	$$ = $50–$99
$$$ = $100–$149	$$$$ = $150+

Eagle River Inn

HC 1, Box 621, Eagle River, MI 49950; tel: 906-337-0666 or 800-352-9228.

The inn's 12 rooms overlook Lake Superior. Guests are served a continental breakfast, and a restaurant is on the premises. A condominium with full kitchen is also available. $$–$$$$

King Copper Motel

P.O. Box 68, Copper Harbor, MI 49918; tel: 906-289-4214 or 800-833-2470.

Located next to the Isle Royale boat dock, this motel has 34 rooms overlooking Lake Superior. $$

Old Shore Beach Bed-and-Breakfast

1434 Old Shore Road, Grand Marais, MN 55604; tel: 218-387-9707 or 888-387-9707.

Guests stay in four rooms with private baths and are served a full breakfast. Amenities include use of a private beach on Lake Superior. $$–$$$

Rock Harbor Lodge

National Park Concessions, P.O. Box 605, Houghton MI 49931; tel: 906-337-4993 (summer), 270-773-2191 (winter).

The only accommodations in the park, this lodge has four buildings along the shore at Rock Harbor. Sixty rooms have harbor and island views. There are also 20 cottages with kitchens. A dining room is on the premises. $$$

TOURS AND OUTFITTERS

Cascade Kayaks

P.O. Box 215, Grand Marais, MN 55604; tel: 218-387-2360 or 800-720-2809.

During six-day trips to Isle Royale, paddlers explore the park on water and on foot, spending each night camping or staying in trail shelters. For beginners, the focus is on learning paddling and safety skills. Rentals are also available.

Keweenaw Adventure Company

P.O. Box 70, Copper Harbor, MI 49918; tel: 906-289-4303.

Five-day guided trips to the national park take paddlers to the small islands and coves. Time is also spent hiking, swimming, wildlife watching, photographing, and exploring local fishing settlements and lighthouses. Keweenaw Adventure rents kayaks to visitors traveling on their own and provides paddling and safety instruction. A wide array of camping gear is also available for rent.

National Park Concessions

P.O. Box 605, Houghton MI 49931; tel: 906-337-4993 (summer), 270-773-2191 (winter).

The Rock Harbor Lodge water taxi provides drop-off and pick-up services between Rock Harbor and docks on the northeast part of the island. Canoe rentals are available at Windigo and Rock Harbor.

Excursions

Boundary Waters Canoe Area Wilderness

Superior National Forest, 8901 Grand Avenue Place, Duluth, MN 55808; tel: 218-626-4300.

The 1,200 miles of canoe trails dwarf the length of hiking trails in this vast wilderness consisting of lakes and streams joined by portages and peppered with more than 2,000 campsites. Paddling through the boreal forest is the best way to observe its inhabitants, which include moose, black bears, beavers, and otters. Bordering the Boundary Waters is Voyageurs National Park (see below) in Minnesota and Quetico Provincial Park in Canada. Together, the three preserves offer 2.5 million acres to explore by canoe or kayak.

Voyageurs National Park

3131 Highway 53, International Falls, MN 56649-8904; tel: 218-283-9821.

Named for the French fur traders who plied the canoe routes of the Great Lakes region in the 17th and 18th centuries, this park is a maze of islands and waterways on and around the Kabetogama Peninsula. Travel in the park is limited to boating and hiking. Canoe trips range from an afternoon of paddling near the Kabetogama Visitor Center to a 70-mile loop around the peninsula. The Cruiser Lake Trail, one of the few long overland routes, runs about 10 miles across the peninsula, with numerous side trails. Resident timber wolves are seldom seen, though hikers may hear them howling or find their tracks.

St. Croix National Scenic Riverway

P.O. Box 708, St. Croix Falls, WI 54024; tel: 715-483-3284.

Rising in northwest Wisconsin, the St. Croix forms a portion of the Wisconsin–Minnesota border before flowing into the Mississippi. More than 250 miles of the river meander along sandstone banks and through forests of maple, birch, aspen, and pines. Paddlers can navigate parts or all of the riverway, stopping to camp as well as to hike the various trails along the way. Two trails are groomed in winter for cross-country skiers.

Theodore Roosevelt National Park

North Dakota

CHAPTER 13

Snowcapped and skirted with forest, the mountains to the west beckon hikers. To the east, Minnesota's pine-rimmed wilderness lakes lure canoeists. Sandwiched between them is North Dakota's Theodore Roosevelt National Park. What could this park in the Great Prairie offer those who crave a backcountry trek? ◆ Perhaps it's the chance to feel the prairie's vastness as the Lakota Sioux once did, or to experience what early pioneer families in lumbering wagons called the "Great American Desert." Or the prospect of seeing the grassland's remnant herds of bison and the fantastically carved badlands that enthralled Theodore Roosevelt. Or maybe to benefit from the same body-healing, mind-strengthening properties of the land that Roosevelt credited with giving him the fortitude to become president of the United States. ◆ **Theodore Roosevelt National Park** is all this – hardscrabble badlands, rolling grasslands, and tree-lined bottomlands. The landscape, though beautiful and wild, was once thought unfit for inclusion in the National Park System. Only through much political maneuvering did it become a memorial park named after Roosevelt in 1947, and only in 1978 was it given full national park status. ◆ Today's park encompasses 70,448 acres, divided into two major units, the North and South. **The Little Missouri River**, which winds through western North Dakota, links the two units. A great deal of the land around the park is also publicly held – within the Little Missouri National Grasslands, managed by the U.S. Forest Service. The park's third site preserves Elkhorn Ranch, Roosevelt's second cattle ranch in the area. ◆ Much of the park's

Colorful badlands, torn from the prairie by thousands of years of erosion, lure hikers with dramatic landscapes, varied trails, and bountiful wildlife.

Tiger swallowtails feed on the thistles that grow throughout the prairie. The park also supports 200 species of birds, from songbirds to raptors.

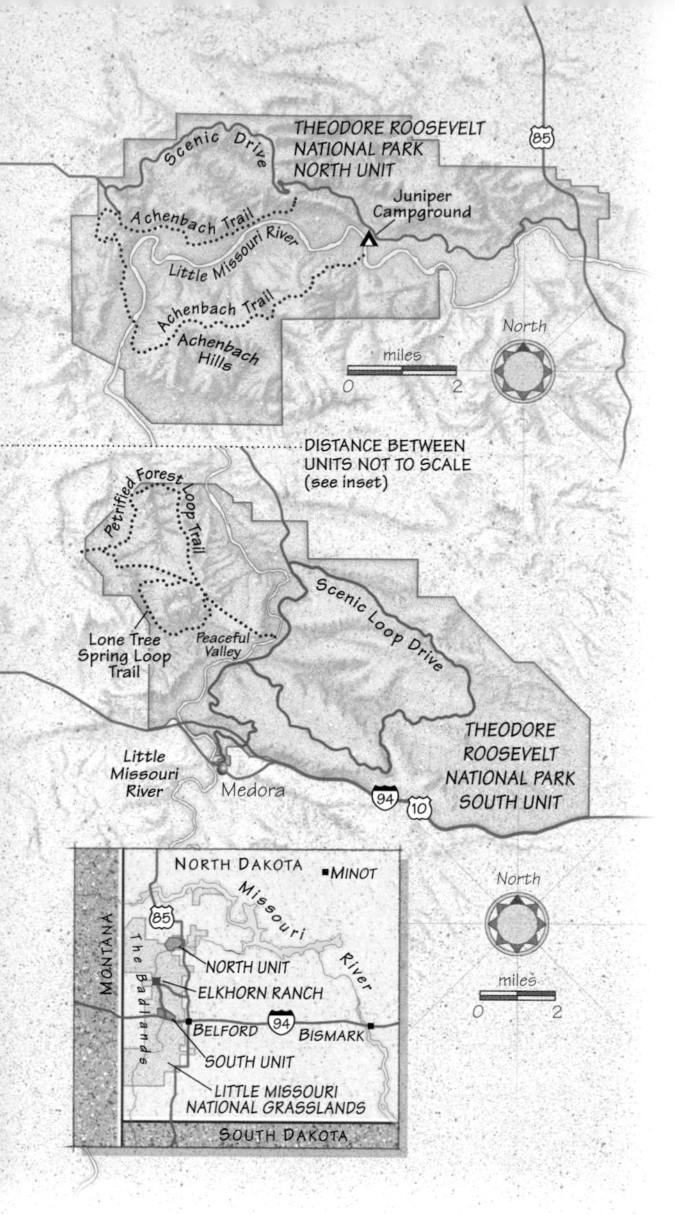

grandeur lies in its least hospitable places – the badlands. These wildly colored buttes and coulees are spectacular examples of the power of water and wind to shape the land. Simply gorgeous when lighted by the setting or rising sun, the hot, dry badlands you see today are the exposed bed of a vast alluvial plain formed by water flowing from the Rocky Mountains as the range was thrust up some 60 million years ago.

The ancient badlands were anything but dry: forests, marshes, and freshwater lakes lay on this land, building layer upon layer of silt and plant matter. The region teemed with wildlife, such as *Champsosaurus laramiensis*, a crocodilelike reptile that lived here when the climate was similar to that of present-day Florida. The fossil remains of numerous mollusks, crocodiles, alligators, turtles, and fish, plus extinct plants, are embedded in these now-exposed sediments, adding an interesting paleontological component to an exploration of the park.

Balancing the rugged contours of the badlands are the broad sweeps of prairie grasslands. The same geologic forces that lifted the Rocky Mountains raised the plains 2,500 feet above sea level. These high plains receive less than 15 inches of precipitation each year, and the wind blows relentlessly, but the mixed grasses thrive, as do the animals adapted to this environment.

River Baptism

In this national park, you won't find backcountry in which you can wander for weeks. But maybe that's just as well. Winter on the prairie is harsh, and summer can broil your brain with temperatures frequently in the 90s and occasionally topping 100°F. The in-between periods – spring through early summer, as well as September – are best for hiking. In addition, because there is no potable water to be found in the interior, park personnel suggest you carry enough for your entire trip. Experienced hikers know how heavy a three- or four-day supply would be, so breaking your explorations down into a series of overnight trips keeps your water needs to a minimum.

These constraints should not deter you, for the trail system is designed to allow hikers to explore the park's two main units in bite-sized treks. Of particular interest to hikers who want to immerse themselves in the backcountry are two overnight hikes – one in the North Unit, the other in the South Unit – that can be extended into longer stays.

The South Unit's 16-mile-long **Petrified Forest Loop Trail** can be reached from the west side of **Scenic Loop Drive** at **Peaceful Valley**. Departing from here, you'll need to ford the Little Missouri River, which at times is only ankle- to knee-deep but may be impossible to cross in the spring or after heavy rainfall. If fording isn't an option, the Petrified Forest loop can be accessed from the park's western boundary or from Interstate 94 via the **Lone Tree Spring Loop**, which will add about five miles to your hike.

In the North Unit, you'll find a hike of similar length – the **Achenbach Trail** – beginning at the **Juniper** campground. It, too, requires a quick ford of the river almost immediately upon departing from the campground, cooling you off before you begin your journey up the 500-foot incline to the rugged bluffs of the **Achenbach Hills**. The North Unit hike is slightly more challenging than the South, but both areas offer similar backcountry experiences.

Perhaps it is appropriate to begin either hike with an impromptu baptism in the Little Missouri, for this river is the lifeblood of the park and was responsible for contouring the badlands. Nearly dry in some years while churning in others, this sinuous, sediment-laden river flows through a broad valley of its own making. Green with grass and sage, the valley is crowded in places by a narrow forest of tall cottonwoods and willows. This lowland habitat is favored by the park's white-tailed deer. Once through

A bison (left) is coated with frost on a frigid winter morning. The creatures were nearly exterminated in the late 1800s.

Prairie ponds like this one near the Scenic Loop Drive (below) are magnets for wildlife.

Evening primrose (opposite), prickly-pear cactus, and other flowering plants paint the landscape from spring to fall.

The Roosevelt Legacy

Teddy Roosevelt, on the left, poses with conservationist John Muir in 1903 (right). Two decades earlier, Roosevelt acquired his first North Dakota cabin (below).

Pronghorns (bottom) can reach speeds in excess of 40 miles per hour.

Erosion (opposite, top) exposes the petrified remains of an ancient forest.

A stand of green ash (opposite, bottom) fronts a view of the badlands.

Before he became, at age 42, the youngest president ever to hold the office, Theodore Roosevelt traveled the American West in search of big game and adventure. In 1883, at just 24, he came to the badlands, bagged a bison, and purchased his first cattle ranch, the Maltese Cross.

When spending time afield, Roosevelt was a serious student of all aspects of the natural world – biology, geology, and forestry. The three years he spent as a working cowboy and his numerous explorations had also instilled in him a great love and respect for nature. "The joy of living is his who has the heart to demand it," he wrote. "The beauty and charm of the wilderness are his for the asking, for the edges of wilderness lie close beside the beaten roads." Few presidents have been so in touch with the land, and no other president ever accomplished as much for its conservation.

As a public official, Roosevelt crusaded to protect wild places. He knew that future generations would need natural resources to fuel a growing nation and to find the same significant connection with the land that he had experienced. Vast reserves of public land, open to everyone, would be the cornerstone of his project. During his two terms as president, Roosevelt established the U.S. Forest Service, signed a bill that designated 18 national monuments, and protected millions of acres in more than 200 national forests, parks, and refuges.

Without Roosevelt, America would be a vastly different place, diminished in natural heritage and bereft of the spirit of exploration that Americans feel when they set foot on "their" land – Roosevelt's legacy.

the trees, you move through grassland dominated by blue grama, little bluestem, and other hardy native plants.

A Close-up View

Stepping up like stairs from the river are the badlands, their raw, red shoulders made of a natural red brick known as clinker, formed when heat from burning underground coal seams baked the minerals in the soil. As you climb and gain a vantage point, look back down over the trail; you may see herds of buffalo – black specks on the plains – sharing the grasslands with elk, wild horses, and pronghorn antelope.

This magical and almost chaotic landscape is a geological marvel. Thin black layers of lignite coal stripe the hillsides between clay and sandstone. Contrasting sands and silts, vertically carved by rain and wind, stain the hillsides tan and brown. The green vegetation, muted silts, and orange-red clinker are often complemented by broad swaths of purple-blue clay called bentonite. This puffy, crumbly clay swells dramatically when exposed to rain, becoming a slippery gumbo that makes for treacherous footing.

Scattered along both hikes, but concentrated along the Petrified Forest trail, are the remains of ancient forests buried by flood debris and later mineralized. Exposed by erosion, some specimens of petrified logs are so well preserved that their growth rings can still be counted.

As you scale the ridges of the badlands,

note that the south slopes support grass and sage, while the moister north slopes give rise to clumps of Rocky Mountain juniper and green ash. Gullies, protected from the wind and trapping brief rains, sustain more vegetation than the ridges. Mule deer, with their pogo-stick gait, clatter up the shrubby slopes, and California bighorn sheep (introduced to the North Unit to replace the extinct native Audubon bighorns) scramble on dry inclines. The damp air near the river gives way to the pungent smell of sagebrush and the ginlike aroma of juniper berries. Instead of sensing the gentle brushing of tall grasses against your legs, you may now feel the prick of scattered clumps of prickly pear cactus. In just a few hundred feet, you've climbed from one ecosystem into another.

Once atop the ridges, you command a view much like that sought by the golden eagles, which nest on the bluffs and scan the sage lands for the movement of jackrabbits or cruise over the towns of black-tailed prairie dogs. These small mammals are also hunted by the swift coyote, whose mournful song echoes off the hills on still prairie nights. The vistas are startling – the glinting, brown river and green ribbon of trees below framed by yellow and rust grasses, the layered hills piling up toward their red peaks, split by long ridges of sandstone, yellow in the sun.

Wet and cool in the bottomlands and dry and hot in the badlands, this geological wonderland chronicling millions of years invites you to walk through time. As you do, you will begin to understand why Theodore Roosevelt was so struck by this region. While most tourists will come away with only a snapshot from a roadside overlook or a postcard from the visitor center, a backcountry hiker can expect to be enriched by the land's beauty and grandeur and to tap into the same soul-replenishing energy that transformed the park's namesake.

TRAVEL TIPS

DETAILS

How to Get There

The airports closest to the national park are in Dickinson, North Dakota, 50 miles east of Medora, and Bismarck, North Dakota, 140 miles east. Rental cars are available at both airports.

When to Go

The park is most popular in June, July, and August; visitation is lowest in December and January. Daytime summer temperatures vary widely and generally range from the low 80s to the mid-90s, sometimes reaching 110°F or higher; nights are in the 50s. Visitors should expect thunderstorms in July and August. Cooler temperatures bring enjoyable backcountry travel in September and October and in April and May before the summer heat returns. By November, temperatures fall below freezing. Winter receives 12 to 18 inches of snow, which often blows into deep drifts. Snow occasionally falls in March or April.

What to Do

Backcountry visitors may explore the park on more than 85 miles of trails and also hike cross-country. Bicycles are allowed on the park's roads, but not off-road or on trails. The Little Missouri River can be floated by canoe or kayak in April and May, even later in years of abundant rainfall. In winter, the river freezes over and collects snow, making it an ideal route for cross-country skiers and snowshoers. The 120-mile Maah Daah Hey Trail, which connects the North and South Units of the national park, may be traveled on foot, by mountain bike, or on horseback. Passing through Missouri National Grasslands, the trail has six overnight campsites.

Backcountry Permits

Backcountry permits are required for all overnight stays in the park and may be obtained at the visitor centers in the park's North and South Units. Call 701-623-4466 for information.

Special Planning

Weather in the region is highly changeable. Temperatures can suddenly drop 30°F or more, or thunderstorms with potentially dangerous lightning strikes can move in. Reliable raingear and extra clothing should be in every hiker's pack. Backcountry travelers must use portable gas stoves rather than build campfires, and each hiker in the party needs to carry one gallon of water per day. The park advises hikers to be cautious when crossing the Little Missouri River, which can be treacherous in early spring and after substantial rains.

Car Camping

The park has two campgrounds, Cottonwood in the South Unit and Juniper in the North Unit. The 158 sites are available on a first-come, first-served basis. Private campgrounds are located outside the park in Medora and Dickinson.

INFORMATION

Theodore Roosevelt National Park

P.O. Box 7, Medora ND 58645; tel: 701-623-4466.

Theodore Roosevelt Nature and History Association

P.O. Box 167, Medora, ND 58645; tel: 701-623-4884.

Little Missouri Grassland

U.S. Forest Service, HC02, Box 8, Watford City, ND 58854; tel: 701-623-5151 for Medora Ranger District or 701-842-2393 for Mckenzie Ranger District.

Dickinson Convention and Visitors Bureau

24 Second Street West, Dickinson, ND 58601; tel: 701-483-4988 OR 800-279-7391.

McKenzie County Tourism Bureau

P.O. Box 699, Watford City, ND 58854; tel: 800-701-2804 or 701-842-2804.

Medora Chamber of Commerce

P.O. Box 186, Medora, ND 58645; tel: 701-623-4910.

LODGING

PRICE GUIDE – double occupancy

$ = up to $49	$$ = $50–$99
$$$ = $100–$149	$$$$ = $150+

Americinn Motel and Suites

75 East River Road South, Medora, ND 58645; tel: 701-623-4800 or 800-634-3444.

The Americinn has 36 standard rooms and 20 rooms with special features such as living areas, kitchens, saunas, hot tubs, or fireplaces. Guests are served a continental breakfast. $$–$$$

Custer's Cottage

156 East River Road South, P.O. Box 174, Medora, ND 58645; tel: 701-623-4378 or 888-383-2574.

Each of the cottage's two furnished units has a separate entrance, private bath, living room, and fully equipped kitchen. One unit has four bedrooms; the other has two bedrooms. $–$$

Dakotah Lodge Guest Ranch

P.O. Box 465, Medora, ND 58645; tel: 800-508-4897 or 701-623-4897.

Situated south of the national park along the Little Missouri River, the ranch has two types of accommodations: four rustic cabins and a three-room lodge. Meals are served in the ranch bunkhouse. Guests may ride horseback on day-trips or arrange to take two-, three-, or four-day pack trips on the ranch grounds. Horseback riding is available to nonguests who make prior reservations. $$–$$$$

Little Missouri Bed and Corral

P.O. Box 8, Medora, ND 58645; tel: 701-623-4496.

Set just south of Medora on the Little Missouri River, this cabin has two bedrooms, kitchen, and living room. There is also a campsite on the property, which has easy access to the Maah Daah Hey Trail. $$

Roosevelt Inn and Suites

P.O. Box 1003, Watford City, ND 58854; tel: 701-842-3686.

In addition to 42 standard rooms, the inn has eight suites with microwaves and refrigerators; there is also a two-room unit. $–$$

TOURS AND OUTFITTERS

Medora Convenience Store

200 Pacific Avenue, P.O. Box 515, Medora, ND 58645; tel: 701-623-4479.

Paddlers may rent canoes to float the Lower Missouri River. Multiday rentals are available for travelers intending to cover the stretch of river from Medora to the park's North Unit. The outfitter can arrange shuttle services and pickups.

Peaceful Valley Trail Rides

Shadow Country Outfitters, P.O. Box 308, Medora, ND 58645; tel: 701-623-4568 or 218-937-5686 (September–May).

Set on the Little Missouri River just inside the national park, this outfitter takes visitors through the badlands to see the landscape and its wildlife. The guided trail rides range from one to three days.

Excursions

Badlands National Park

P.O. Box 6, Interior, SD 57750-0006; tel: 605-433-5361.

A half-million years of erosion by wind and water have shaped the furrowed cliffs, gnarled spires, and deep, branching ravines of the Badlands. The park also contains the largest protected expanse of mixed-grass prairie in the United States. More than 64,000 acres are within the Sage Creek Wilderness, where backpackers hike cross-country, camp among the wondrous geological formations, and observe a wide range of wildlife including raptors, pronghorn, bison, coyotes, and bighorn sheep.

Black Hills National Forest

RR 2, Box 200, Custer, SD 57730-9501; tel: 606-673-2251.

Most tourists come here to marvel at the four famous visages carved into the granite of Mount Rushmore, but wilderness lovers seek out the area for its interesting ecology and backcountry opportunities. The Black Hills, which rise 4,000 feet above the surrounding prairie, are a crossroads where the Great Plains meet the mountains and where creatures from both habitats roam. Within the 1.2-million-acre national forest are 600 miles of trails open to hikers, horseback riders, and skiers.

Niobrara National Scenic River

P.O. Box 591, O'Neill, NE 68763; tel: 402-336-3970.

Paddling the gently flowing Niobrara River, canoeists drift through a region where boreal forest meets eastern and western woodlands, where ponderosa pines are seen alongside paper birches, giving way to expanses of short and mixed-grass prairie. The river's first nine miles pass through the Fort Niobrara Wildlife Refuge, inhabited by elk, bison, and antelope. The best section to float is the upper third. Paddlers spend the night in campgrounds along the river.

Bob Marshall Wilderness

Montana

At first, so much goes unseen. The narrow trail pushes gently uphill beneath dripping cedars and firs. The early-morning sun catches droplets as they fall. Patches of mist, fleeing skyward, dissipate against the blue. The path is carpeted with delicate plants, some in bloom – a sure sign that few hikers or horses come this way. Tracks report only the passing of occasional elk and deer. Hermit thrushes call from the treetops, their flutelike songs spiraling upward. You walk slowly, lulled by the quiet beauty of the morning. ◆ But then, where the path crosses a small muddy depression, you find something different: a clear, rounded footprint punctuated on its leading edge by five long claws. So that explains the flattened plants you've been seeing in the trail. A grizzly is walking somewhere up ahead, and suddenly you're fully awake. ◆ Thank heaven for grizzlies. And for wolves, mountain lions, wolverines, lynx, eagles, and all the other splendid creatures that prosper only in big, wild places. And thank heaven we have a few places left where a person can slip behind the curtain of modern industrial society and experience the natural world undiminished, unharnessed, and untrammeled. America has wilderness areas of all sizes: some small and gemlike and filled with valuable things that must not be lost, and some big, still thundering with power and mystery, still capable of raising the hair on the backs of our necks, testing our mettle, provoking thoughts of creatures and ideas bigger than ourselves. ◆ Montana's **Bob Marshall Wilderness** is such a place. It's not only big, and loaded with high mountains, deep forests, and strong

The Continental Divide runs like a crooked spine through a rugged mountain stronghold in the northern Rockies.

A hiker scans distant mountains for wildlife, hoping to spot mountain goats, bighorn sheep, or soaring raptors such as golden eagles or peregrine falcons.

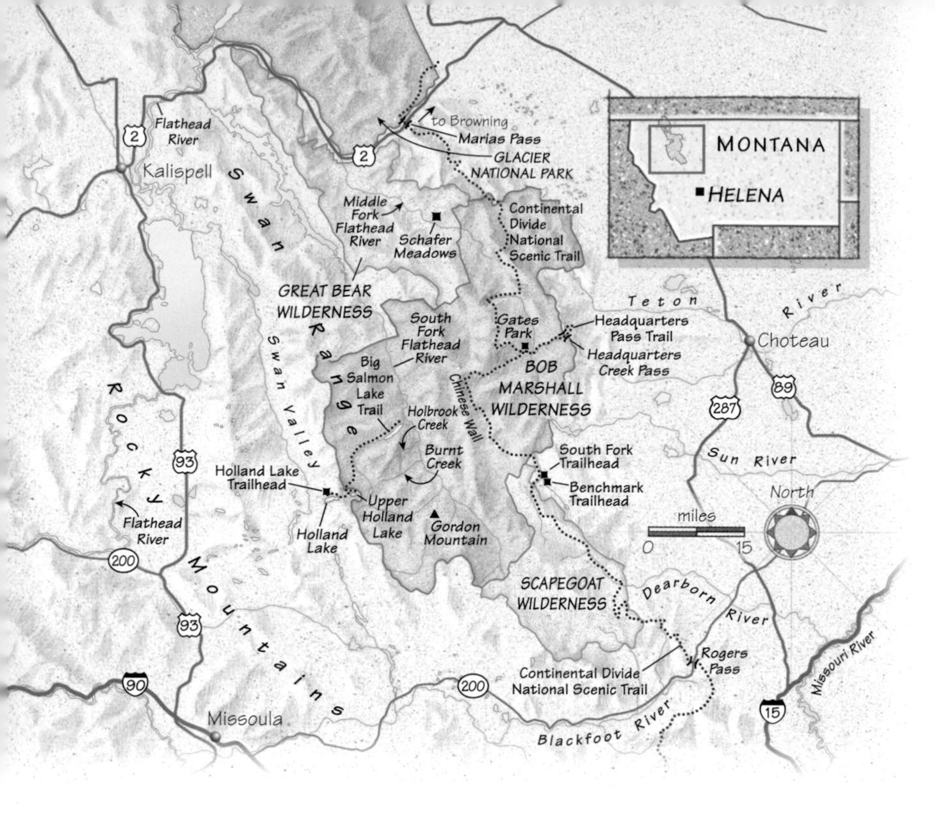

rivers; it is fully alive with the species that conjure up images of wilderness. Anything that walked there 150 years ago still does, including people. Like those before us, we humans still sit beside campfires and marvel at the beauty of the natural world and ponder its reassuring message of continuity. This may be the most important lesson wilderness has to teach us: that the land has been this way for hundreds of years and might survive for many hundreds more if only given the chance.

Together with the adjacent **Great Bear** and **Scapegoat Wilderness Areas**, the

"Bob," as locals fondly refer to the designated wilderness and its surrounding region, takes up more than 1.5 million acres. It is a country of wilderness – practically an independent wilderness nation, surrounded on all sides by forest lands, large tracts of which remain roadless. It's hard country to get a grip on, geographically speaking. On a highway map, the Bob looks simple enough – a rough oval sprawled across the Continental Divide south of Glacier National Park measuring some 65 miles wide and about 100 miles long. But if you look closer, you find no single unifying crest, no overriding structural theme.

Of course, this is a good thing. Size and complexity reinforce each other. The Bob is a tangled, roundabout country that includes not only mountains piled grandly on top of one another but also big, open valleys and gentle, rolling foothills. You can burrow for days through tunnels in the forest or follow high traverses above timberline. Some trails climb steeply for thousands of feet; others mosey peacefully through meadows beside clear streams. None is short. As one gray-bearded outfitter put it when asked about short day-trips, "The only short trail in the Bob is one you turned around and came back on."

Rocky Mountain Geography

Here's an attempt at an overview of Bob Marshall country. Start on U.S. 89 between Choteau and Browning, Montana, and look west. That billowing line of snowy peaks is one section of the **Rocky Mountain Front**. Like a fortress wall thousands of feet high, it runs for hundreds of miles from the rolling prairies of western Montana and far into Canada. Behind it lies an archipelago of wilderness preserves including the world-famous national parks of Jasper, Banff, Waterton, and Glacier.

Trails in the Bob cross the Continental Divide (opposite), making for rigorous and challenging hiking.

A backcountry trekker (left) cools off in an ice-cold mountain stream.

The Chinese Wall (below), an ancient limestone reef embedded with fossils, rises above a meadow filled with bear grass blossoms.

The Bob is part of the same geography, in many ways equally spectacular but less traveled. Roughly speaking, it consists of three parallel mountain ranges and the valleys that lie between them.

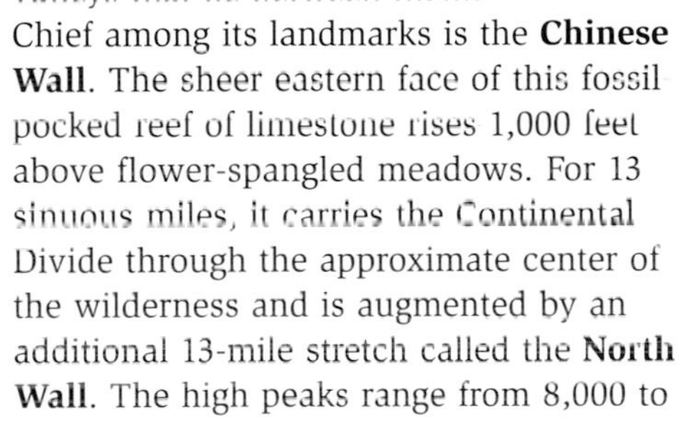

Chief among its landmarks is the **Chinese Wall**. The sheer eastern face of this fossil pocked reef of limestone rises 1,000 feet above flower-spangled meadows. For 13 sinuous miles, it carries the Continental Divide through the approximate center of the wilderness and is augmented by an additional 13-mile stretch called the **North Wall**. The high peaks range from 8,000 to 9,400 feet in elevation, while major interior valleys lie between 3,500 to 4,500 feet.

Although the land is rugged, it has breathing space. Valleys tend to be broad with big trees and open meadows. Distances are long, ideal for travel by horseback. Of the interior valleys, the longest one is drained by the South Fork of the Flathead River. Another spills into the Middle Fork of

the Flathead. Both those rivers flow northwest toward Kalispell; both are designated wild and scenic. Other drainages include the Blackfoot, Teton, Sun, and Dearborn Rivers. All achieve substantial size before leaving the wilderness.

The mountains of the Bob, especially the Rocky Mountain Front, are generally steeper on the east than the west. They seem to be surging toward the plains, like waves about to break against a flat sand beach. In fact, the analogy is not too far off. These ranges are part of the Overthrust Belt that stretches from Alaska to Mexico. The Bob's parallel mountain ranges took up their positions between 55 and 70 million years ago, when vast slabs of sedimentary rock plowed tens of miles eastward before finally grinding to a halt.

In general, Bob Marshall country is well watered. Most moisture comes in the winter, with an annual average snowfall of 300 to 500 inches, depending on elevation and aspect. The east is the drier side, nestled in the rain shadow of the Continental Divide. It's also the colder side in winter; the lowest official temperature ever recorded in the Lower 48 states, -70°F, was at Rogers Pass in 1954. It might have been colder; the thermometer in question could go no lower.

All the celebrity Rocky Mountain species are found here. Grizzlies dig up meadows and pulverize logs in search of rodents and other small edibles. Black bears keep more to the deep forest. Fishers and pine martens, along with lynx, make life difficult for red squirrels. Mountain lions prefer rugged terrain, where they hunt deer, both mule and white-tailed. After years of persecution, gray wolves are gradually reestablishing themselves. Elk number around 10,000. Moose are less common, but they find good habitat in the moist forests of the western slope. Bighorn sheep and mountain goats stake out the high country. Peregrine falcons haunt the cliffs, along with golden eagles and other birds of prey. Great gray owls drift like ghosts along meadow edges at dusk. Bald eagles and osprey stay near water and sometimes tussle over the same fish.

The big-name animals set a high tone, but the smaller and less rare creatures weave themselves into the fabric of one's experience. In spring, the flute tones of hermit thrushes mingle with the clear, operatic whistles of ruby-crowned kinglets and the sweet, persistent calls of chickadees. A blend of conifers – larch, fir, spruce, lodgepole – perfumes the air. Pikas call among the boulder fields of the alpine zone. Marmots lend their comic pomposity to meadows at all elevations. Trout take mayflies from shadowed streams, and mosquitoes make life a torment for a few weeks every summer.

Plan of Attack

As in all northern mountains, summer is brief here. The hiking season begins in May to a very limited degree, because passes

Horses (opposite, top) are an excellent way to travel in the Bob. Pack trains allow visitors to make extended trips into the high country.

Male elk (opposite, bottom) call to potential mates with an eerie, high-pitched "bugle."

Bob Marshall (below) advocated the establishment of federal wilderness areas.

Wilderness Advocate

Bob Marshall maintained that a proper wilderness area should be big enough for a person to walk two weeks without retracing or crossing his or her path. He'd be happy with the size of the wilderness that carries his name.

Born to a prosperous eastern family in 1901, he studied forestry and then, in 1925, came west to join the U.S. Forest Service in Missoula, Montana. It was a time when few foresters thought seriously about preservation. They were interested mostly in cutting timber and maximizing the harvest.

Marshall represented a new way of thinking, one that valued trees and other resources for more than their commercial worth. He recognized wilderness as a spiritual entity that could have a powerful impact on people but that was easily damaged and therefore required strict protection.

Having begun as a forest scientist, he eventually became the first recreation chief of the Forest Service and a founder of the Wilderness Society. A tireless advocate for the preservation of wild land, he wrote that for those who love wild country, "the enjoyment of solitude, complete independence, and the beauty of undefiled panoramas is absolutely essential to happiness."

By all accounts, Marshall enjoyed life and lived it fully. Hefting a canvas pack and wearing sneakers, he commonly logged 30 to 40 miles a day, sometimes more. Nothing pleased him more than walking a trail through wild country.

Although he died in 1939 at the young age of 38, apparently from a heart attack, he covered enough miles and accomplished enough of his passionately held goals to fill several lifetimes. The wilderness that bears his name was designated one year after he died. It looks much the same as it did when he traveled its valleys and peaks, which is exactly what he would have wanted. For Marshall, the best monument would be a footpath threading deep into the mountains that gave him such joy.

generally remain blocked by snow until early or mid-July. Experienced climbers might get over the snowdrifts with crampons and an ice ax, but those tools aren't much use when it comes to streams flooded with icy water. In this respect, the Bob is a true wilderness; bridges are rare, and streams in spring runoff are as big as rivers and can be impassable. Summer thunderstorms can raise water levels high enough to stop hikers, and snow can fall at any time of the year. Backpackers are advised to carry a few extra days' worth of food in case of detours or delays.

The only way into the wilderness is by foot or horseback. Roads come close, but even they stop well short of the boundary. There are numerous trailheads around the perimeter, some heavily used and some virtually ignored. They all connect to a tangled web of trails that, when you first look at them on a map, can be mighty confusing. It seems as though half a dozen routes lead to every destination, and deciding on the wrong one can yield serious consequences. Trails with low maintenance priority become choked with vegetation. Others turn into mud bogs under the pressure of heavy stock use.

That said, it makes sense to begin your exploration with major trails and branch off from them. Whatever a man on horseback might say, there are plenty of short hikes. Some of the trailheads – notably **Holland Lake** on the west and **South Fork Teton** on the east – are located within several miles of high passes where a day hiker can get a taste of the country and a view of the interior. In some cases, alpine lakes set in high glaciated cirques can be reached in a few hours.

Backpackers' Delight

Yet, in a place this big, thoughts naturally turn to longer trips that traverse the entire complex. Among the foremost options is the **Continental Divide National Scenic Trail**, which wends its way for 155 miles from north to south, beginning at **Marias Pass** (where it comes out of Glacier National Park) and ending at **Rogers Pass** on Highway 200. The trail sticks close to the divide but follows the actual crest only in a few dramatic sections, including several miles along the base of the Chinese Wall. It stays in wilderness or roadless country almost the entire distance, touching at several trailheads along the way. You can backpack sections of it or tie parts of it into other itineraries.

Another splendid option combines a backpacking excursion from the southern end of the wilderness, starting on the Continental Divide National Scenic Trail or one of its variants, with a whitewater float on the **Middle Fork of the Flathead**. The wild and scenic Middle Fork is a popular whitewater run and, because it begins in wilderness, has no road access. Rafters generally fly their gear to a back-country airstrip and launch site at Schafer Meadows. You can set up a rendezvous with an outfitter and spend the last few days of a long trip with your feet in cool water.

The east-west traverse is shorter. One classic route runs between Holland Lake in the **Swan Valley** and **Headquarters Creek Pass** on the east slope. Beginning at the lake, the trail starts out hard, climbing steeply for nearly 4,000 feet to the crest of the **Swan Range** before setting off on a long, mostly wooded trek to the **South Fork of the Flathead**. From there, it's up and over the Chinese Wall and down the other side to the Sun River drainage. At Gates Park, the **Headquarters Creek Pass Trail** takes off northeast, crests the pass just north of Rocky Mountain, and skids 2,000 feet down to the eastern trailhead. Another popular option uses **Benchmark Trailhead** as the eastern terminus.

The whole trip is about 80 miles, depending on which of the many possible variations you follow. The direct route goes via Upper Holland Lake, where it picks up the **Big Salmon Lake Trail** to the South Fork. But the lower end of that trail can be a boggy mess in wet weather when horses have been through it, and the scenery for much of the way is limited by trees. Some hikers choose less-traveled routes along Holbrook or Burnt Creeks, or the strenuous but glorious ridgetop trek over Gordon Mountain.

Such choices are typical of the Bob, where every trail leads to another. That's precisely what Bob Marshall, the wilderness's namesake, had in mind.

Muddy trails (left) often slow down hikers after the spring thaw.

Bobcats (opposite) give birth in spring. The kittens are usually fed small, live rodents after two months and are hunting on their own by fall.

Rafters muscle their way through the rapids of the Middle Fork of the Flathead River (below).

TRAVEL TIPS

DETAILS

How to Get There

Three Montana airports are within easy reach of the Bob Marshall Wilderness complex: Kalispell, to the northwest; Missoula, to the west; Helena, to the south; and Great Falls, to the east. Rental cars are available at all airports.

When to Go

Late July through early September is the time of peak visitation. Although some trails open in May, passes can remain covered in snow until early to mid-July. Weather varies, depending on elevation; temperatures can drop below freezing at any time. Summer temperatures generally range from the low 40s to the low 80s. Beginning in mid-July, late-afternoon thunderstorms are a daily occurrence. Fall lows are usually below freezing; highs are in the mid-60s. Snow can fall at any time.

What to Do

Backpackers may hike thousands of miles of trails in the three wilderness areas of the Bob Marshall complex – Bob Marshall, Scapegoat, and Great Bear – or travel on most trails by horseback, either self-guided or on pack trips. Fishing is permitted on the numerous lakes and streams. Experienced backcountry travelers cross-country ski and snowshoe in the Bob from late fall through spring.

Backcountry Permits

Visitors do not need permits to hike and camp in the wilderness but should check on regulations governing size of groups, length of stay, and trail and campsite closures.

Special Planning

The Bob is a vast area where travelers without guides should have confidence in their back-country skills, including navigation and first aid. They are also advised to be prepared for sudden changes in weather by carrying high-quality raingear and warm clothing. Portable gas stoves must be used in areas where fires are not allowed or when fire danger is high. To reduce encounters with bears, food and garbage should be suspended from a tree at least 10 feet off the ground and four feet away from the trunk, or stored in a bear-resistant container. Hikers visiting during spring runoff should check trail conditions; because stream crossings may be dangerous from mid-May to early July, trips may need to be planned around the location of bridges.

Car Camping

Numerous campgrounds are in the national forests outside the wilderness areas; call the ranger districts below for detailed information.

INFORMATION

The Bob Marshall Wilderness Complex consists of three wilderness areas that overlap several national forests. The Bob Marshall Wilderness is administered by Flathead and Lewis and Clark National Forests; the Great Bear Wilderness is administered by Flathead National Forest; the Scapegoat Wilderness is administered by Helena, Lolo, and Lewis and Clark National Forests.

Flathead National Forest

Hungry Horse Ranger District, P.O. Box 190340, Hungry Horse, MT 59919; tel: 406-387-3800.

Flathead National Forest

Spotted Bear Ranger District, P.O. Box 190310, Hungry Horse, MT 59919; tel: 406-758-5376 (summer) or 406-387-3800 (winter).

Helena National Forest

Lincoln Ranger District, P.O. Box 219, Lincoln, MT 59639; tel: 406-362-4265.

Lewis and Clark National Forest

Rocky Mountain Ranger District, P.O. Box 340, Choteau, MT 59422; tel: 406-466-5341.

Lolo National Forest

Seeley Lake Ranger District, HC 31, Box 3200, Seeley Lake, MT 59868; tel: 406-677-2233.

LODGING

PRICE GUIDE – double occupancy

$ = up to $49 | $$ = $50–$99
$$$ = $100–$149 | $$$$ = $150+

Big Sky Motel

209 South Main Avenue, Choteau, MT 59422; tel: 406-466-5318.

This motel has nine rooms with small refrigerators and microwaves. There are also two rooms with kitchenettes, and two suites with kitchens. $$

Glacier Raft Company

P.O. Box 210C, West Glacier, MT 59936; tel: 800-235-6781 or 406-888-5454.

Three cabins located a half mile from the entrance to Glacier National Park accommodate six to 14 guests. Each has separate sleeping and living areas, and a fully equipped kitchen. $$$–$$$$

Tamaracks Resort

P.O. Box 812, Seeley Lake, MT 59868; tel: 406-677-2433.

The resort's 13 cabins overlook Lake Seeley and are surrounded by the Lolo National Forest. Some are one-room cabins. Others have multiple bedrooms; the largest sleeps 10. All have kitchen facilities. $$–$$$$

TOURS AND OUTFITTERS

Glacier Raft Company

P.O. Box 210D, West Glacier, MT 59936; tel: 800-235-6781 or 406-888-5454.

The Middle Fork of the Flathead River is the destination of multi-day trips that combine camping, rafting, fishing, and wildlife watching in the Great Bear Wilderness. Visitors are flown to a remote airstrip or ride horses into the backcountry.

Montana Safaris

21 Airport Road, Choteau, MT 59422; tel: 406-466-2004.

Horse and mule trips head for the alpine lakes of the Bob in summer. From base camp, travelers spend their time fishing, hiking, and watching wildlife.

Novak Llama Company

P.O. Box 182, Seeley Lake, MT 59868; tel: 406-677-2113.

Visitors bring their own gear, and llamas carry it into the Bob on two- to four-day trips offered from July 1 through mid-September. Novak Llama provides guides and food. Hikers can also rent llamas and follow their own itinerary.

Rich Ranch/Double Arrow Outfitters

P.O. Box 495, Seeley Lake, MT 59868; tel: 406-677-2317.

From June to early September, visitors join "roving" pack trips into the Bob Marshall Wilderness. Parties move every other day and establish a base camp for exploring the area on day hikes or fishing alpine lakes and streams.

Scapegoat Wilderness Outfitters

P.O. Box 824, Fort Benton, MT 59442; tel: 800-242-4868 or 406-622-3210.

Pack trips on horseback go into the Scapegoat Wilderness and along the Continental Divide. Itineraries and length of trips are customized to suit a traveler's interests, be it hiking, camping, fishing, or photography. All meals and outdoor gear are provided.

Excursions

Bridger Wilderness

Bridger–Teton National Forest, P.O. Box 220, Pinedale, WY 82941; tel: 307-367-4326.

The heart of this roadless wilderness on the western side of the Continental Divide can be reached only on foot and by horseback via a 600-mile network of trails. Backcountry travelers discover a landscape shaped by glaciers – in fact, seven of the 10 largest glaciers in the Lower 48 states are found here in the Wind River Range. Forty-eight of the range's summits are higher than 12,500 feet, including Gannett Peak, Wyoming's highest point. Scattered throughout the wilderness are some 1,300 lakes.

Frank Church–River of No Return Wilderness

Bureau of Land Management, 1808 North Third Street, Coeur d'Alene, ID 83814; tel: 208-769-5000.

A backcountry traveler would need a lifetime to explore fully this 2.3-million-acre wilderness area in central Idaho, one of the largest in the Lower 48. Countless mountains and expanses of coniferous forests – as well as lakes and streams filled with trout – beckon backpackers traveling on their own or on pack trips. Paddlers enjoy whitewater thrills on the wild and scenic Salmon River and its Middle Fork, which rush through sheer-walled canyons.

Yellowstone National Park

P.O. Box 168, Yellowstone National Park, WY 82190; tel: 307-344-7381.

Yellowstone's natural attractions are legendary: bison, grizzly bears, wolves, and other megafauna; geysers and other geothermal wonders; lakes and streams known for their world-class trout fishing. This popular park has 2.2 million acres and 1,000 miles of trails that enable backpackers to enjoy these wonders and find solitude. Yellowstone's creatures and geysers are also active in winter, when visitors can travel on cross-country skis and snowshoes.

Grand Staircase–Escalante National Monument

Utah

CHAPTER 15

"Yup! You Gotta Get Wet." The sign on the north bank of the **Escalante River** elicits big grins. Get wet? No problem. On any desert pilgrimage to southern Utah's famed **Escalante Canyons**, a river baptism is the price of admission to heaven. There'll be additional toll-takers later on: deep sand to slog through, bushwhacking through willow thickets along waterways, rock scrambling, squeezing through water-carved narrows, friction-walking over slickrock, heart-pounding climbs to rim country. ◆ No one here would want it any other way. **Grand Staircase–Escalante National Monument** in Utah, as its guardians, the Bureau of Land Management, will readily tell you, is and always will be remote, wild country. In other words, it's just the place to have an adventure. ◆ This was one of the last regions in the Lower 48 to be mapped, when members of John Wesley Powell's second expedition to the West traveled overland from Kanab to survey the area. They named the Escalante River after the 1776 Spanish Dominguez-Escalante expedition, although Father Silvestre Velez de Escalante never saw the river. Even today, despite a sprinkling of Mormon ranching and farming communities on the periphery, the area remains essentially pristine, joined by the national parks of Capitol Reef on the northeast, Glen Canyon on the southeast, and Bryce Canyon on the west. ◆ The scientific implications of such a vast, intact ecosystem have become increasingly clear in recent decades. In September 1996, Grand Staircase–Escalante National Monument was set aside to protect the area's natural and cultural resources from development.

Follow a river corridor through spellbinding red-rock canyons rich with desert life and adorned with ancient pictographs.

The undulating walls of aptly named Zebra Canyon were sculpted over thousands of years by water cutting through beds of Navajo sandstone.

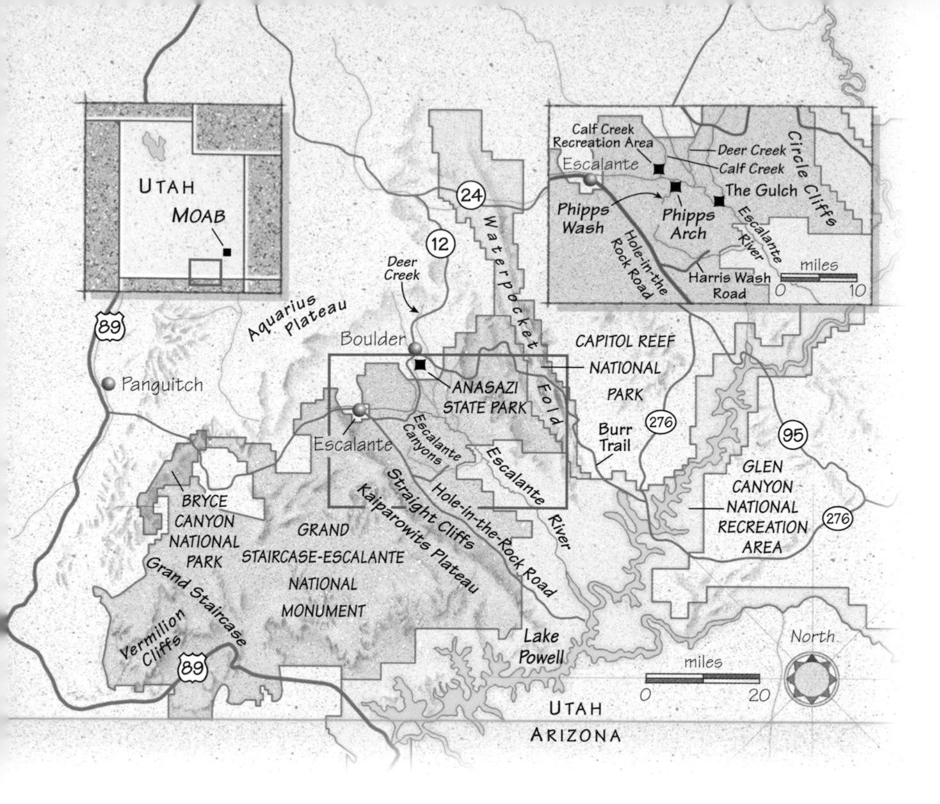

At 1.9 million acres, this is the largest national monument in the contiguous United States. Within its boundaries is an almost intact fossil record in beautifully exposed, relatively undeformed geological formations; flora and fauna adapted to cool and warm deserts, five life zones, and numerous microenvironments; and thousands of pristine archaeological sites.

You'll barely have to leave one of the monument's graded roads to find yourself surrounded by the most rugged terrain imaginable. There's only one designated short trail; all other "trails" are unmarked routes through desert canyons along rivers, streams, and washes. A compass, topographical map, and route-finding ability are essential. Spring and fall offer cooler hiking temperatures, blessedly free of biting flies, mosquitoes, and no-see-ums. Too much or too little water is the norm here, and what there is, is notoriously unreliable or contaminated by chemicals. To be safe, plan on carrying a gallon of water per person per day. On the other hand, watch out for flash flooding year-round, especially in summer when daily thunderstorms send surges through the narrow canyons.

Stop at one of the monument's ranger stations to pick up permits, plan your route, and ask about current conditions. And be sure to let someone know where you're going. It may seem romantic to head alone into the wildest place in America and take your chances, like young adventurer Everett Ruess, who disappeared here in the 1930s. But you really want to live to tell your tales of derring-do, don't you?

The skeleton of a juniper tree (right) is a ghostly presence in Long Canyon on the Burr Trail.

Walking along the Escalante River (opposite, top) is an easy and safe way for hikers to travel deep into Canyon Country.

An abandoned movie set (opposite, bottom) was built at the site of a real ghost town, originally settled by Mormons in 1873.

Red-Rock Maze

For a first multiday trip into Grand Staircase-Escalante, consider hiring a local outfitter to introduce you to the area and help pack your gear. You can go the traditional route with horses, but a more unusual option is to use llamas, which need far less water than horses and can carry up to 120 pounds of gear. With their cushiony, two-toed feet, they have about as much impact on fragile desert soils as deer and are possessed of remarkably docile temperaments. Bucktoothed and haughty in profile, they like to hum as they work – just a little sighing tune below the breath that lets you know they're thinking of herd and home. It's not quite *Lawrence of Arabia*, but the whimsy quotient matches practicality well enough to ensure a lot of fun.

Of the three different sections of the monument – **Grand Staircase**, **Kaiparowits Plateau**, and **Escalante Canyons** – the last offers the most delightful backpacking experience. The **Escalante Basin** begins east of **Escalante**, between the 1,100-foot Straight Cliffs of the remote Kaiparowits Plateau and the great dropoff of the Waterpocket Fold. On either side of Highway 12, the torqued and twisted knobs and buttes of Navajo sandstone rimrock roiling to the horizon are almost enough to bring on seasickness.

Near its Calf Creek confluence, the **Escalante River** appears in a blaze of preternaturally green vegetation at the feet of ruddy sandstone. It's about 10 feet wide and usually only knee-deep, but don't laugh – this qualifies as a river in Canyon Country. Its headwaters are on the 11,000-foot Aquarius Plateau, from whence the Escalante drops 6,000 feet toward its conjunction with Lake Powell. If the water gods had their way, this would be a straight shot, but Mother Earth has shrugged her shoulders at such plans and wrinkled the area in a series of uplifts, or monoclines, that have forced the river and its tributaries to cut deep, labyrinthine canyon courses. It's the maze to end all mazes.

If you stick close to the Escalante River,

Horse packers (left) water their mounts at a natural sandstone basin.

Penstemon and claret cup cactus (below) grow side by side along the Escalante River.

A hiker squeezes through narrow Peekaboo Gulch (opposite).

you won't have to sprinkle bread crumbs to find your way back. Cattle have pounded out a trail along the riverbank that's easy to follow. You'll ford the silty river numerous times, so wear good river sandals or light boots and bring spare footwear, dry socks, and cover-ups. A number of side canyons lead into and out of the canyons. On the north side, **Deer Creek** and **The Gulch** are popular access points. They join the **Burr Trail**, an old rancher's road that starts in **Boulder** and crosses the Circle Cliffs and Waterpocket Fold in Capitol Reef. On the south side, **Harris Wash** is a popular route in from the 60-mile **Hole in the Rock Road**, which was blasted by Mormon pioneers in the winter of 1879 on their epic mission to colonize southeastern Utah.

River's Path

An easy, 14.9-mile overnight trip can be made along the **Escalante River** between the town of **Escalante** and **Calf Creek** for great views of an arch, a natural bridge, and Indian granaries and rock art. Continue downcanyon for longer trips – a trip of four or five days will allow you to reach the Glen Canyon National Recreation Area boundary, explore side canyons, then head out.

Water and other erosional forces have sculpted sandstone into myriad cliffs, alcoves, arches, bridges, slots, and hoodoos. Cross-bedded Navajo sandstone, the remnant of a vast, ancient sand-dune desert, reaches precipitously to the rim and catches fire at sunrise and sunset. Beneath the rosy Navajo, the maroon Kayenta siltstone erodes into ledges, forcing the canyon to step back in terraces and benches. Even more dramatic than the Navajo (if that's possible) is the fiery orange Wingate sandstone, which appears deeper in the canyon and reaches its most stunning expression in the fractured **Circle Cliffs** to the northeast. Lengthening shadows bring out the tapestry effect on sandstone. Pouroffs have washed out manganese and iron in the rock, creating desert varnish fixed to cliff faces by bacteria.

The eye is constantly drawn up to the cliffs, then back down to the feet, where your passage may send a dozing lizard scurrying from the undergrowth or crickets jumping. Watch out for cryptobiotic crusts in sandy areas. These dark, castlelike biological soil crusts are made up of strands of cyanobacteria, lichen, and algae that hold moisture and nitrogen in the soil and prevent erosion. This is where life begins in the desert, but it's easily destroyed by careless feet. To avoid "crypto," walk in washes or on slickrock. Where walking on it is unavoidable, travel single file to minimize impact.

The bank of the Escalante River is a grabby tangle of exotic tamarisk, willow, box elder, and thorny Russian olive. Scouring rushes and horsetails poke up from the shallows. Growing along the trail are woody Great Basin Desert big sagebrush, rabbitbrush, greasewood, and four-wing saltbush interspersed with orange-red globemallow, vermilion Indian paintbrush, scarlet gilia, skyrocket, and purple-headed woolly vetch. On higher ledges, dwarf pinyon and juniper, gambel oak, old man sage, and roundleaf buffaloberry find purchase in soil pockets.

Over the joyous burbling of the river, listen for the descant serenade of the canyon wren accompanied by the fluting notes of robins. Egrets and herons visit at times, along with dainty water ouzels that dip for insects in the shallows. Graceful white-throated swifts swoop down from cliff nests to the river in long, acrobatic swallow dives. The cliffs are also home to more than 20 raptor species, which use tree snags and ledges as staging areas for skyline sorties. Perhaps you'll be lucky enough to see a golden eagle soaring into the early morning sun and follow its shadow twin on a cliff face as it spirals. Big though they are, these majestic birds are no match for peregine falcons (which, along with condors released along the Vermilion Cliffs, are the great comeback story here). It's not unknown for lightning-fast peregrines to attack and kill slower eagles. More than three-quarters of the monument's plants and animals use riparian corridors like this one.

In side canyons, giant Fremont cottonwoods wrap rubbery limbs around boulders like gymnasts and stretch toe roots into warm pools skittering with water striders and polliwogs. When you least expect it, you'll happen upon miniature Hanging Gardens of Babylon of moss, ferns, and eye-dazzling columbines, monkeyflowers, and shooting stars crowding around dripping springs in the canyon walls. The water percolates

down through porous Navajo sandstone and exits as springlines above the impervious Kayenta siltstone. The constant dripping undermines the overlying sandstone cliffs, which crack along joints, then peel away like an onion, leaving behind huge alcoves that will one day become arches. Various creatures find refuge here: rarely seen bighorn sheep, timid mountain lions scanning for deer, coyotes sniffing around for cottontails and jackrabbits, and rodents like the desert-adapted kangaroo rat, which recycles all its water from seeds.

About two miles downcanyon from the Highway 12 bridge, a side canyon to the south follows **Phipps Wash**. Head east in a box canyon to view 40-foot-high **Phipps Arch**, a magnificent natural span. You'll need to scramble up several hundred feet of crumbly ledges and slickrock to reach the arch, but it's worth the effort. This is a great place for a picnic or for heart-to-hearts with the turkey vultures and red-tailed hawks that waft past on thermals at eye level.

Vanishing Treasures

Some of the most memorable sights in the canyons are the dwellings, granaries, stone-working sites, and rock art panels left

Rafters (above) float the Escalante River when water levels are high enough.

Dawn illuminates the sheer face of the Vermilion Cliffs (below) in Arizona.

A gnarled juniper (opposite, top) frames a view of Calf Creek Canyon.

Fremont pictographs (opposite, bottom) of animals and humanlike figures are found in remote canyons throughout the monument.

Plateau Panorama

It's a name that often baffles visitors who arrive in the western section of Grand Staircase–Escalante National Monument prepared to puff their way up a large set of man-made stairs. You do need to be a giant to negotiate these steps, because the **Grand Staircase** is actually a series of progressively higher and younger Technicolor plateaus – dubbed the Vermilion, White, Gray, and Pink Cliffs – that were uplifted along faults some 15 million years ago. Spanning elevations of 5,500 to 9,000 feet and 200 million years of Earth's history, the Grand Staircase supports five life zones, from desert scrub to coniferous forest, making this one of the monument's most diverse areas.

For a closer look, drive east from **Kanab** along Highway 89, then turn north on Johnson Canyon Road through sagebrush range. Surrounding you is the brilliant red Moenkopi sandstone of the **Vermilion Cliffs** underlaid by the fossil-rich Chinle Formation. Marching northward are the creamy-pink Navajo sandstone of the **White Cliffs**, the paler marine-formed Carmel Formation of the **Gray Cliffs**, and finally the towering orange-red lakebed sediments of Claron Formation that make up the **Pink Cliffs**.

To the east is the **Cockscomb**, a huge, jagged monocline that separates the Grand Staircase from the remote, rarely traveled **Kaiparowits Plateau**. The Cockscomb, accessed via Cottonwood Canyon Road, does indeed look like the red comb of a rooster. **Cottonwood Slot**, a narrows carved by Cottonwood Wash, makes an interesting day hike, about 25 miles north of Highway 89. For a longer trip into canyon narrows, head for the area's main drainage, the **Paria River**. The Paria's southern section is heavily traveled, but you can find some solitude in its upper reaches.

behind by the Fremont and Kayenta Anasazi peoples who lived here between the first century A.D. and 1300. The two cultures mingled to such a degree that archaeologists jokingly dub them the Frem-Azi.

The Fremont dug snug pithouses with warm southern exposures on deer and elk migration routes, gathered plants seasonally, raised corn, and appear to have subsisted on water from *tinajas*, or potholes. The Kayenta Anasazi were pueblo builders who erected the large Coombs Site now preserved in **Anasazi State Park** in nearby **Boulder**. It's estimated that 19,000 to 100,000 archaeological sites lie on the monument, many protected by inaccessibility.

Pecked and painted rock art panels display strong Fremont characteristics – wide-shouldered anthropomorphs with round shields, headdresses, and ear bobs, accompanied by bighorn sheep, animal tracks, handprints, joined-hand figures, and concentric circles. It's hard not to admire the resourcefulness and artistry of such a people and to wonder about the threads of human connection that link us to them. But not everyone here has been so reverent, as is heartbreakingly obvious when you come upon sites desecrated by thoughtless vandalism. With every hand that touches, chips away at, or defaces a panel, we see our connection to the past slip away and are a little the lesser for it.

A greater sense of connection is what visiting wilderness is all about. "Music has been in my heart all the time, and poetry in my thoughts," wrote Everett Ruess of his experiences in the Escalante Canyons before he disappeared in 1934. "Alone on the open desert, I have made up songs of wild, poignant rejoicing and transcendent melancholy. The world has seemed more beautiful to me than ever before .... I have rejoiced to set out, to be going somewhere, and I have felt a still sublimity .... I have really lived." Lying under a star-studded sky in an alcove with just the breath of a wind wafting through the canyons, you know exactly what he meant.

TRAVEL TIPS

DETAILS

How to Get There

Major airlines serve airports in Salt Lake City, five hours north of the town of Escalante, Utah; Grand Junction, Colorado, five hours east of Escalante; and Las Vegas, Nevada, six hours to the southwest. Rental cars are available at all airports.

When to Go

The most popular times for backcountry travel are April to May and September to October. The monument receives the fewest visitors in winter. Daytime spring temperatures are in the 70s and 80s; temperatures at night can drop to freezing. Winter storms can occur in spring. Summer days are in the mid- and upper 90s. Thunderstorms are daily occurrences from July to September, and rainfall brings cool nights in the 60s. Rain tapers off by mid-September. Winter brings snow and subzero weather.

What to Do

Backpackers hike on their own or join guided pack trips. Mountain biking is allowed on designated trails and backroads; routes range from short, easy trips to longer routes allowing for overnight stays at campsites. Visitors can also fish the monument's streams. Though winter weather is unpredictable and may make roads impassable, visitors can arrange to take guided hiking, camping, and four-wheel-drive trips.

Backcountry Permits

Permits are required for overnight stays in the monument; call 435-644-4300 for details.

Special Planning

Backcountry travelers are advised to plan their trips in consultation with monument staff. Because most hiking in Grand Staircase–Escalante is on unmarked routes, visitors must have confidence in their backcountry skills, including navigation and first aid. They need to carry a minimum of one gallon of water per person per day, as well as portable gas stoves for cooking. Narrow canyons, prone to flash flooding, should be avoided if a storm is approaching, and camp should always be made on high ground. Roads are often impassable in wet weather; conditions should be checked with monument headquarters.

Car Camping

The monument has two developed campgrounds and a number of primitive campsites. Other campgrounds are located in national forests to the north and south.

INFORMATION

Grand Staircase–Escalante National Monument

180 West 300 North, Kanab, UT 84741; tel: 435-644-4300.

Anasazi State Park

P.O. Box 1429, Boulder, UT 84716; tel: 435-335-7382.

Dixie Interpretive Association

755 West Main, P.O. Box 246, Escalante, UT 84726; tel: 435-826-5499.

The association maintains eight outlets, including one in Escalante, where visitors may obtain books (see Resource Directory) and maps related to the monument.

Escalante Interagency Visitor Center

755 West Main, P.O. Box 246, Escalante, UT 84726; tel: 435-826-5499.

Kanab Field Office

318 North First East, Kanab, UT 84741; tel: 435-644-2672.

LODGING

PRICE GUIDE – double occupancy

$ = up to $49 $$ = $50–$99

$$$ = $100–$149 $$$$ = $150+

Boulder Mountain Lodge

P.O. Box 1397, Boulder, UT 84716; tel: 801-335-7460.

Eleven of the lodge's 15 acres are a waterfowl sanctuary. Three main buildings hold 20 rooms, and those on the top floors have balconies and views. Two rooms have kitchenettes, and a restaurant is on the premises. $$–$$$

Capital Reef Inn

360 West Main Street, Torrey, UT 84775; tel: 435-425-3271.

The inn has 10 rooms with small refrigerators. A restaurant is on the premises. $

Escalante Outfitters

310 West Main, P.O. Box 570, Escalante, UT 84726; tel: 435-826-4266.

Seven cabins each accommodate two people; guests share bath facilities. Escalante Outfitters carries topo maps, guidebooks, backpacking food, and other camping supplies. $

TOURS AND OUTFITTERS

Boulder Outdoor Survival School

P.O. Box 1590, Boulder, CO 80306; tel: 303-444-9779.

BOSS courses teach participants about the tools and skills they need to survive in the wilderness. Programs in southern Utah, running from late May until early September, include one-, two-, and four-week sessions in the field.

Escalante Canyon Outfitters

P.O. Box 1330, 842 West Highway 12, Boulder, UT 84716; tel: 435-335-7311 or 888-326-4453.

Guided horse-pack trips focus on the region's plants, animals, geology, and native history.

Treks ranging from four to six days go into the Escalante River Canyon, Navajo Gorges, and other canyons.

Hondoo Rivers and Trails

P.O. Box 98, Torrey, UT 84775; tel: 435-425-3519.

Backcountry travelers ride horses on five-day camping trips into the Escalante River Canyon and elsewhere to experience the area's geology, history, and rock art. Overnight stays in lodges, shorter trips, and four-wheel-drive explorations may also be arranged.

J. F. Parker Flyfishing

P.O. Box 245, Orderville, UT 84758; tel: 435-648-2868.

Anglers of all ability levels are taken to the monument's small streams to fish for rainbow, brown, and brook trout, plus native cutthroats.

Red Rock 'N' Llamas

P.O. Box 1304, Boulder, UT 84716; tel: 435-335-7325.

Guides knowledgeable about geology, archaeology, and natural history show visitors the Escalante River Canyon and other areas of the monument. All equipment and food are provided; llamas carry everything.

Tag-A-Long Expeditions

452 North Main Street, Moab, UT 84532; tel: 800-453-3292.

Four wheel drive vehicles transport passengers into the Escalante and Maze areas of the monument. After a night of camping, travelers strike out on long day hikes.

Western Spirit Cycling

478 Mill Creek Drive, Moab, UT 84532; tel: 435-259-8732.

Guided mountain-biking trips follow the Burr Trail to Capitol Reef National Park and through the Abajo Mountains. Western Spirit designs customized itineraries, obtains permits for visitors, and provides naturalists and archaeologists as guides.

Excursions

High Uintas Wilderness

Wasatch–Cache National Forest, 8236 Federal Building, 1255 South State Street, Salt Lake City, UT 84138; tel: 801-524-3900.

At 460,000 acres, this is the largest wilderness in Utah. Among its other distinguishing features, it includes the highest peak in the state – 13,528-foot Kings Peak – which is part of the Uintas Mountains, the most prominent east-west range in the contiguous states. Hiking the high elevation terrain can be challenging. Lower trails lead backcountry users on foot and horseback to alpine lakes and meadows, and through glacier scoured canyons and forests of spruce, fir, and pine.

Jarbridge Wilderness

Humboldt National Forest, 2035 Last Chance Road, Elko, NV 89801; tel: 702-738-5171.

Tucked into the remote northeast corner of Nevada, this 113,000-acre wilderness spreads across a seven-mile mountain crest with eight peaks over 10,000 feet tall. The area is known for its pristine air, and from high elevations, hikers have clear views of the canyons and sagebrush flats below. Backcountry travelers have access to 150 miles of trails, including routes that take them to two alpine lakes, Jarbridge and Emerald.

Zion National Park

Springdale, UT 84767; tel: 801-772-3256.

There are enough natural splendors in this park to satisfy every backcountry hiker's interests. The range of habitats, including hanging gardens, forested canyons, and imposing mesas, supports 800 native plant species, the richest diversity in Utah. Wildlife in the park – including 75 mammals and 271 birds – is equally abundant. Trails also allow visitors to investigate geological wonders from colorfully sedimented canyons to sandstone formations sculpted by the elements over thousands of years. Spring is the time to see wildflowers in bloom; fall colors peak in September in the high country, a month or more later in Zion Canyon.

San Juan Mountains
Colorado

CHAPTER 16

Sprawling between the humpy Elk Mountains of central Colorado and the mesas and canyons of the Four Corners region, the **San Juan Mountains** reign with craggy majesty – crowned in white well past the long winter, bejeweled with wildflowers from snowmelt through summer, and mantled in gold when the aspens turn in autumn. As Theodore Roosevelt said of Colorado's natural splendor, "The scenery bankrupts the English language." ◆ The San Juans don't look all that impressive on a road map – just a big patch of green. You need a topographic map to get a hint of their rugged nature. In some places, contour lines are so close together that they appear almost solid, denoting the sheer cliffs, deep gorges, and skyscraping summits that characterize this stunning range. Of Colorado's 54 "fourteeners," the local parlance for peaks 14,000 feet or higher, 13 are in the San Juans. In fact, 29 of the state's 100 highest peaks are here. The **Continental Divide**, which meanders nearly 700 miles through Colorado, reaches its westernmost point in the San Juans, where it is part of the **Weminuche Wilderness**, an area of nearly 500,000 acres. ◆ Scores of creeks and rivers course through the mountains, roiling and frothing as hundreds of inches of melted snow churn through steep-sided canyons and deep valleys. The best-known river is the **Rio Grande**. Its headwaters are just under the brow of the Continental Divide, roughly 30 miles northwest of the town of **Creede**. As it squeezes through Wagon Wheel Gap, with the Rio Grande Palisades looming above like a wall, it bears no resemblance to the wide, wadable

Backcountry trails, many of them former mining roads, lead backpackers and bicyclists to alpine lakes, aspen groves, and boulder-strewn peaks.

A party of backpackers heads high into the San Juan Mountains, where more than a dozen peaks top out at 14,000 feet or higher.

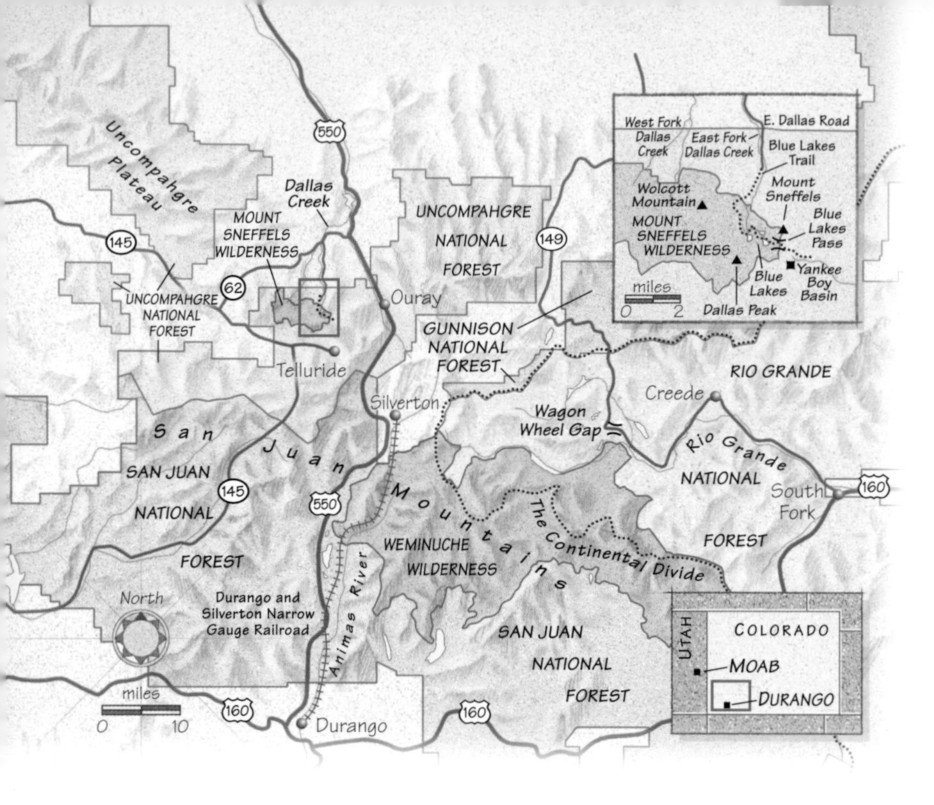

flanked by deep forests and soaring mountains.

Mountain Seasons

Too big to be just one place, the San Juans sort themselves into subranges: the San Miguel, Sneffels, Grenadier, La Plata, Rio Grande, San Luis, Silverton, Lake City, and Needle and West Needle groups, each one wild and beautiful. Administratively, the San Juans are parceled out among three national forests: Uncompahgre, Rio Grande, and San Juan. They include 11 designated wilderness and roadless areas, with room to spare.

river at the U.S.–Mexico border. Most of it is navigable only by raft or kayak, but a 22.5-mile stretch near the town of **South Fork** is Colorado's second-longest Gold Medal Stream, so designated for its excellent fishing and large trout. The **Animas**, the westernmost of the San Juans' significant rivers, is best seen from a raft or aboard the Durango-Silverton Narrow Gauge Railroad, a steam train that passes through a stunning gorge

In these grand mountains, the seasons are intense. Autumn is a palette of deep green conifers, golden aspen leaves, mountain meadows turning tawny, and achingly blue skies. It's a spectacular show but all too brief. Winter comes early and stays late. As early as October, storms roll in, bringing rain or sleet to the valleys and frosting the mountaintops. Serious cold sets in by mid-November, and the snow line steadily drops lower and lower, until even the valley floors are covered in white. With average annual snowfalls of 400 to 500 inches, the San Juans are prone to avalanches, and backcountry travel is advisable only for knowledgeable and well-equipped skiers and snowshoers.

Come spring, the snow melts quickly from the south-facing slopes but lingers until June in shady spots and remains in some sheltered

basins and chutes year-round. Summer is brief but intense. Wildflowers carpet all but the rockiest talus slopes and steepest cliff walls. Hibernating animals emerge from their dens, elk and deer return to the high country to graze, and mountain goats and bighorn sheep have an easier time negotiating rocky ledges. Wildflower season begins with the brilliant yellow glacier lilies that pop up in the wake of retreating snowfields in spring and ends when the blue-violet petals of late-blooming harebells finally succumb to the first snows.

Alpine Spectacle

Returning to the road map, you'll see that two federal highways, U.S. 550 and U.S. 160, and several state highways pass through the range. More important for backcountry trekkers are the dozens of dotted lines that appear on the map—mostly old mining roads built to reach remote mountain camps before the concept of "wilderness" was even a gleam in the government's eye. These roads, along with trails once used to move livestock to and from high pastures, are now recreational byways. Some may be used by mountain bikes and four-wheel-drive vehicles; others lead toward wilderness areas and dead end where only hikers, horseback riders, and llama trekkers are permitted to tread.

But hiking the San Juans is not for the unprepared. Many trailheads are located at

Numerous creeks and rivers pour out of the mountains, making irresistible campsites (left).

A climber (below) ascends a wall of ice. The San Juans draw winter adventurers who savor the challenges of ice climbing, cross-country skiing, and snowshoeing.

Aspens ablaze with autumn color provide a sheltered place to hang a hammock (opposite).

8,000 or 9,000 feet or even higher, and often rise with breath-sapping steepness. Rain, hail, and even snow can fall any day of the year – and you can just about count on short afternoon downpours in August. Thunderstorms are not uncommon, and lightning is a threat, particularly at high elevations. This makes backpacking a challenge, for in these mountains there is no such thing as traveling light. Tent camping is a must at high elevations, because nights are downright cold.

Given these concerns, the **Blue Lakes**, a trio of stunning alpine tarns at and above timberline, are a good destination for beginning and intermediate backpackers. The lakes are nestled in the southwest side of 14,150-foot **Mount Sneffels**, which mountaineer Louis W. Dawson II has described as "undeniably the most spectacular peak in the San Juans." While most mountains in the Colorado Rockies were shaped by a combination of geological uplifting and glacial erosion, Sneffels was born of fire. This steep-sided volcanic cone is best viewed from the north side, where Dallas Creek emerges.

The **Blue Lakes Trailhead**, at an elevation of 9,400 feet, is at the end of the East Fork Dallas Creek Road. There are no campgrounds with facilities, but you can camp along the road once it enters the national forest. From the best spots, you wake to early-morning views of Mount Sneffels, with the sun peeking over the mountains. Get going early, because any bad weather that rolls in is likely to do so in mid- to late afternoon.

Your hike starts relatively gently, paralleling Dallas Creek as you climb gradually toward the southwest and contour along a hillside covered with spruce trees. The trail then becomes steeper, but a series of switchbacks not only eases the ascent but also controls erosion. As you climb, flower-filled clearings and small meadows alternate with stands of trees.

In just over a mile, you reach the

Biking Hut to Hut

In 1889, Butch Cassidy and his gang completed their first bank transaction in Telluride, a jewel of a town nestled in the San Juan Mountains. They outran the law by spurring their horses northwest to Moab, Utah. You can follow their path, but mountain bikes are now the transport of choice. San Juan Hut Systems operates six backcountry cabins strung along the 206-mile route.

The huts each accommodate eight people and are stocked with food, fuel, and sleeping bags. Riders should be equipped with the legs and lungs of a Tour de France cyclist, the route-finding ability of Sacajawea (or at least good map and compass skills), and the mechanical aptitude of Inspector Gadget to make emergency bike repairs. To do this weeklong trip and stay in a hut each night, you ride about 35 miles a day over rough logging, ranching, and mining roads at an average elevation of 9,000 feet. Shorter trips can also be arranged.

The trail begins near **Telluride**, which still possesses some buildings that Butch and the boys would recognize, and ends in **Moab**, a former uranium-mining town regarded as the mountain-biking capital of the West.

Beginning in the shadow of the **Sneffels Range**, you spend two days deep in the San Juans – where every crank of the pedals brings a new panorama of snow-kissed mountains, wildflower meadows, aspen groves amid evergreen forests, and cascading mountain streams – and two days crossing the **Uncompahgre Plateau**, a 90-mile mesa between the San Juans and the Colorado River. This curious name is Ute for "rocks made red by water" or "rocks that make the water red." The final two days' ride leads down through stark, arid canyon country, a landscape that feels light-years removed from the mountains.

A mountain biker (left) pedals through a stand of aspens. Hundreds of miles of biking trails loop through the mountains.

Rock climbing (opposite, top) is popular throughout the San Juans; guides offer instruction to novices.

Countless creeks (opposite, bottom) drain the mountains and swell dramatically during the spring runoff.

Mount Sneffels Wilderness boundary. The trail crosses a creek, then bends due south. Before you is a brilliant wildflower meadow, while filling the horizon to the west is the huge cirque of Wolcott Mountain. The trail enters the forest one more time and heads upward, curving toward the southeast. When you emerge from the trees, stop to catch your breath and gaze at the spectacular panorama splayed before you. The **Blue Lakes** nestle in a vast basin that is now your universe. The north-facing ridge connecting Mount Sneffels and beefy Dallas Peak is daunting. If you spot anyone on Dallas's 13,809-foot summit, allow yourself to be impressed, because this is considered one of the hardest climbs in Colorado.

Watery Gems

The Blue Lakes are examples of what early explorers called Pater Noster lakes. Set one above another in lofty alpine basins with creeks running between them, the lakes reminded the apparently devout mountaineers of rosary beads, which in turn called to mind the Lord's Prayer, or Pater Noster.

The trail climbs steeply toward **Lower Blue Lake**, the largest of the group, situated at 11,000 feet in a beautiful basin just below the treeline, where you can make camp. No matter how hot it is below and no matter how brightly the sun is shining, you can expect cool air and stiff breezes at such elevations. Above the lake, you are in alpine tundra, a dramatic ecosystem of hardy, deep-rooted plants that have evolved to withstand long, harsh winters. If you go no farther than Lower Blue Lake, you can still consider your hike a considerable achievement; you will have walked three

Mountain goats (right) are adept at foraging on the rocky terrain above treeline. Their hooves are adapted to grip the ice and slick rock surfaces found at high altitudes.

Backpackers (below) hike toward Silex Peak in the Weminuche Wilderness, the largest wilderness area in Colorado.

Showy daisies carpet a meadow in the La Plata Range (opposite).

and a half miles and ascended 1,600 vertical feet.

If you are fit and the weather is fine, you can continue up another 700 vertical feet of ever steeper trails and thinner air to **Middle Blue** and **Upper Blue Lakes**. To reach them, backtrack about 100 yards along the main trail from the northern shore to a faint side trail on the right. Cross a small bridge and continue hiking along a cliff toward Mount Sneffels's muscular western shoulder.

These lakes sit in pristine splendor on a high, flower-filled plateau that exemplifies nature's best efforts at showy gardening, with a profusion of low-growing species of Indian paintbrush, Arctic gentian, saxifrage, primrose, daisy, and aster. Mount Sneffels dominates the skyline and your consciousness, while Lower Blue Lake, which you labored mightily to reach, now looks small and distant in the basin below. From Upper Blue Lake, a faint trail threads rocky cliffs to **Blue Lakes Pass** at 12,960 feet above sea level.

An alternate route to the Blue Lakes approaches from **Yankee Boy Basin**, southeast of Blue Lakes Pass. The hike, only about two miles, may seem easier, but most people find it more difficult since it requires crossing the pass, and the trail on both sides is steep. Yankee Boy is a popular four-wheel-drive destination because a rough road reaches 11,800 feet. It also attracts nature lovers who come for one of Colorado's finest wildflower displays, at peak splendor between late July and late August.

Locals often arrange a car shuttle or key exchange. For a shuttle hike, park one vehicle at Yankee Boy Basin, then start your backpacking trip at the Blue Lakes Trailhead, stopping to make camp and explore along the way. Your hike over Blue Lakes Pass will cover more than six miles, with a 3,200-foot ascent and a 1,200-foot descent. For a key exchange, you team up with another party. Each group parks at one of the trailheads, and both parties meet in the middle, perhaps at Lower Blue Lake, to trade keys – and share tales of the journey.

TRAVEL TIPS

DETAILS

How to Get There

Airports are located in Telluride, in the center of the San Juans; Montrose, 90 minutes north of Telluride; and Durango, two and a half hours south. Rental cars are available at all airports.

When to Go

Backcountry travel is most enjoyable from mid-June through August. Because snow can linger at high altitudes well into June, trails may not open until early July. Summer days are in the 60s and 70s; nights are in the 50s. Temperatures vary considerably, depending on the elevation, and at high elevations can drop to freezing at night and in early morning. Rain falls nearly every afternoon in August. Snow can accumulate by November. Average annual snowfall is 390 inches.

What to Do

The San Juan Mountains encompass three national forests, including a number of wilderness areas, with hundreds of miles of trails for backpackers as well as horse and llama packers. On designated roads and trails outside the wilderness areas, visitors may explore the San Juans by mountain bike and four-wheel-drive vehicle. Fishing is permitted on lakes and streams, and several rivers are ideal for trips by raft or kayak. Visitors come from late fall through early spring for cross-country skiing, snowshoeing, and other winter activities.

Backcountry Permits

Permits are not required in the national forests and wilderness areas. Backcountry users should check with the appropriate national forest office for regulations governing the size of groups and length of stay in any one area.

Special Planning

Some wilderness areas receive heavy use in peak season; visitors may want to schedule their trips for midweek and avoid holiday weekends. Travelers should be prepared for sudden changes in weather by carrying reliable raingear and warm clothing. Portable gas stoves must be used in areas where fires are not allowed. To reduce encounters with black bears, food and garbage should be suspended in a tree at least 10 feet off the ground and four feet away from the trunk, or stored in a bear-resistant container. Skiers and snowshoers are advised to check on avalanche conditions before venturing into the backcountry.

Car Camping

Numerous campgrounds are in the Rio Grande National Forest (719-852-5944); San Juan National Forest (970-247-4874); and Uncompahgre National Forest (970-240-5367). Call for specific information on locations and reservations.

INFORMATION

Rio Grande National Forest

1803 West Highway 160, Monte Vista, CO 81144; tel: 719-852-5944.

San Juan National Forest

15 Burnett Court, Durango, CO 81301; tel: 970-247-4874.

Uncompahgre National Forest

2505 South Townsend, Montrose, CO 81401; tel: 970-240-5367.

Durango–Silverton Narrow Gauge Railroad Company

479 Main Avenue, Durango, CO 81301; tel: 970-247-2733 or 888-872-4607.

The train offers drop-off services for backcountry visitors entering the Weminuche Wilderness at the Elk Park and Needleton Trailheads.

San Juan Mountains Association

P.O. Box 2261, Durango, CO 81302; tel: 970-385-1210.

The association's catalog features a comprehensive selection of guidebooks covering hiking, mountaineering, mountain biking, fly-fishing, and other activities (see Resource Directory), plus maps indispensable for backcountry travelers.

LODGING

PRICE GUIDE – double occupancy

$ = up to $49	$$ = $50–$99
$$$ = $100–$149	$$$$ = $150+

Chipeta Sun Lodge and Suites

304 South Lena, Ridgway, CO 81432; tel: 970-626-3737 or 800-633-5868.

Surrounded by Uncompahgre National Forest, the Chipeta has a variety of rooms with views of the San Juan Mountains. Lodge guests are served a full breakfast. The suites have full kitchens. $$–$$$$

Johnstone Inn

P.O. Box 546, Telluride, CO 81435; tel: 800-752-1901 or 970-728-3316.

The Johnstone has eight rooms, each with private bath. Guests are served a full breakfast. $$–$$$

Riverside Inn and Cabins

Box 342, Ouray, CO 81427; tel: 800-432-4170.

The inn has 18 motel rooms with kitchenettes, plus rustic cabins along the Uncompahgre River. The Riverside is open year-round. $–$$$

TOURS AND OUTFITTERS

La Garita Llamas

32995 County Road 41 G, Del Norte, CO 81132; tel: 719-754-3345.

Llamas carry travelers' gear on overnight trips in the San Juan

Mountains and surrounding area. Itineraries include treks on the Continental Divide and into the San Juan Wilderness. There are also special trips for women and seniors.

San Juan Hut Systems

P.O. Box 1663, Telluride, CO 81435; tel: 970-728-6935.

In addition to operating six backcountry cabins for mountain bikers, San Juan Hut Systems maintains five cabins for skiers on another route in the San Juan Mountains. Huts on the mountain-biking trail are open June 1 to October 1; winter huts are open December 1 through April 15. Cyclists can also take five-day, four-night trips from Telluride to Gateway. Shuttle service can be arranged.

San Juan Mountain Guides

P.O. Box 895, Ouray, CO 81427, tel. 970-325-4925.

Visitors who want to try mountain climbing in the San Juans can get instruction from this outfitter; guide services are available for experienced mountain and ice climbers.

San Juan Outfitting

186 County Road 228, Durango, CO 81301; tel: 970-259-6259.

Horses carry travelers and their gear into the Weminuche Wilderness. From base camp, participants explore the high country of the Continental Divide, fish at alpine lakes, and photograph the scenery. Eight-day pack trips follow the Divide, setting up camp at a different location each night.

Telluride Outside

P.O. Box 685, Telluride, CO 81435; tel: 800-831-6230 or 970-728-3895.

Backpackers can arrange San Juan trips from one night to a week. Guides also take climbers to a base camp, then proceed on a guided ascent of one of the area's 14,000-foot peaks.

Excursions

Bandelier National Monument

HCR 1, Box 1, Los Alamos, NM 87544; tel: 505-672-3861.

Centuries before European settlers came to the continent, the Anasazi people inhabited cliff dwellings on Pajarito Plateau, a landscape formed by volcanic eruptions a million years ago and now protected in this national monument. Visitors today can see ancient Anasazi ruins at Frijoles Canyon and other sites and also take extended trips into the backcountry. More than 70 miles of trails wind through verdant canyons and ponderosa pine woodlands and onto mesas that top out at 10,000 feet in elevation.

El Malpais National Monument

P.O. Box 939, Grants, NM 87020; tel: 505-285-4641.

Spanish for "badlands," El Malpais is a wonderland of volcanic formations, from cinder cones above the ground to lava flows beneath the earth. To see this impressive geologic display, visitors venture into the backcountry on hiking trails and on designated four-wheel-drive roads, mountain-biking routes, and horseback-riding trails. Cavers have plenty of territory to explore, including Junction Cave, a 3,000-foot-long lava tube. It is not unusual to discover pottery chips, rock cairns, and petroglyphs – evidence of ancient Puebloan peoples.

Rocky Mountain National Park

Estes Park, CO 80571; tel: 970-586-1206.

Snow-capped peaks, high-altitude tundra, gemlike alpine lakes, lushly forested valleys, and meadows carpeted with wildflowers make this park a spectacular backcountry destination. Nearly a third of the 266,000 acres are above treeline, a habitat supporting plants that also thrive in the Arctic. Traveling the more than 350 miles of trails, backpackers may see elk, moose, bighorn sheep, black bears, and mountain lions. Winter visitors enjoy cross-country skiing, snowshoeing, and snow camping.

Big Bend National Park

Texas

CHAPTER 17

E*l país despoblado*. The land without people. That's what early Spanish explorers named the desert wilderness around a broad bend in the Rio Grande about midway in the river's course to the Gulf of Mexico. Then, as now, it struck travelers as an unforgiving country, its broken-tooth mountains rising from sere desert flats, its sparse vegetation bristling with spines and needles. Miners, farmers, and ranchers settled here in the late 19th and early 20th centuries, but only a handful remained. Today, the region is still lightly populated, with fewer than 9,000 people in an area larger than Connecticut. ◆ **Big Bend National Park** encompasses more than 800,000 acres at the heart of this arid land, most of it Chihuahuan Desert. Despite first impressions, the park isn't all cactus and creosote bush. Willow and cottonwood crowd the Rio Grande, whose waters slide through spectacular, sheer-walled canyons along the U.S.–Mexican border. In the center of the park rise the **Chisos Mountains**, whose wooded slopes are topped by 7,825-foot **Emory Peak**. Here, in shady canyons of tough volcanic rock only a few miles from the desert floor, grow stands of maple, oak, ash, aspen, and the southernmost ponderosa pines in the United States. ◆ The Chisos can be up to 20°F cooler than the desert below and, not surprisingly, are the site of the park's most popular hiking routes. From the **Basin**, a bowl-shaped depression ringed with cliffs in the center of the mountains, trails lead to some of the finest panoramas in

Birdsong may be your only companion in the desert heights and river canyons of the "land without people."

Popular trails in Big Bend meander through canyons and meadows and ascend the Chisos highlands, where hikers have views of distant mountains across the border in Mexico.

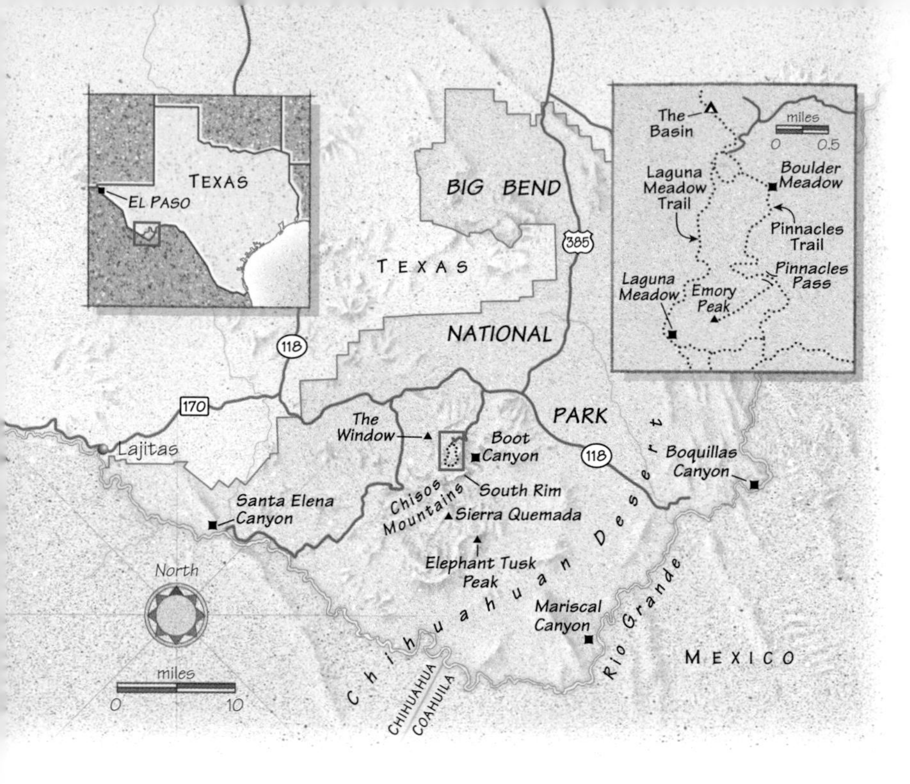

Texas, including a wonderful sunset lookout called the Window. You'll find perhaps the best view in the park along the **South Rim**, reached by heading south from the Basin on either the **Laguna Meadow Trail** or the **Pinnacles Trail**. From this escarpment nearly half a mile above the desert, you can see the mountains of Mexico beyond the Rio Grande to the south, as well as the closer Sierra Quemada – "burned mountains," for their reddish brown color – and such distinctive features as sharp-pointed Elephant Tusk peak, five miles away.

Depending on your route, it's a 13- to 15-mile round-trip to South Rim, with designated campsites along the way. The Laguna Meadow Trail climbs gradually up a wide canyon to a grassy, sometimes marshy area where Native Americans once camped. Look around and you'll see signs of a fire that swept through this part of the park in 1980.

The Pinnacles Trail passes through **Boulder Meadow**, where oaks and pinyon pines grow amid striking boulders. The trail quickly gains a great deal of elevation in a series of switchbacks up to **Pinnacles Pass**; take a breather here and enjoy the tremendous view back into the Basin, with its rocky, castlelike towers on every side. From just east of Pinnacles Pass, a one-mile spur ascends to the summit of Emory Peak, a climb that entails some strenuous boulder-scrambling at the end but offers superlative views in all directions.

It won't take you long to see where nearby **Boot Canyon**, east of the peak, got its name: an eroded rock spire rising across the canyon from the trail looks exactly like a gigantic, upside-down cowboy boot, as if wind and rain had conspired to create a comical surprise for every hiker who has climbed this far.

If you're in Boot Canyon between mid-April and early summer, you'll probably run across at least one group of people carrying binoculars and gazing intently into the oaks along the trail. With its combination of

Glorious views of Juniper Canyon (left) reward those who make the strenuous hike to Lost Mine Peak.

A lone rider (opposite, top) crosses the Rio Grande at sunset; the river forms the southern boundary of the park.

Havard agaves (opposite, below) have adapted to the arid conditions of the Chihuahuan Desert, blooming only once in their lifetime.

habitats, Big Bend ranks among North America's most popular birding areas. Some 450 bird species have been recorded here, more than at any other national park. One of the area's major avian attractions is the Colima warbler, a small, gray-and-yellow bird that nests in Chisos canyons, the only place to see it in the United States. If you camp in Boot Canyon, after dark you may hear the deep, hoarse hoot of a flammulated owl, an uncommon and much sought-after species among birders.

Ancient Ocean Remnants

No one hiking in the Chisos could possibly miss the thick and spiky leaves of the Havard agave, which grows in clusters about three feet tall. This astonishing plant blooms only once and soon dies – but it makes a memorable exit. The agave sends up a thick stalk that can be 20 feet tall and as thick as a lamppost, bearing an enormous "candelabra" of nectar-laden yellow flowers that attract hummingbirds and other animals. The agave may live 20 years or more before its one and only blossoming, which accounts for its somewhat exaggerated common

name: the century plant.

If by chance you look up and spot a soaring golden eagle, take a moment and imagine an animal with a wingspan 10 times larger sailing overhead. In 1971, a scientist working at Big Bend discovered the wing bone of a flying reptile called a pterosaur, whose wings measured at least 36 feet from tip to tip, making it the largest flying creature known to have ever existed. Big Bend has provided a rich lode of other fossils as well, from clams and sea turtles (dating from 135 million years ago, when an ocean covered this region) to a crocodile almost 50 feet long.

The animals that range through Big Bend today don't quite approach that monstrous size. Both white-tailed and mule deer live here (the former higher in the mountains than the latter), along with the piglike collared peccary, occasionally seen in the lower and middle elevations of the park. Black bears roam the Chisos highlands, and campers should use lockers provided at backcountry campsites to store food and avoid unwelcome nocturnal visits.

A glance at a map will reveal the identity of the park's most famous wild resident: Panther Junction, Panther Pass, and several other sites take the name of the big cat more properly known as a mountain lion. More than 20 lions are thought to live in the park, though the odds of seeing one are slim.

Desert Florescence

Backpackers in the Chisos Mountains camp at assigned backcountry sites, but hikers who obtain a permit for desert camping are free to pitch a tent nearly anywhere within a designated zone. This allows more freedom but also requires a greater degree of prudence. Particularly in the hotter months, when temperatures commonly

Floating the Rio

Over the course of millions of years, the relentless erosive power of the silt-laden Rio Grande has carved three spectacular canyons along the southern edge of Big Bend National Park. In **Santa Elena, Mariscal**, and **Boquillas Canyons**, limestone cliffs tower up to 1,500 feet over the river's edge, creating chasms of truly breathtaking grandeur. Short hiking trails leading into Santa Elena and Boquillas Canyons allow a glimpse of these wonders, but the best way to discover the canyons is on a raft, canoe, or kayak trip.

Local outfitters lead river journeys ranging from a few hours to several days in length. Overnight trips provide a genuine wilderness experience during which floaters get a sense of the solitude encountered by the U.S. Geological Survey expedition that made the first trip through the canyons in 1899. Camping along the Rio Grande in splendid isolation beneath sheer cliffs, you'll have a chance to spot a peregrine falcon zooming along the rock face high above. The haunting songs of canyon wrens ring out everywhere, echoing between the narrow rock walls.

Depending on water level, the Rio Grande presents a wide range of boating challenges. The famed Rock Slide rapids in Santa Elena Canyon often rate as a Class IV, requiring preliminary scouting and skilled navigation. Boquillas Canyon has no rapids above Class II and makes a great float for beginners. But any trip – whether a relaxing paddle along a calm stretch or an exhilarating run through rapids – will reveal the beauty that inspired the Rio Grande's designation as a national wild and scenic river along its 196-mile route through Big Bend country.

A kayaker (above) inspects the fluted walls of Mariscal Canyon.

Pyrrhuloxias (opposite, top), a relative of the northern cardinal, inhabit mesquite thickets and arid canyons.

The limestone walls of Santa Elena Canyon (opposite, bottom) rise more than 1,000 feet above the Rio Grande.

exceed 100°F and shade can be almost nonexistent, desert travel is for experienced backpackers only.

Desert washes can make good backcountry routes and are also excellent places to observe wildlife like peccary and such birds as the noisy and abundant cactus wren and gorgeous varied bunting. Keep in mind, however, that sudden and severe afternoon thunderstorms in late summer and early fall can turn a dry streambed into a roaring torrent in a matter of minutes. While this can be an exciting phenomenon to observe from a distance, don't allow yourself to become trapped in a wash, and never camp in one.

Dangers aside, the Big Bend desert has as much to offer backcountry explorers as do the imposing Chisos: the stunning landscape, the delightful coolness of a desert dawn, the trill of a lesser nighthawk, the *check-churrr* of a scaled quail. In spring, especially after rainy winters, the "barren" Chihuahuan Desert can be a vibrantly colored quilt of flowers. Verbenas, bluebonnets, prickly poppies, and sunflowers contribute their hues, but many of the most beautiful flowers are those of the cacti. From the desert to the high Chisos, these spiny plants bloom in colors from brilliant red and vivid yellow to a deep, rich purple.

Big Bend's variety of terrain makes it a year-round destination: Hiking in the desert is better from fall through spring, while the Chisos are seen at their best from spring through fall, though winter weather is often mild even in the mountains. It's virtually impossible to cover the entire park in a single visit. Once you've had a taste, it's a safe bet that you'll want to return again and again.

TRAVEL TIPS

DETAILS

How to Get There

The nearest commercial airports are in Midland, 230 miles northeast of Big Bend, and El Paso, 325 miles northwest of the park. There is no public transportation to the park. Car rentals are available at both airports.

When to Go

Most visitors come to Big Bend in March and April, and in December. The park receives the fewest visitors in August and September. Spring temperatures are comfortable, with highs ranging from 75° to 90°F and lows from 45° to 60°F. Summer is considerably hotter, with highs exceeding 100°F, sometimes up to 115°F, though the humidity is low. Winter temperatures often drop below freezing. Expect temperatures 10 to 20 degrees cooler at high elevations. During the rainy season, from mid-June through October, thunderstorms can be heavy but usually are brief. Snowfall is rare.

What to Do

Approximately 200 miles of trails are open to backpackers, who stay in 42 designated campsites in the Chisos Mountains but can choose their own sites in the desert. Mountain bikers and visitors with high-clearance or four-wheel-drive vehicles explore the park on more than 150 miles of unpaved backroads; mountain bikers may also use the park's paved roads (off-road vehicle travel and bicycling on hiking trails are not allowed). Horseback riders may travel cross-country and on the unpaved back roads. The Rio Grande borders the park, offering opportunities for float trips by raft, canoe, or kayak.

Backcountry Permits

A permit is required for all overnight backcountry camping and must be obtained in person up to 24 hours in advance of arrival. Visitors also need a permit to stay at backcountry roadside campsites. Paddlers using their own equipment on the Rio Grande must have a permit, issued in person up to 24 hours in advance of a trip.

Special Planning

Trail conditions can be unpredictable; backpackers should contact the park in advance to plan an itinerary. Because backcountry water supply is unreliable, hikers should not plan their trips around springs and are advised to carry at least one gallon of water per day per person. Visitors driving backcountry roads should check conditions in advance, make sure their vehicles are properly serviced, and carry survival gear, including food and plenty of water.

Car Camping

The park has three campgrounds with nearly 200 sites available on a first-come, first-served basis: Chisos Basin, Cottonwood, and Rio Grande Village. For information on these campgrounds and others outside the park, call 915-477-2251.

INFORMATION

Big Bend National Park

Big Bend National Park, TX 79834; tel. 915-477-2251.

Big Bend Natural History Association

P.O. Box 196, Big Bend National Park, TX 79834; tel: 915-477-2236.

The association publishes field, trail, and river guides. Other publications, as well as trail and topo maps, are also available (see Resource Directory).

LODGING

PRICE GUIDE – double occupancy

$ = up to $49 $$ = $50–$99

$$$ = $100–$149 $$$$ = $150+

Big Bend Motor Inn/ Mission Lodge

P.O. Box 336, Terlingua, TX 79852; tel: 915-371-2218.

This inn, just west of the park, has 80 rooms, some with kitchenettes. A restaurant, a gas station, and tent sites are on the property. $$

Chisos Mountains Lodge

Basin Station, Big Bend National Park, TX 79834; tel: 915-477-2291.

Situated in the center of the park, this concessionaire has four types of accommodations: Casa Grand Motor Lodge with 38 rooms; a motel with 20 rooms; a small lodge with eight rooms; and five stone cottages. All are available year-round. A restaurant is also on the property. $$

Terlingua Ranch

HC 65, Box 220, Alpine, TX 79830; tel: 915-371-2416.

Located one hour from the national park, this ranch offers 31 motel rooms. A restaurant and a swimming pool are on the premises. $

TOURS AND OUTFITTERS

Big Bend Natural History Association

P.O. Box 196, Big Bend National Park, TX 79834; tel: 915-477-2236.

Desert survival, geology, and history are among the topics covered in seminars held year-round at the national park. Workshops, which often include field trips, are generally limited to 15 participants. Those attending multiday seminars camp in the park free of charge.

Big Bend River Tours
Box 317, Lajitas, TX 79852; tel: 800-545-4240 or 915-424-3219.

Specific itineraries and custom-designed trips feature floats down the Rio Grande and tours of the backcountry, including canyons in and around the park. Trips range from a half day to 10 days and emphasize the region's wildlife, geology, and history.

Desert Sports
P.O. Box 448, Terlingua, TX 79852; tel: 888-989-6900 or 915-371-2727.

Desert Sports offers scheduled and custom-designed multiday trips for backpackers, mountain bikers, and paddlers in the park and nearby areas. Extended excursions combine activities such as paddling and backpacking. Visitors can also rent equipment for self-guided trips and arrange shuttle services.

Far Flung Adventures
P.O. Box 377, Terlingua,TX 79852; tel: 800-359-4138 or 915-371-2489.

Trips on the Rio Grande by canoe or raft range from one to 10 days. Far Flung has access to 225 miles of river, including five stretches of canyon.

Rio Grande Adventures
P.O. Box 229, Terlingua, TX 790852; tel: 800-343-1640 or 915-371-2567.

Travelers may choose float trips with stops to hike remote canyons or four-wheel-drive tours of the backcountry. All equipment and food, as well as guides, are provided. Rio Grande Adventures also rents camping gear, canoes, and rafts, and offers a shuttle service. Customized itineraries and self-guided trips can be arranged.

Texas River and Jeep Expeditions
P.O. Box 583, Terlingua, TX 79852; tel: 800-839-7238 or 915-371-2633.

Guides take visitors by jeep to explore the natural history of Big Bend and on floats down the Rio Grande for a different view of the park's topography and wildlife.

Excursions

Carlsbad Caverns National Park

3225 National Parks Highway, Carlsbad, NM 88220; tel: 505-785-2232.

Carlsbad is famous for its large network of caves and underground chambers and for the Mexican free-tail bats that leave the caves at night in large numbers. Of the park's nearly 47,000 aboveground acres, three-fourths make up a wilderness area where backpackers can hike through the Chihuahuan Desert, at an elevation of 3,500 feet, up to conifer forests at 6,300 feet. These habitats support 64 species of mammals and 330 kinds of birds.

Gila National Forest

3005 East Camino del Bosque, Silver City, NM 88061; tel: 505-388-8201.

Encompassing mountains more than 10,000 feet tall, impressive river canyons, conifer forests, and grassy foothills, this half-million-acre national forest is a mecca for backpackers. One of the Gila's wilderness areas, named after renowned conservationist and author Aldo Leopold, straddles the Black Range, whose dramatic elevation gains challenge hikers but reward them with vistas of deep canyons. Visitors come in winter to enjoy cross-country skiing and snowshoeing.

Guadalupe Mountains National Park

HC 60, Box 400, Salt Flat, TX 79847; tel: 915-828-3251.

Contributing to the rugged terrain of this 86,416-acre park is Guadalupe Peak, 8,749 feet in elevation, the highest peak in the state. Also in the park is a stretch of Capitan Reef, buried eons ago underneath an ancient sea and now fossilized and exposed to view. One of the park's trails ascends the peak. Others are less strenuous, allowing visitors to observe the park's more than 1,500 species of plants from small button cactus to huge ponderosa pines, and an abundance of blooming wildflowers in all colors of the spectrum.

Mazatzal Wilderness

Arizona

"Is that what you intend to wear on your feet?" asked the packer as he dubiously eyed the woman shod in Birkenstock sandals. No, she assured him – her hiking boots were in the truck. The question was a reasonable one, for here they were, standing by the corral near the U.S. Forest Service office in Payson, Arizona, about to set out on a four-day horseback expedition through the **Mazatzal Mountains**. Birkenstocks just wouldn't cut it. ◆ There's a reason, the packer explained, why riders wear slick-bottomed cowboy boots. If a horse throws you, your feet won't get hung up in the stirrups. It sounded like well-earned advice, coming from a packer who had tallied nearly two decades deep in the Mazatzals and who would be leading the group. Distrustful of horses, he always rides a mule. Another little tidbit to tuck away. ◆ And lest a greenhorn have to prove any more saddle savvy, it behooves a person right at the start to adhere to the local vernacular. Though *Mazatzal* is the correct spelling, anyone who has spent time in the Mogollon Rim country of central Arizona knows it's pronounced *MAT-a-zal.* ◆ Whatever they're called, these mountains showcase some of the roughest, toughest territory in the state. They rise up in a massive north-south bulwark near Payson, about 90 miles north of Phoenix. Pink and gold peaks of granite and quartzite tower to nearly 8,000 feet. Brush-choked canyons topple down in every direction, through hardscrabble land speared with agave, cactus, and manzanita. With nearly 6,000 feet of elevation difference from base to crest, the Mazatzals show off a fantastic display of plant life – stately saguaro cactus and prickly pear, buckbrush and scrub

Saddle up for a journey into the heart of a rugged desert range.

Horseback riding is the best way to travel through the remote canyons and over the precipitous heights of the Mazatzal Mountains.

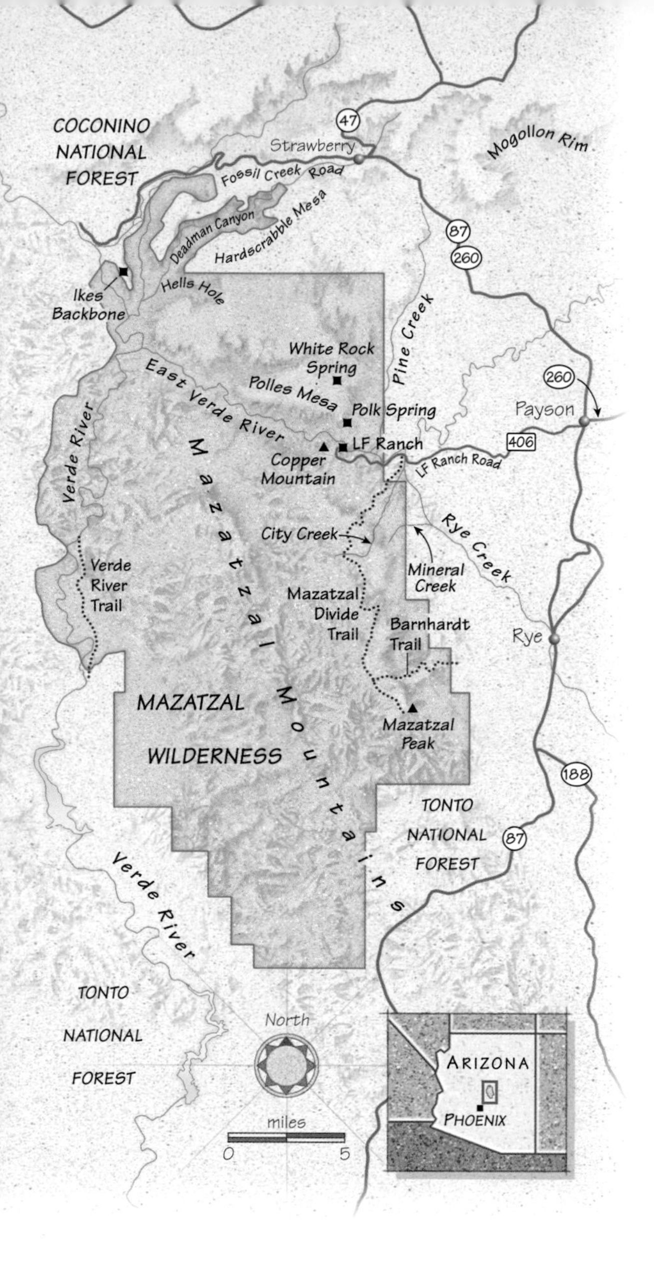

oak, tall pines and giant alligator junipers. More than 252,000 acres of the Mazatzals within Tonto National Forest were officially designated wilderness in 1940. It was one of the first such areas in the nation, long before the federal Wilderness Act was passed in 1964.

Riding High

The Mazatzals were made for long horseback trips, which afford a pleasant way to see a big chunk of the range. One of the most popular entry points is the 6.2-mile **Barnhardt Trail**, on the east side of the mountains down by the little town of **Rye**. Saddled up with plenty of feed for the animals and a gallon canteen strapped on each saddle horn, the riders proceed on the steady climb up the rocky route beside searingly steep mountainsides.

On the first day out, a few hours in the saddle is plenty for most folks. With camp chosen, the horses are unsaddled and fed, the fire gets started, and dinner is cooked. At dark, a common poorwill calls, stars pop out all at once in the clear sky, and eyelids droop before the soft firelight and murmured stories of black bears coming out of side canyons. The morning after is another story. For those whose knees and backsides are unaccustomed to a long stint on a hard saddle, it's hard to imagine mounting that cayuse and enduring another 10 to 15 miles in a day. But it's off after breakfast, with **Mazatzal Peak** presiding over the scene. Below, sheer drops yawn into giant voids as riders stay alert and ever mindful of a horse that might decide to wander off the trail.

The Barnhardt Trail joins the 29-mile **Mazatzal Divide Trail**, which runs along the crest of the Mazatzals and has been incorporated into the **Arizona Trail**, a path that eventually will stretch the length of the state, 750 miles from Mexico to the Utah border. Continuing on the Divide Trail, the riders drop into **City Creek**, named for Mazatzal City, a bustling mining town in the 1880s. Up and then down, rocky and then brushy, the trail is edged by plants that exude a heady scent when the riders' leather

Rafters (right) on the Verde River pass through a rich riparian environment lined with patches of cottonwood, sycamore, and willow.

The side-blotched lizard (opposite, top) is sometimes seen on boulders basking in the sun.

Riders (opposite, below) head for the Mazatzal Divide Trail, which follows the crest of the range.

chaps sweep over them. All along the crest, the views are stupendous – to the south, the Sierra Ancha, and far to the north, the soaring San Francisco Peaks by the town of Flagstaff.

By the next night out, pitching camp is routine – find an inviting clearing near a granite-lined pool of water, hobble the horses and mules or tie them to a picket line, serve them their dinner of oats and alfalfa pellets, and feed their riders, who then rest their bones. Morning finds a little Coues white-tailed deer sneaking through camp. Besides deer, the Mazatzal wilderness is a sanctuary for all kinds of creatures: mountain lions, bears, bobcats, ringtail cats, jackrabbits, javelina, birds, lizards. It's onward and downward in a long, steep descent over dark volcanic terrain to the **East Verde River**. At river's edge reposes the **LF Ranch**, where the jovial caretaker sweeps the group into the ranchhouse and extends a generous invitation to a hearty lunch. Outside, the windmill creaks in the breeze, and cottonwoods in fresh April leaf shade the stream. Peregrine falcons, golden eagles, and river otters ply the glistening waterway. In many ways, this feels like the heart of Arizona, and indeed, not far away, where Pine Creek enters the East Verde, is the geographic center of the state. That night, after dinner, the visitors sleep out under the western sky, hung with a perfect sliver of a quarter moon.

History's Imprint

That moon recalls an old tale of the Mazatzals. In 1864, two prospectors, addled by thirst, heard a tinkling sound and then spied the source – a hard-worn mule with a bell around its neck. The mule led the pair up to a spring, where they found a man's body, apparently crushed by a boulder. They dutifully buried him, then continued to follow the mule, or at least the bewitching sound of its bell. Campers near the spot, called Haunted Spring in Deadman's Canyon, say they still hear the ghost mule's bell when the moon is in its last quarter.

Though officially a "wilderness," these mountains have witnessed the imprint of humans for at least 5,000 years. First were

The Noble Agave

Magnificent agaves adorn the slopes of the Mazatzal Mountains, as they do many other places throughout the Southwest's deserts, grasslands, and woodlands. The word *agave* comes from the Greek for "noble" or "admirable," and especially fine specimens of this family well earn that description.

Agaves are also commonly called century plants, because they seem to take a century before they bloom. For 20 to 50 years, they display stiff, sharp-leaved rosettes. Then the plant sends up a stout central stalk that looks like a big spear of asparagus. Abundant golden chalices of flowers rise from branches off the center stalk. But once the agave has bloomed, its life is over.

For thousands of years, humans have enjoyed a symbiotic relationship with agaves, which provide food, fiber, medicine, drink, and shelter. "The uses of agaves," international agave authority Howard Scott Gentry writes, "are as many as the arts of man have found it convenient to devise."

The fleshy stalk, which can grow a foot a day, was an extremely important food source for the Apaches, other American Indians, and Mexicans. The hearts of the stalks were harvested, then roasted for a day or two in a large rock-lined pit. After baking, the hearts were dried for later consumption. High in sugar, the sweet agave hearts are said to taste something like pineapple. Roasting pits were used year after year, and hikers may notice them piled high with blackened rocks.

Agave fiber was woven into cloth, basketry, and cordage. The Apaches even manufactured a stringed musical instrument from the fiber and hollow stems. Some agave species were fermented to produce the potent alcoholic drink called mescal.

Agaves (left) produce flower stalks eight to 25 feet high, culminating in blooms that are usually shades of yellow.

A campfire (opposite, top) warms a traveler in one of the mountains' deep, shady canyons.

The Verde River (opposite, below) winds through the wilderness; backpackers find the river corridor less rugged than the highlands.

hunters, who stayed on the move in search of game. Those who left more permanent traces were the Hohokam, desert farmers who entered the area around A.D. 900. Later, another culture, called the Salado, developed in central Arizona. Between 1200 and 1400, they settled down in these mountains in small farmsteads and larger villages. Sometime in the early 1500s, Native Americans known as the Yavapais entered and took advantage of the abundant foods available in the Mazatzals.

In the 1800s, as miners, ranchers, and homesteaders claimed the land and its resources, the U.S. Army sequestered the Yavapais and the Tonto Apaches, who lived mostly to the east, on reservations to make way for the newcomers. And though the newcomers faced Indian hostilities for a time, General George Crook staged a campaign in 1873 that led to the final Apache surrender.

That latest influx of people is marked in the names of places in the Mazatzals – Copper Mountain and Mineral Creek, a band of high cliffs called Ike's Backbone, and Polle's Mesa for Napoleon Bonaparte Polle of the NB Ranch. Hardscrabble Mesa and Hells Hole say something about the reaction of these settlers to this raw-boned land. Now, except for a few inholdings like the LF Ranch, the Mazatzals see only visitors.

Trail's End, Hikers' Options

Back at the ranch, the horseback riders rise at five in the morning, getting an early start to cover the last miles of the trip. The horses have to be coaxed back into their bridles and gently urged to cross the river. After a brief stop at **Polk Spring**, adorned with cool, green watercress, it's a slow trudge over the chunky basalt boulders that cover **Polle's Mesa**. It's on to White Rock Spring, where cliff rose is in bloom, following fresh bear tracks left by an animal the packer thinks may have just come out of hibernation. Trail's end is at the little town of **Strawberry**, where roads and other signs are sudden reminders of civilization.

Woven with nearly 240 miles of trails, the Mazatzals also offer abundant opportunities to those who wish to go on their own two feet – from extended backpack trips to shuttle hikes along the 28-mile **Verde River Trail** that follows along a wild and scenic stretch of the **Verde River** on the western side of the range. The **Divide Trail** along the crest, the main through route, is well defined and heavily used, at least by Mazatzal standards. Several east-west trails join it, giving access from the lower elevations and allowing for loop hikes.

But the rigors of hiking here should never be underestimated, for this is demanding, unforgiving terrain. Even equipped with the best gear and years of experience, backpackers face plenty of challenges, both physical and mental. Extremes are the norm. A hiker may set off in the balmy warmth of the desert, only to encounter winter at the high elevations. Or heat may persist, anticipated water sources may be dry, trails can be dim or poorly marked, and rock cairns can be easily missed.

One outdoorsman who has been lost in the Mazatzals declares, "This is mean country, all right hellishly fickle between snows and rains, bristling with all manner of spines and thorns, treacherous at all times for someone afoot." Yet, as he and anyone else who's been to these mountains know, that's their ultimate attraction.

TRAVEL TIPS

DETAILS

How to Get There

Commercial airlines serve Phoenix, 70 miles south of the wilderness. Rental cars are available at the airport.

When to Go

The best times to visit the wilderness are spring and fall, when daytime temperatures are moderate, from the 50s to the 70s, and nights are in the 40s, sometimes lower at high elevations. Summer days are often in the 90s and can exceed 100°F, even 110°F. Lightning storms are common in summer, particularly during July and August. Winter temperatures range from lows in the 30s to highs in the 60s and 70s. Temperatures are lower and snow is common at high elevations, restricting travel.

What to Do

Hikers and horseback riders have use of 240 miles of trails, including the 29-mile Mazatzal Divide Trail and a 28-mile segment of the Verde River Trail. The river, which is designated wild and scenic, can be floated by raft and kayak. Fishing is also permitted in the Verde. Mountain bikes or other motorized vehicles are not allowed in the wilderness.

Backcountry Permits

Permits are not required for overnight stays in the wilderness. Backcountry users should check with national forest headquarters or individual ranger districts for regulations governing the size of groups and length of stay in any one area.

Special Planning

Trips should be carefully planned around sources of water. In the absence of reliable sources, each traveler should carry two gallons of water per day. Sudden storms can cause dangerous flash floods; at the slightest indication of rain, hikers should avoid walking or camping in dry washes. Very high temperatures can occur at low elevations, and rain and wind at high elevations can cause a sudden drop in temperature. Visitors should, therefore, be vigilant for the signs of heat exhaustion or heat stroke, and should carry reliable raingear and extra layers of clothing. Backcountry travelers are also advised to bring a portable gas stove for use in areas where campfires are prohibited.

Car Camping

Campsites are located throughout Tonto National Forest; call 602-225-5200 for specific locations.

INFORMATION

Tonto National Forest

2324 East McDowell Road, Phoenix, AZ 85006; tel: 602-225-5200.

Cave Creek Ranger District

40202 North Cave Creek Road, Scottsdale, AZ 85262; tel: 480-595-3300.

Payson Ranger District

1009 East Highway 260, Payson, AZ 85541; tel: 520-474-7900.

Arizona Trail

Kaibab National Forest, 800 South Sixth Street, Williams, AZ 86046; tel: 602-635-2681

Southwest Parks and Monuments Association

221 North Court, Tucson, AZ 85701; tel: 520-622-1999.

The association carries books about the flora, fauna, and human history of Arizona (see Resource Directory), as well as trail maps.

Apache Junction Chamber of Commerce

P.O. Box 1747, Apache Junction, AZ 85217; tel: 480-982-3141.

Rim Country Regional Chamber of Commerce

P.O. Box 1380, Payson, AZ 85547; tel: 800-672-9766 or 520-474-4515.

LODGING

PRICE GUIDE – double occupancy

$ = up to $49	$$ = $50–$99
$$$ = $100–$149	$$$$ = $150+

Fossil Creek Llamas

10379 West Fossil Creek Road, Strawberry, AZ 85544; tel: 520-476-5178.

Guests sleep on futons in a teepee that accommodates four or in a room in a log home, and are served breakfast the next morning. The 15-acre ranch is surrounded by Tonto National Forest, where visitors can hike and see Indian ruins. Fossil Creek is open year-round. $$

Grey Hackle Lodge

HC 2, Box 145, Payson, AZ 85541; tel:520-478-4392.

Eleven cabins are set on four acres just east of Payson. Some are one-room cabins with kitchenettes; others are two-story cabins with full kitchens and fireplaces. $$–$$$

Mountain Meadows Cabins

HC 2, Box 162E, Payson, AZ 85541; tel: 520-478-4415.

Seven cabins are situated east of Payson under the Mogollon Rim at an elevation of 6,400 feet. Each has a private bath, kitchen, and fireplace. Most of the land surrounding the cabins is national forest. $$–$$$

Strawberry Hill Cabins

HC 1, Box 302, Strawberry, AZ 85544; tel: 520-800-637-6604.

These cabins have kitchens, wood-burning fireplaces, and front and back decks with views of the surrounding national forest. $$–$$$$

TOURS AND OUTFITTERS

Apache Junction Parks and Recreation Department

1001 North Idaho Road, Apache Junction, AZ 85219; tel: 480-983-2181.

Two hiking trips are scheduled each year into the Mazatzals. A guide leads participants on the Barnhardt Trail, pointing out flora and fauna and discussing the region's human history.

Chaparral Guides and Outfitters

P.O. Box 1332, Payson, AZ 85547; tel: 520-474-9693.

Guided pack trips of varying duration take backcountry travelers into the wilderness area from late spring through early fall.

Cimarron River Company

7902 East Pierce, Scottsdale, AZ 85257; tel: 480-994-1199.

Forty-mile float trips of three days or more navigate the wild and scenic Verde River. Rafts are used in early spring, inflatable kayaks for the remainder of the year.

Fossil Creek Llamas

10379 West Fossil Creek Road, Strawberry, AZ 85544; tel: 520-476-5178.

Fossil Creek's guides go into the Mazatzals and other areas of the Tonto National Forest on overnight and day trips. On extended treks, llamas carry travelers' gear, and the outfitter supplies all necessary supplies, including tents and food.

Payson Adventures, Inc.

408A South Beeline Highway, Payson, AZ 85541; tel: 888-746-3545 or 520-474-8808.

Customized trips take visitors by foot or on horseback into the Mazatzal Wilderness, along the base of the Mazatzal Mountains, and to nearby areas such as the Mogollon Rim. Trips vary in length and include transportation by four-wheel-drive into the backcountry.

Excursions

Coronado National Forest

Federal Building, 300 West Congress, Tucson, AZ 85701; tel: 520-670-4552.

The 12 sections of this 1.7-million-acre national forest protect isolated mountain ranges that rise 10,000 feet or more above the surrounding desert. Hikers exploring these "sky islands" start their journey among abundant varieties of cacti, climb through steep, cottonwood-lined canyons, and arrive at pine forests and alpine meadows. Coues deer, black bears, gray foxes, desert tortoises, and more than a dozen hummingbird species inhabit this biologically diverse area, where the Chihuahuan and Sonoran Deserts meet the Rocky Mountains and Sierra Madre.

Grand Canyon National Park

P.O. Box 129, Grand Canyon, AZ 86023; tel: 520-638-7888.

Hike or float? That is the question facing back-country travelers headed for the Grand Canyon. The Colorado River, which carved this chasm over millions of years, winds for 277 miles through the canyon. Guided whitewater trips begin at Lees Ferry and last as long as three weeks. Hiking from rim to river allows a more leisurely appreciation of the canyon's enormity and its fascinating geology. Pack trips by mule can also be arranged.

Pinacate and Grand Desert Biosphere Preserve

Apartado Postal No. 125, Puerto Peñasco, Sonora, Mexico 83550; tel: 011-62-159864.

A three-hour drive south of Phoenix, Arizona, takes travelers to the largest area of desert and dunes found in Mexico, also the home of a hardy desert beetle, the *pinacate*, honored in the preserve's name. To the south of the dunes lies a landscape of gigantic calderas, cinder cones, and dormant volcanoes. Javelinas, coatimundis, and Sonoran pronghorns are among the creatures that backcountry hikers will encounter. February and March are the months to see wildflowers and cacti in bloom.

Joshua Tree National Park

California

Hikers at **Joshua Tree National Park** quickly learn to be connoisseurs of shade. It is a basic lesson, more instinctual than cerebral. The wild creatures know it by heart, from the lizards that spend their days sidling in and out of rock fissures to the birds Mary Austin described in her 1902 California desert classic, *The Land of Little Rain.* "There was a fence in that country shutting in a cattle range, and along its fifteen miles of posts one would be sure of finding a bird or two in every strip of shadow, sometimes the sparrow and the hawk, with wings trailed and beaks parted, drooping in the white truce of noon." ◆ Fence posts aren't much good to wilting hikers, of course, and there aren't many fences in Joshua Tree, anyway. About 75 percent of the park is congressionally designated wilderness. Fortunately, some natural objects in this vast expanse of desert can shelter bulky human visitors. Monzonite boulders that loom from ridges and valley floors give good shade, although it gets a bit narrow toward noon. Joshua trees, those giant gesticulating members of the lily family, cast a deep if spotty shade along dry washes, where groundwater makes their foliage unusually full. Juniper shade is even as well as deep, but it tends to be airless because the little trees grow so close to the ground. The taller pinyon pine casts the park's best shade - even and airy, lasting through the heat of the day. ◆ Pinyon pines and junipers are in fair supply along the park's 35-mile **California Riding and Hiking Trail**, which runs through the relatively high-elevation **Mojave Desert** of the northwest half. One of the shadier sections is the 12 miles

Adapting to the ways of the desert, backpackers encounter dramatic geology, curious plants, and creatures that emerge only at night.

Climbers of all abilities test their skills on cliffs and boulders of monzonite, a type of granite that is particularly well suited for rock climbing.

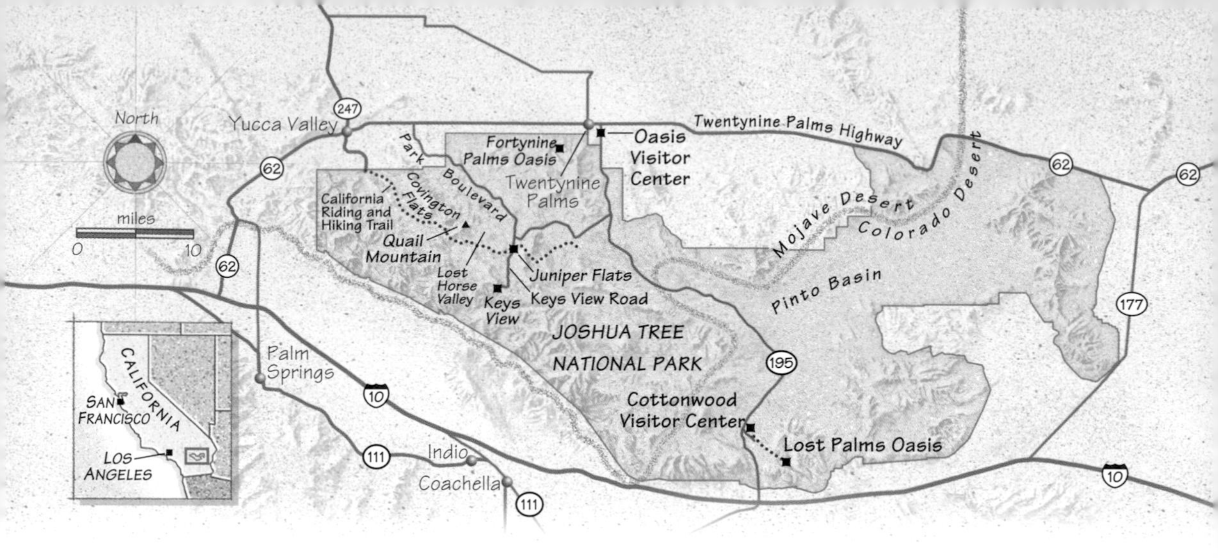

between Keys View Road and Covington Flats, making for a pleasant backpack. The trail is clearly marked, and there are good campsites at Juniper Flats, about five miles from the Keys View trailhead. The going gets steep and rocky between Juniper and Covington, but that's because the trail traverses some of the park's best scenery, with Quail Mountain to the north and a nameless canyon to the southwest. Mule deer and bighorn sheep are often seen. The vegetation is about as rich as the Mojave Desert's gets, with various odd, ingenious shrubs like the purple-blossomed *Salazaria mexicana*, called "paper bag bush" for its bladderlike calyxes, which blow away and disperse its seeds. In spring, cactuses and Mojave yuccas (the Joshua tree's smaller congener) are flowering, and the showy orange blooms of desert globe mallow dot the yellow grass.

Desert Lessons

The desert sets some restrictions even on these deluxe accommodations. Surface water is seldom present, and the Park Service

A backpacker (left) surveys the landscape.

A weathered marker (opposite, top) commemorates a fatal gunfight; it was made by the killer, Bill Keys, after he was released from prison.

The Joshua tree (opposite, bottom) was named by Mormons who thought its shaggy leaves resembled the beard of an Old Testament patriarch. Other trailblazers took a dimmer view. Explorer John C. Fremont called it the most repulsive tree in the vegetable kingdom.

recommends that each hiker carry at least a gallon of water per day, two gallons in the May–October hot season. This might seem excessive. Because the park's northwest half is largely above 4,000 feet, the heat isn't too uncomfortable – but the Mojave Desert can be deceptive. The breezy altitude that cools backpackers also extracts moisture and gives little protection against ultraviolet rays, so an exhilarating morning can become an exhausted afternoon. Exhilaration can lead to another misperception. The scenery invites off-trail wandering, and although getting lost may seem unlikely in such open terrain, an absentminded stroller may awaken suddenly to unrecognizable surroundings.

These lessons are less applicable to the **Colorado Desert**, which occupies the park's southeastern half below 3,000 feet. Shade is

less of an issue, because there is less of it. There are boulders, to be sure, but no Joshua trees or pinyon pines. There are not even many boulders in the 200-square-mile **Pinto Basin**, only the meager shadows of smoke trees and desert willows (which aren't real willows) along dry washes. The olive-drab creosote bushes that dot the flats cast just about enough shade for a coiled rattlesnake.

As for wandering absentmindedly off-trail, the Pinto Basin's blazing expanse should make the most foolhardy stroller think twice, and anyway, there are no clearly marked hiking trails in the Basin. Not surprisingly, backpackers are less common in the park's Colorado Desert than in its Mojave. The only maintained trail of any length is a four-mile track from the **Cottonwood Visitor Center** to spectacular **Lost Palms Oasis** through a labyrinth of monzonite canyons and ocotillo-dotted flats.

The whole backcountry is open to experienced off-trail hikers and horse packers. Survival supersedes liberty in some respects even here. Visitors must leave vehicles at designated registration points so that rangers will know where to look for people who don't return. Human survival is not the only consideration. The few more or less permanent surface water sites are reserved for wildlife, particularly threatened California bighorns, which easily can be scared away from a drink they've traveled miles to reach. Such sites, like Lost Palm Oasis, are located in day-use areas where camping is prohibited. Another lies just south of Juniper Flats, which is why bighorns and mule deer are often seen along that stretch of the California Riding and Hiking Trail.

Creatures Bold and Reclusive

Despite the strictures the desert puts on its creatures, many thrive in the ostensibly inhospitable terrain. "Go as far as you dare in the heart of a lonely land," Mary Austin wrote, "you cannot go so far that life and death are not with you." The landscape may seem utterly still at dusk, when the wind has died, but then a hummingbird zips overhead or a kangaroo rat bounces like a tennis ball across the darkening sand. Some of the life is surprisingly suburban. Mourning doves and scrub jays are common. Honeybees throng the white flowers of Mojave yucca. Some is strictly dryland, like the antelope ground squirrels that scramble unconcerned over cholla cactuses, or the black-throated sparrows whose sweet, tinkling song can be heard in the remotest, blast-furnace flats. When the Mojave is heating up in late May, black-throated sparrows are just building their nests, deep cups of plant fibers in junipers or other shady plants.

Some of the life is spectacular. At **Lost Horse Valley**, a prairie falcon squabbles with a pair of loggerhead shrikes, driving them to shelter in a Joshua tree, then circling around to buzz them again. (Shrikes can be nest robbers.) Near **Juniper Flats**, a large and colorful horned lizard struts about the grass beside a dry wash like a miniature ceratopsian dinosaur. It seems undaunted by human presence, though it climbs on a fallen Joshua trunk as if to even the height differential between itself and the looming intruder.

Desert animals don't have to be seen to be evident. The desiccated landscape is a museum of tracks, scats, burrows, nests, and other such evidence. Mary Austin devoted a chapter of *The Land of Little Rain* to the signs animals leave as they travel in search of water. Some evidence tells the story not simply of individuals, but of generations. Desert pack rat "middens" of cactus spines, leaves, twigs, bones, and other objects accumulate in the cracks of boulder piles over long periods. Paleontologists have used middens thousands of years old to learn what the region was like at the end of the last ice age. The middens seem to show, for one thing, that the now-ubiquitous creosote bush (*Larrea tridentata*) did not occupy North American

Twilight at the Oasis

The desert mirage has become a cliché, but **Fortynine Palms Oasis** does look like one from a distance – a patch of glossy green fronds tucked into a mountain wall of bare gray monzonite. Reddish barrel cactuses are the largest other plants in sight. Not even Joshua trees grow at the roughly 2,500-foot elevation on the park's north edge. The palms seem unreal in this austere landscape, and their presence is extraordinary. Along with the nearby Oasis of Mara at Twentynine Palms, this is the northernmost natural occurrence of *Washingtonia filifera*, the western fan palm, a species perhaps left over from a time when subtropical woodland covered these mountains.

The oasis comes in and out of sight as the trail approaches it over a boulder-strewn ridge. Fat, foot-long chuckwalla lizards sprawl on the boulders, absorbing the warmth of a sun already nearing the western horizon. As the trail descends, fire-blackened trunks become visible under the palm fronds, then give way to a tangle of lighter greenery – mesquite, cottonwood, and other water-loving plants.

At trail's end, the canyon bottom is already in shade, but the granite walls still reflect a reddish light. Under the palms, the bare ridges now seem distant, and it's easy to believe that woodland once covered them. The air is full of humid smells and colorful birds. A pair of black-headed grosbeaks gobbles palm fruits. An oriole flits past, then a western tanager. Gambel's quail are everywhere, even in the palm tops. The quacking of California tree frogs and the trilling of red-spotted toads sound at intervals from pools that dot the streambed.

The toads will reach a full chorus after dark, and many other creatures will haunt the oasis then. Western yellow bats will emerge from palm tops where they've spent the day roosting, and perhaps a bobcat or a group of bighorns will come to drink. They will do so unobserved by human visitors, who must walk back to the parking lot by eight, leaving the oasis to the creatures of the desert night.

Fan palms (above) are among the tallest North American palms, growing up to 75 feet and weighing as much as three tons.

California tree frogs (left), inhabitants of Joshua Tree oases, can be heard making an unusual quacking sound.

A climber (opposite, left) has a tenuous hold on Headstone Rock, a popular climbing spot near the Sheep Pass campground. There are thousands of climbing routes in the park; private climbing schools offer guide services and instruction.

Beaver tail cactus (opposite, right), a member of the prickly-pear family, is named for its broad, flat pads. Birds and butterflies feed on the flowers.

California poppies and goldfields (left) bloom in spring, when wildflowers reach their peak.

Roadrunners (below) use their powerful legs, rather than their wings, to chase down reptiles and other prey, sometimes reaching 15 miles per hour.

Granite spheres, (opposite), smoothed by erosion, were left stranded atop other rocks after the earth around them gradually washed away.

deserts until that time. Migrating birds may have transported creosote bush seeds from South America, where a closely related species occurs.

The Park's Namesake

A now-dominant shrub that arrived in a bird's gut an evolutionary instant ago seems typical of the desert's deceptiveness, its discontinuities and incongruities. Certainly, the desert's recent history has had such qualities. In the 1860s, a small band of Native Americans called the Serrano were the sole inhabitants of what is now Joshua Tree. Today, freeways and fast-growing towns surround it and seem to belie its austerities. They doubtless would be inside the park if a botany-loving Pasadena matron named Minerva Hoyt (perhaps the original "little old lady from") hadn't convinced President Franklin D. Roosevelt to proclaim an 825,000-acre national monument in 1936. Commercial interests got this reduced to 560,000 acres in 1950, but the California Desert Act of 1994 upgraded the monument to a national park and enlarged it to 795,000 acres.

This recent history speaks of the different ways that humans have adapted to the desert: that of the Serrano, who left arrowheads, clay pots, and pictographs in what is now the park; that of miners and ranchers, who left dams, tunnels, roads, buildings, and garbage dumps; and that of backpackers, who leave nothing permanent if they obey park rules. The backpackers' way seems an ambitious one – trying to survive so gently in the desert, even temporarily, that they leave less trace than a pack rat or a black-throated sparrow. Yet, with its rigors and complexities, the desert encourages ambitious adaptations. Maybe it requires them.

TRAVEL TIPS

DETAILS

How to Get There

The closest airport is in Palm Springs, one hour from the park. Airports are also located in Ontario, 90 minutes from the park, and Los Angeles, nearly four hours away. Rental cars are available at all airports.

When to Go

The park receives the most visitors in March and April, the fewest in January and July. Backcountry travel is the most comfortable in spring and fall, when daytime temperatures are in the 70s and 80s and nights are in the 50s. Summer is hot, with temperatures over 100°F during the day; nights are rarely cooler than the 60s. July and August receive the most rain – less than one inch – often as intense downpours. Winter brings cooler days, in the 50s or low 60s, and freezing temperatures at night. Snow occasionally falls at high elevations.

What to Do

More than 75 miles of trails may be used by backcountry hikers, who are also permitted to travel cross-country. Bicycles are allowed on both paved and unpaved roads; riding on unpaved routes, where automobile traffic is light, is safer. Cyclists are not permitted on park trails but may stop along bike routes and hike park trails. Joshua Tree is also a mecca for rock climbers.

Backcountry Permits

Visitors staying overnight should register at one of the 12 backcountry boards found throughout the park and marked on official maps. Backcountry users with horses or other stock animals should obtain a permit by calling 760-367-5541.

Special Planning

Because water sources are rare or nonexistent, hikers should carry one gallon of water per person per day – two gallons when weather is hot. A portable gas stove should be used in the backcountry, where fires are not permitted. Dry washes are prone to flash flooding and should be avoided after thunderstorms or severe weather. Temperatures can rise or fall 40 degrees within 24 hours; visitors should have clothing that they can layer on or off as conditions change.

Car Camping

The park's nine campgrounds have almost 500 sites. Most are available on a first-come, first-served basis; other can be reserved in advance. Call 760-367-5500 for details.

INFORMATION

Joshua Tree National Park

74485 National Park Drive, Twentynine Palms, CA 92277; tel: 760-367-5500.

Joshua Tree National Park Association

74485 National Park Drive, Twentynine Palms, CA 92277; tel: 760-367-5525.

The association carries books and maps related to the national park, plus a selection of publications about desert life (see Resource Directory).

Joshua Tree Chamber of Commerce

P.O. Box 600, Joshua Tree, CA 92252; tel: 760-366-3723.

Twentynine Palms Chamber of Commerce

6455 Mesquite Avenue, Unit A, Twentynine Palms, CA 92277; tel: 760-367-3445.

LODGING

PRICE GUIDE – double occupancy

$ = up to $49 $$ = $50–$99
$$$ = $100–$149 $$$$ = $150+

Homestead Inn Bed-and-Breakfast

74153 Two Mile Road, Twentynine Palms, CA 92277; tel: 760-367-0030.

This inn, located on 15 acres, has a variety of accommodations, many with private patios and views. Guests are served breakfast. Dinner and picnic lunches can be arranged. $$–$$$

29 Palms Inn

73950 Inn Avenue, Twentynine Palms, CA 92277; tel: 760-367-3505.

Guests stay in adobe bungalows dating from the 1930s or in cabins and suites. Some accommodations have kitchen facilities. $$–$$$

Yucca Inn and Suites

7500 Camino Del Cielo, Yucca Valley, CA 92284; tel: 760-365-3311 or 800-989-7644.

The inn has 55 standard rooms and 18 apartments, each with separate bedrooms and living and dining areas, plus a fully equipped kitchen. A pool is on the premises. $–$$

TOURS AND OUTFITTERS

Adventure 16

4620 Alvarado Canyon Road, San Diego, CA 92120; tel: 619-283-2362, extension 156, or 310-473-4574.

This outdoor-equipment supplier with several outlets in Southern California offers an extensive selection of wilderness outings. Two- and three-day backpacking trips at Joshua Tree are preceded by classes covering route planning, gear selection, backcountry cooking, cross-country navigation, and other survival skills. Families can sign up for outings that combine climbing and backpacking in the national park. Other seminars in climbing instruction are aimed at both beginning and experienced climbers. Also offered are women-only and photography trips.

Joshua Tree Rock Climbing School

P.O. Box 29, Joshua Tree, CA 92252; tel: 760-366-4745 or 800-890-4745.

From September through June, instruction for all levels of rock climbers is held in Joshua Tree National Park, which has more than 4,000 climbing routes. Beginning courses are scheduled every weekend; intermediate instruction is given every other weekend. Climbers from neophytes to experts can also arrange for private guiding services.

Mountain Adventures Seminars

P.O. Box 5450, Bear Valley, CA 95223; tel: 209-753-6556.

Climbers with belaying skills can sign up for the Joshua Tree Rock Camp, where they learn about climbing equipment and rappelling techniques, as well as climbing safety and backcountry ethics. Participants camp in the park during the three- to five-day camps, and the outfitter provides meals and camping and climbing equipment. Individual guiding services are also available.

Trail Discovery

P.O. Box 8394, Palm Springs, CA 92263; tel: 888-324-4453 or 760-325-4453.

Hikers explore the flora and fauna of Joshua Tree, as well as the area's history, on a variety of guided treks. Visitors can ascend Ryan Mountain for a panoramic view of the park or go to the Desert Queen Mine, where they will see the ruins of a large gold mine and a scattering of abandoned shaft mines. Trail Discovery tailors trips to suit hikers' interests.

Excursions

Anza–Borrego Desert State Park

200 Palm Canyon Drive, Borrego Springs, CA 92004; tel: 760-767-5311.

The largest state park in California occupies a 600,000-acre chunk of the Colorado Desert that backcountry travelers may access on foot or by four-wheel-drive vehicle. The terrain ranges from badlands with stunning sandstone formations, to fan palm oases and riparian canyons, to pinyon pine forest at high elevations. April, the peak time for blooming cacti and wildflowers, lures birds and other wildlife, as well as visitors, in abundance.

Death Valley National Park

P.O. Box 579, Death Valley, CA 92328; tel: 760-786-2331

A gigantic museum of geology, Death Valley's landscape was shaped over millions of years as tectonic plates beneath the earth shifted and the land aboveground was carved by rain and wind. On display are canyons with huge alluvial fans opening onto the valley floor, curious badlands tinted by mineral deposits, fields of sand dunes and salt flats, and a deeply furrowed volcanic crater. Most hiking is cross-country; visitors may also explore the backcountry by four-wheel-drive vehicle, on horseback, or by bicycle.

Mojave National Preserve

222 East Main Street, Suite 202, Barstow, CA 92311; tel: 760-255-8800.

In size – an astounding 1.4 million acres – this preserve rivals those in Alaska, but its natural features couldn't be more different. The preserve is the meeting place of three deserts – the Mojave, Great Basin, and Sonoran – with elevations from 900 to 8,000 feet. Traveling on foot, by four-wheel-drive, or on horseback allows visitors to see volcanic formations such as cinder cones and lava fields, rose quartz sand dunes, plants from all three desert systems, and wildlife including lizards, snakes, desert bighorn sheep, and bobcats.

Sequoia and Kings Canyon National Parks

California

Yosemite National Park is apt to appall as well as inspire the nature lover. For all its splendor, it is simply too popular for its own good. But there is a place in the Central Sierra where people are scarce and wildlife is abundant, where a vast wilderness encompassing a rich array of different habitats beckons from all points of the compass, where the predominant sounds are the sough of the wind through giant sequoias and the coursing of white water down granite canyons, not revving cars and tour buses. ◆ **Sequoia and Kings Canyon National Parks,** about 50 miles south of Yosemite, are contiguous parks often viewed as a single entity. Their 9,420 square miles receive far fewer visitors, have far less in the way of developed amenities, and provide a far more accurate insight into the nature of the pristine Sierra Nevada, the Sierra that existed prior to European exploration and settlement. ◆ The parks' lower elevations – 3,000 to 7,000 feet – support great stands of old-growth trees. Here is the eponymous giant sequoia, the world's largest living thing. The biggest of these big trees is the General Sherman Tree, located in the **Giant Forest** in Sequoia National Park. Its vital statistics: 275 feet tall, 103 feet in circumference at the base, 1,385 tons in weight, and 2,100 years in age. There are also huge sugar pines, ponderosa pines, Jeffrey pines, and red firs. This ancient coniferous forest comprises one of the country's rarest ecosystems, and numerous uncommon and reclusive animals inhabit it, including the California spotted owl, northern goshawk, fisher, marten, and possibly wolverine. ◆ Alluring as the big trees are, the parks'

Twin parks hold classic Sierra wonders – breathtaking canyons, cathedral-like forests, and granite peaks, including the highest mountain in California.

A backpacker pauses to savor a canyon panorama along a trail that leads ever higher toward the crest of the Sierra Nevada.

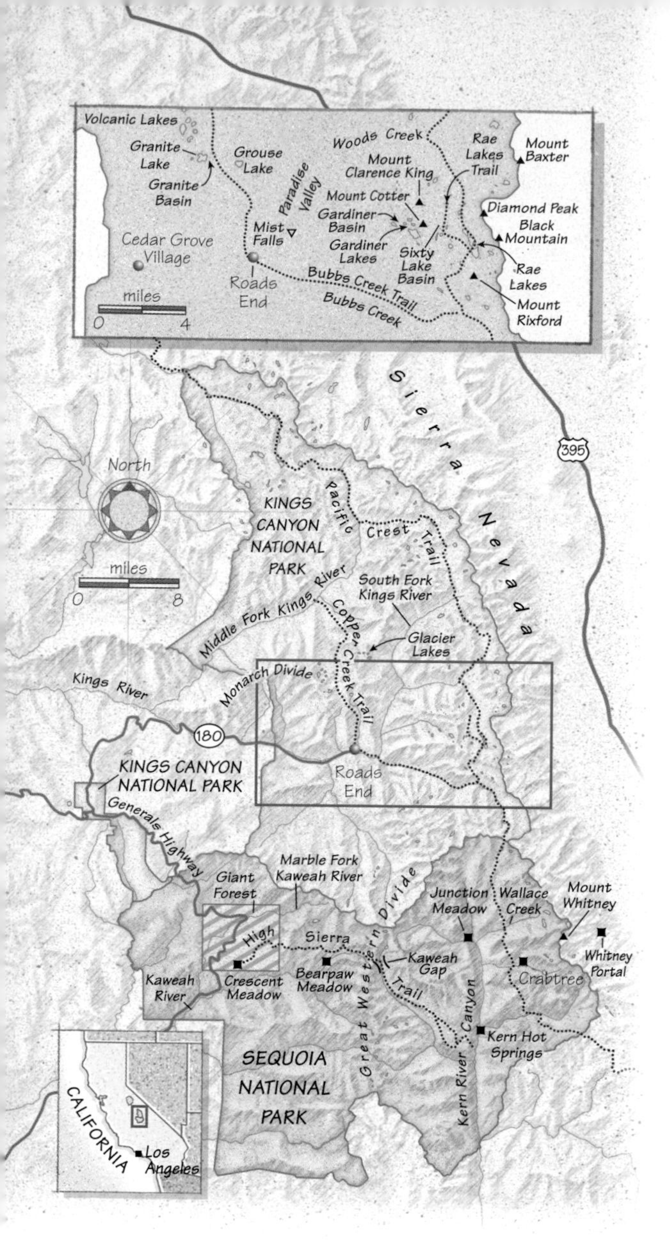

high-elevation terrain is the primary draw for backpackers. The Kings Canyon and Sequoia backcountry conjoin with several contiguous wilderness areas to form one of the largest tracts of roadless wildland in the Lower 48 states. This is immensely beautiful and immensely rugged country – a fastness of rock shield and peaks, meadows and lakes, creeks lined with wildflowers, and groves of alpine fir and hemlock. Most backpackers opt for trips ranging from three days to a week, but a decade of summers could be spent here, and there would still be country left to see.

Peak Experience

If the parks have a grand tour, it has to be the **High Sierra Trail**, a 70-mile route that begins at **Crescent Meadow** and tops out – literally – at the summit of 14,494-foot **Mount Whitney**, the highest peak in the contiguous 48 states. This well-designed and well-maintained trail, one of the first fully trans-Sierra trails constructed, takes seven to 10 days to traverse; a shorter option is to hike one or two days to **Bearpaw Meadow** or slightly beyond, then return to the trailhead. Even this truncated trek provides splendid vistas of classic Sierra alpine terrain.

The trail begins at 6,800 feet above the **Marble Fork of the Kaweah River**, at the upper margins of the ancient coniferous forests, then climbs gradually about 12 miles to **Bearpaw Meadow**. About six miles farther is **Kaweah Gap**, a 10,600-foot-high pass that affords views of the **Great Western Divide**, a bulwark of granite peaks guarding the heart of the parks' interior wilderness. On the east slope of the divide, the trail descends into the **Kern River Canyon**. One of the wildest and most beautiful of the Sierra's rivers, the Kern carves a great valley right through the granite heart. Wildflowers and copses of incense cedar, white fir, and ponderosa frame turbulent white water and deep, green pools burgeoning with trout. There's good fishing in the Kern, so pack a rod.

Junction Meadow, about eight miles up the Kern, is a stellar place to camp, though a little crowded during midsummer. Still, this traditional layover spot is an ideal place to recuperate from the rigors of conquering the Great Western Divide. You can fish, swim – and soak in **Kern Hot Springs**, a partially developed vent of luxuriously hot, mineralized water downstream from the meadow. The springs are particularly enjoyable at night, when the Milky Way blazes down from the sky and the only sounds are the murmur of the Kern and the occasional muted hoot of an owl.

The trail traverses east up **Wallace Creek** to connect with the **Pacific Crest Trail**, then cuts south to **Crabtree**. Lay over here for a night to get acclimatized, then strike out for Whitney in the morning. The final eight-and-a-half-mile stretch is rigorous due to the altitude, but it requires no technical climbing skills. The vantage is spectacular, affording perhaps the premier view of the spine of the Sierra and the sere deserts that lap against the cordillera's east slope. After topping out, backpackers usually hike to the **Whitney Portal** trailhead, the standard dropoff point for shuttle vehicles.

The **Rae Lakes** route is another classic Central Sierra hike, a 40-mile loop that covers big timber to alpine meadows. The trailhead is at **Roads End**, east of **Cedar Grove Village** in Kings Canyon National Park. The trail wends through the sheer, magisterial gorge of the **South Fork of the Kings River** – popularly known as "the" Kings Canyon, though it is but one of the several great declivities of this canyon system. The route skirts northward by **Mist Falls**, an impressive, broad cataract, and through the aptly named **Paradise Valley**, a wide, three-mile-long vale framed by sheer, soaring cliffs. At the northern terminus of the valley, the trail follows **Woods Creek**, slowly gaining altitude and ultimately connecting with the Pacific Crest Trail.

Here the route turns south through some of the loveliest country in the High Sierra, the **Rae Lakes Basin**. Almost 10 large lakes are set into the granite, like sapphires in silver, some 20 more lie just to the east in **Sixty Lake Basin** and **Gardiner Basin**. Framing them all is a diadem of peaks: Mount Clarence King, Mount Cotter, Mount Rixford, Black Mountain, Diamond Peak, and Mount

A juniper (above) is gnarled by severe winds and snowpack above timberline. Stunted trees, known as krummholz, can be several centuries old.

Pockets of snow (left) linger on the peaks surrounding the Rae Lakes.

Pikas (opposite) live in colonies and spend daylight hours gathering and storing grasses for the winter. Hikers often hear them bleating from within their dens.

Matching the Hatch

On a backcountry trip in Sequoia and Kings Canyon, a fly rod should be considered essential gear, for the parks offer some of the best trout fishing in the Sierra Nevada.

The Middle and South Forks of the Kings River are gold-medal fisheries. The Middle Fork is almost exclusively a rainbow-trout river; the South Fork contains both browns and rainbows. There is a short stonefly hatch in spring, and the fish feed eagerly on the big bugs. Nymph patterns work well, with local flyfishers favoring size six and eight imitations. Caddis flies hatch throughout the year, so have a wide array of patterns in sizes 12 to 16. Emerging nymphs are particularly effective, as are attractor flies.

The forks of the Kings are dangerous during high water and should be fished with care through June. The best fishing is in midsummer, when the water is relatively low. Cast into the pocket water and the riffles at the heads of pools, where the trout tend to stack up with their noses pointed upstream, waiting for insects to wash down.

High Sierra lakes have a short ice-free season and are extremely low in nutrients. Because food is relatively hard to come by, fish often strike fast and furiously at both dry and wet flies, particularly in lakes seldom visited by anglers. Brook trout, non-natives, are extremely common in the lakes and creeks of the High Sierra. Backcountry waters also hold native golden trout, a beautiful rainbow subspecies with flanks of burnished gold, lavender, and crimson. Brookies, viewed as competitors to rainbows, can be kept for the frying pan, but golden trout should be released. Efforts are under way to re-establish these jewel-like fish throughout their historic range in the Central Sierra.

An angler (left) fishes for trout in a high-country river.

Sequoias (opposite), the largest living things on the planet, are also among the oldest.

A backpacker (below) takes in the view from the John Muir Trail.

Baxter, to name the most eminent. The basin offers almost endless possibilities for day hikes and fishing. The trail continues south past the lakes, hooking up with the **Bubbs Creek Trail**. A 15-mile hike returns backpackers to their cars at Roads End.

High-Elevation Inhabitants

For a short, sharp ingress to the high country, try the **Copper Creek Trail**, which also starts at Roads End east of **Cedar Grove**. Don't attempt this route if you can't handle steep trails with a full pack – Copper Creek gains 5,000 feet in about eight miles. It's worth the effort, though, ultimately debouching into the alpine vastness of the **Monarch Divide** area, a sprawling tableland between the **South Fork** and **Middle Fork of the Kings**.

The first few miles can be particularly challenging during summer. The trail is on a south-facing slope with little shade, and most of the vegetation consists of manzanita, chamise, and scrub oak. The sun pounds unrelentingly on the route, making for hot, parched hiking. An early start is therefore recommended – at sunrise, if possible. Timber at the higher elevations affords some midday relief.

The trail exits timberline at **Granite Basin**, where backpackers have a number of choices. To the west lie the Volcanic Lakes and Granite Lake; to the east are the Glacier Lakes, Kid Lakes, and Grouse Lake. Great meadows of wildflowers, lasting well into August, frame them all. There are no maintained trails to the lakes, but cross-country hiking, with topo map and compass, is easy in this open country.

The Monarch Divide area is favored habitat for yellow-bellied marmots and pikas, the dominant herbivores of the High Sierra. Similar in appearance to woodchucks, marmots are large, ocher-and-brown rodents that often sun on boulders and scree overlooking meadows. When disturbed, they emit shrill whistles – something they do with particular enthusiasm when golden eagles, their primary predators, are in the area.

Pikas – or "rock rabbits" as they are sometimes known – are, in fact, related to rabbits, though they look more like fat, tailless gerbils with oversized ears. They live in small colonies and are provident to a degree unusual in animals: they spend most of the summer in front of their burrows cutting and drying grass and herbs, which they store as hay for winter consumption.

Myriad varieties of wildlife thrive throughout the parks. Spotted owls are doing quite well, and the parks and surrounding Sequoia National Forest support the largest population of fishers in the Sierra Nevada and southern Cascades.

More common species are, well, common. The Sierra's top mammals, black bears and mountain lions, are abundant. The parks contain some of the best songbird habitat in California, with riparian areas and woodland-meadow transition zones constituting the prime places to observe the spring and fall migrations.

It is something of a puzzle that Sequoia and Kings Canyon National Parks have remained the best-kept secret in the Sierra. Then again, they hold little appeal for people with a theme-park frame of mind. There are no guided jitney tours, no bicycle concessions, no ice-skating rinks. There is only the Sierra itself – a beautiful and remote kingdom of forest, meadow, and rock, beckoning those who ascribe to the simple philosophy that human endeavor cannot improve upon nature.

TRAVEL TIPS

DETAILS

How to Get There

The only road access to Sequoia and Kings Canyon is from the west side of the Sierra Nevada. The nearest airports are in Fresno, about an hour and a half from Grant Grove, and Visalia, about an hour and a half from Ash Mountain and two and a half hours from Grant Grove. In the summer, a shuttle operates between General Sherman Tree, Lodgepole, Moro Rock, Crescent Meadow, and Wuksachi Village.

When to Go

Most backcountry travelers visit in summer; July and August are the busiest months. Visitation is lowest in winter. Summer temperatures range from lows in the 40s and 50s to highs in the 70s and 80s. Nighttime temperatures can drop into the 20s and low 30s at high elevations. By late fall, nights throughout the parks are consistently below freezing. Winter daytime temperatures are in the 30s and 40s. The parks receive 40 to 45 inches of precipitation each year, most of it in winter.

What to Do

Backcountry travelers can hike on 800 miles of trails or explore the parks on guided trips. The streams and lakes are open to anglers. Bicycles may be used on the parks' roads but not on trails. The parks are also a popular mountain-climbing destination. Visitors come in winter to cross-country ski and snowshoe.

Backcountry Permits

A permit is required for all overnight stays in the backcountry and may be reserved in advance by mail or fax. Permit requests should be sent no earlier than March 1 and no later than three weeks before the start of a trip. In summer, a quota system is enforced for popular trailheads. For more information, call the Wilderness Office at 559-565-3708.

Special Planning

Backpackers headed for elevations above 9,000 feet should be prepared for wide swings in temperatures by carrying extra layers of clothing and using a three-season sleeping bag. They should also bring reliable raingear. A portable gas stove should be used in lieu of building campfires. Visitors are advised to rent or buy bear-resistant canisters to hold their food. Otherwise, food must be hung 20 feet aboveground and 10 feet from tree trunks according to the counterbalancing method described in instructions accompanying permits.

Car Camping

Over 800 sites at 12 campgrounds are available on a first-come, first-served basis. The 405 sites at Lodgepole and Dorst campgrounds may be reserved from Memorial Day through September; call 800-365-2267.

INFORMATION

Sequoia and Kings Canyon National Parks

47050 Generals Highway, Three Rivers, CA 93271; tel: 559-565-3341.

Sequoia Natural History Association

HCR 89, Box 10, Three Rivers, CA 93271; tel: 559-565-3759.

The association carries guidebooks on a variety of topics related to the two parks and the Sierra Nevada (see Resource Directory), as well as maps.

LODGING

PRICE GUIDE – double occupancy

$ = up to $49 $$ = $50–$99

$$$ = $100–$149 $$$$ = $150+

Bearpaw Meadow Camp

Delaware Parks Services, P.O. Box 89, Sequoia National Park, CA 93262; tel: 888-252-5757.

Backpackers hike more than 11 miles, with a 1,400-foot elevation gain, to reach this camp where they stay in tents with single beds. The price includes breakfast and dinner. $$$$

Cedar Grove Lodge

Kings Canyon Park Services, P.O. Box 909, Kings Canyon National Park, CA 93633; tel: 559-335-5500.

This lodge located along Kings River has 18 motel-style rooms. $$

Grant Grove Cabins

Kings Canyon Park Services, P.O. Box 909, Kings Canyon National Park, CA 93633; tel: 559-335-5500.

Nine cabins have private baths; one has a refrigerator. There are also 24 rustic cabins with shared shower facilities, plus 23 tent cabins. $–$$

Pear Lake Ski Hut

Sequoia Association, HCR 89, Box 10, Three Rivers, CA 93271; tel: 559-565-3759.

From mid-December through early April, trekkers can ski a steep, six-mile course to this hut located just north of Pear Lake at 9,200 feet. The hut sleeps 10. Reservations are granted by a lottery system. $

TOURS AND OUTFITTERS

High Sierra Pack Station

P.O. Box 1166, Clovis, CA 93613; tel: 559-285-7225.

Horses carry hikers and their gear into Evolution Valley and Goddard Canyon from the western side of the Sierra Nevada. Backpackers may have their gear brought in and can hike out after exploring the area on their own.

Leelin Llama Treks

P.O. Box 2363, Julian, CA 92036; tel: 800-526-2725.

Guided llama expeditions into the twin parks range from four days to nine days covering over 30 miles and ascents over 11,000-foot passes. Trips begin on the west side of the Sierra Nevada at Florence Lake or trailheads inside the parks. Destinations include the John Muir Trail, Mono Hot Springs, and Evolution Valley. The outfitter supplies all gear, including fishing tackle.

Sequoia Kings Pack Trains

P.O. Box 209, Independence, CA 93526; tel: 760-387-2797.

Based in the Onion Valley on the eastern side of the Sierra Nevada, this outfitter leads pack trips over Kearsarge Pass to various destinations in the parks, including the Rae Lakes basin and the John Muir Trail. Treks can be fully guided, or travelers can pack in by horse and hike out. Hikers on the John Muir Trail can arrange to be resupplied.

Sierra Mountain Center

P.O. Box 95, Bishop, CA 93514; tel: 760-873-8526.

In summer, the center's guides take visitors into the parks for rock climbing and peak ascents. In winter, multiday trips on skis traverse the Sierra Nevada from east to west. Return trips by air, which give a view of the mountains, can be arranged.

Excursions

Lassen Volcanic National Park

P.O. Box 100, Mineral, CA 96063; tel: 530-595-4444.

The truncated, snow-capped caldera of 10,457-foot Mount Lassen comes in and out of view as backpackers explore the park's network of trails. The mountain last erupted in the early 1900s and is part of the Cascade Range, which in this national park meets the Sierra Nevada. Large, black cinder cones, impressive lava pinnacles, and steaming fumaroles are among the volcanic features that shape the landscape. The park's only through-road closes in winter and is used by cross-country skiers.

Redwood National Park

111 Second Street, Crescent City, CA 95531; tel: 707-464-6101.

Preserving a 50-mile-long strip of land on the Pacific Ocean, this park is the place to wander among ancient redwoods, investigate the wealth of marine life in tidepools, and from beachside bluffs look for sea lions and migrating gray whales. Trails take backpackers north and south along the coast, as well as inland to prairies and oak woodlands. Three state preserves, Prairie Creek, Jedediah Smith, and Del Norte Coast, are joined in this national park and also offer recreational opportunities for cyclists and horseback riders.

Yosemite National Park

P.O. Box 577, Yosemite, CA 95389; tel: 209-372-0200.

Backcountry travelers' best strategy is to map out routes that take them into the high country of the Sierra Nevada, far from the park's roads and popular attractions. More than 650,000 acres are designated wilderness, where hundreds of miles of trails skirt granite domes, wildflower meadows, and alpine lakes, with plentiful chances to observe Sierra wildlife. A segment of the Pacific Crest Trail and portions of two wild and scenic rivers, the Tuolumne and the Merced, run through the park.

North Cascades National Park

Washington

t sparkles as a seductive reward for flushed faces and ravaged feet, this miniature alpine creek at the end of the **Sahale Arm Trail**, 7,200 feet high in the **North Cascades**. It's been a six-mile, 3,600-foot skyward slog on a warm and humid August day. Half a dozen trail survivors tug off their boots and splash their dogs into the cool stream – and howl in unexpected pain. The creek is a torrent of frigid needles. Small wonder. Fifty feet above is its headwater, the icy toe of **Sahale Glacier**, melting resentfully in the summer sun. ◆ Agony aside, this is the perfect introduction to the **North Cascades National Park** complex. Glaciers are the form-givers here, the gargantuan rasps that sculpted hundreds of jagged mountain peaks, sapphire lakes, and gaping gorges; the reservoirs for the countless waterfalls that make the name "Cascades" so perfect; and ultimately the arbiters of all the life in the neighborhood: the woolly mammoth and saber-toothed cat, among many other species, vanished in the last ice age 10,000 years ago. There are far more glaciers in the North Cascades (more than 300) than in Alaska's Glacier Bay National Park (37), and although they are currently in recession, they will be back in force, marching to the rhythms of geologic time. ◆ Speaking geologically, the **Cascade Range** stretches from southern British Columbia to northern California, a 700-mile-long stegosaurus spine that bedeviled 19th-century explorers and today guarantees cities such as Seattle and Portland long, wet winters. The South Cascades are spiked with volcanoes – Lassen Peak, Mount Hood, Mount St. Helens, Mount Rainier – but the northern reach of the range, extending

Lofty peaks draped with glaciers and waterfalls draw backcountry explorers to this alpine fastness at the Canadian border.

Fall brings a dusting of snow to a ridge in the North Cascades, where winter arrives early and lingers well into spring.

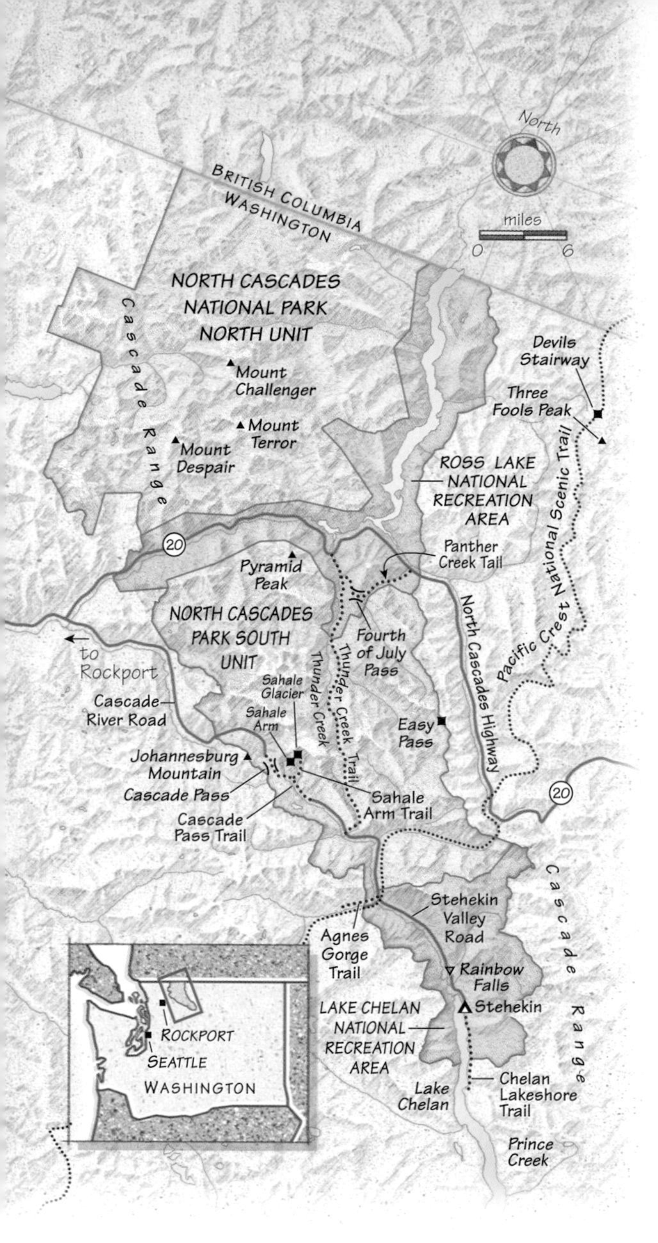

from Washington's Snoqualmie Pass to British Columbia's Mount Garibaldi, is also the product of cataclysmic tectonic forces thrusting and heaving. From the air, the North Cascades are a pandemonium of glacier-choked peaks, many of them 8,000 to 9,000 feet high, separated by imponderable yawns of green-black gorges. Names given these geological features by climbers and explorers evoke their character perfectly: Devils Stairway, Three Fools Peak, Mount Challenger, Mount Despair, and Mount Terror. Easy Pass, by the way, usually requires an ice ax until mid-July.

Nice country for a national park, but it took a while. Agitation for federal protection for these mountains began as early as 1892, but the chaos of claims on them – by loggers, miners, hunters, hydroelectric dam investors, and, finally, conservationists – thwarted agreement until 1968. Today the North Cascades are managed, to varying degrees, by a quilt of federal landlords. North Cascades National Park, the Ross Lake and Lake Chelan National Recreation Areas, and three contiguous national forests comprise 5.13 million acres, an area larger than Massachusetts. Few humans have set foot on much of it.

The Pass to Solitude

Unless you're into mule trains, there are just two gateways into the heart of the North Cascades: the **North Cascades Highway** (Washington State Route 20) and the 50-mile water trip up **Lake Chelan**.

The highway opened in September 1972 and promptly closed two months later, as it has almost every November to April since. The deep snowpack and terrible avalanche hazard make it impractical to keep open year-round. In amenable weather, the park is a two-hour drive from Seattle. At the entrance from the west around the appropriately named town of **Rockport**, the peaks gather into a crowd so vertiginous that just staring up at them seems to threaten nosebleed. Surprise waterfalls crash through the ever-green curtain wall beside the road, while summer cumulus clouds rub noses with glaciers a mile above. For many visitors, this windshield wilderness is spectacle enough.

But hands-on contact with the North Cascades is far better, and despite the government's ever-penurious trail-maintenance budget, more than 100 trails in and around the park offer a vast range of wilderness backpacking experiences and an astonishing variety of scenery. The only limitation is the weather: some years the snow doggedly persists into August in the higher elevations, so hikers, wildflowers, and mosquitoes all have to cram their action into two frenetic months. Cross-country skiers and snowshoers

have more time and solitude, but heads up: the North Cascades are possibly the most avalanche prone mountains in the country.

Many Cascade connoisseurs have a love/hate relationship with one particular trail reached from a gravel spur off the North Cascades Highway: **Cascade Pass/Sahale Arm**. Unspeakably gorgeous, it is also notoriously crowded, just as one would expect of a world-class day hike located only 120 miles from an urban conglomeration of 3.3 million outdoors enthusiasts – who, come July, are stark-raving bonkers after nine months of gray, soggy weather. Tip: Weekdays are better. Also: Most casual hikers go no farther than Cascade Pass, so the backpacking trek up Sahale Arm is sometimes substantially lonelier.

The trail begins at an elevation of 3,600 feet in dense Douglas fir, red cedar, and western hemlock forest, signature conifers of the west slope of the North Cascades. First-time hikers are always surprised at, and sometimes unnerved by, the violence

Mount Shuksan (above) is reflected in a still alpine lake just outside the park in the Mount Baker Wilderness.

A climber traverses Sulfide Glacier (right), one of several that ring 9,131-foot Mount Shuksan in the northwest corner of the park.

regularly occurring across the valley from the parking lot: every few minutes, the glaciers draping 8,065-foot Johannesburg Mountain release an avalanche of ice and snow in a volley that sounds like distant cannons trading rounds in a canyon. Another proper introduction to the North Cascades.

The trail climbs five and a half miles, like a snake with the bends, to 5,400-foot **Cascade Pass**, which is subalpine territory. Trees are stunted at this elevation, and the views open up to horizons defined by a sugar-glazed skyline of impossibly spiky peaks. Valleys sag gracefully below in the characteristic U shapes of glacial gouging (river gorges resemble a V), and wildflower-carpeted meadows stretch fetchingly along **Sahale Arm**. If you choose to continue, the effort is worth it: there may be no other trail in the Pacific Northwest that feels so much like a parkway into the heavens.

This is one polarity of the North Cascades – the exhilarating expanse, the feeling of taking part in the merger of mountain and sky. The opposite experience – the intimate encounter – is equally valuable, and emotionally altogether different.

Forest Ramble

Thunder Creek to **Fourth of July Pass** sounds like a route full of explosive drama, but it's more enchanted forest than visual fireworks. Beside the turquoise creek is almost a rain forest; lower elevations of the west slopes enjoy 80 inches of precipitation a year. Fungi of many varieties thrive on live trees and decaying logs right next to the trail; western red cedars challenge their alleged old-growth height limit of 200 feet.

A party of three backpackers stops to try to encircle one of these cedars; their finger-linked hug fails to surround it by three feet. That would make it about – let's see, 18 feet in circumference and, going by Daniel Mathews's invaluable *Cascade–Olympic*

Backpackers (above) in the high country have dramatic views of glacier-carved valleys and peaks 8,000 to 9,000 feet high.

Wildflower meadows (right) greet hikers from midsummer through September.

Natural History: A Trailside Reference, in the region of 500 years old. And it's certainly worth a moment's reverent contemplation. Rot-resisting red cedar has proven too valuable for its own good; the few big ones left in the Northwest are practically museum specimens.

The trail peels away from the riverbank after two miles and begins climbing fairly relentlessly toward the pass three more miles and 2,300 feet above. The slow hiker's oxlike plod here is perfect; it allows the thoughtful observation of detail. Mottled sunlight struggles through the trees and seems to breathe velvet light on the forest-floor moss at the same time that it accents the roughness of the Douglas fir bark by burnishing its cinnamon ridges and avoiding its black fissures.

And listen to the Cascade Philharmonic. On many west slope hikes, the music of flowing, running, or crashing water is present, and different sources weave a spatial fugue that would astonish and delight Bach. These are not amorphous masses of white noise; each has a distinct character. Thunder Creek provides the vaguely ominous basso continuo a thousand feet below. A seasonal creek around the trail's next bend supplies a polite alto gurgle. A microwaterfall underfoot is a silky rush of soprano sibilants. As you plod, the orchestration shifts constantly in space.

North Cascade wildlife may choose to make its presence known on trails like these. Expect everything from the pika, a pipsqueak rabbit that looks like an overfed rodent, to the ubiquitous black bear. There may be grizzlies roaming the North Cascades – bear biologists estimate the total population at five to 20 – but they're as elusive as UFOs; scientists

Sheer rock walls (right) and glaciers make a challenging combination for the many mountaineers who are drawn to the park.

have found only tracks and fur to confirm their existence. Cougar sightings are on the rise, but it could be that there are just more people in the North Cascades to sight them.

Waterfall's Reward

It is possible to backpack from State Route 20 to **Stehekin**, the stunningly isolated settlement on the east slope of the North Cascades, but nearly everyone takes the path of much less resistance – the 50-mile boat ferry north from **Chelan**.

The town of Chelan is not a fetching destination, despite its resorts and relentless parade of villas marching up the lakefront. But over the two- to three-hour passage, the lakeside landscape matures from brown, arid hills into 8,000-foot glaciated peaks. The lake, third deepest in North America at 1,486 feet, actually fills the lower fifth of America's deepest gorge. If it somehow drained, you could peer down from 8,245-foot Pyramid Peak into a glacier-gouged trough 386 feet below sea level.

Some travelers budget all of 90 minutes for Stehekin, booking same-day return passage on the *Lady of the Lake*. A shuttle on the Stehekin end whisks these sightseers to 312-foot **Rainbow Falls**, the obvious attraction, and returns them to the dock. More deliberate visitors stay at North Cascades Stehekin Lodge, rent a cabin, or claim a campsite. Happily, Stehekin offers a laundry and shower 200 yards up the valley from Stehekin Landing, and shuttle buses regularly rattle up the lone gravel road to the valley's 18 trailheads. Tip: Bring a well-rounded box of food; Stehekin's "general store" is extremely basic.

Stehekin's 100-odd residents are disconnected from the world except for the daily ferry and an occasional supply barge. There are no

A Good Judge of Mountains

Why climb a mountain? Mallory's classic, "Because it is there," is a throwaway line. William O. Douglas, who returned time and again throughout his 36-year career on the Supreme Court to hike his beloved Cascades, had a better answer: "One has the sensation of being part of something much bigger than himself, something great and majestic and wholesome."

Douglas grew up in the lee of the South Cascades, pondering Mount Adams and Mount Rainier from his front porch. On the day of his father's funeral, his eyes flooding with tears, he looked up at Mount Adams, cool and unperturbed in the crushing event of his childhood, and saw it as a spiritual anchor. From that moment, mountains became his friends.

Douglas had childhood polio, but he still devoured alpine peaks like a shark cruising through a school of tuna. In his 20s, he hiked 25 miles a day with a 30-pound pack. In his 60s, hair glacier white and face craggy as a Cascade ridge, he stayed as trim as a straw.

Mountains treated him well. They also shaped a conservation conscience. He constantly joined crusades to save lakes and forests from development. In one opinion, writing as a minority of one, he argued that alpine meadows should have legal standing, like individual citizens, to sue for protection. But he was an environmental elitist. He hated the roads that invaded his Cascades. "Potbellied men," he snorted, "smoking black cigars, who never could climb a hundred feet, were now in the sacred precincts of a great mountain."

Douglas believed that mountains are touchstones of spirituality and that they teach us character impossible to learn within the contrivance of cities. "When man knows how to live dangerously, he is not afraid to die," he wrote in *Of Men and Mountains.* "When he is not afraid to die, he is, strangely, free to live."

William O. Douglas (left) sought comfort and strength in the Cascades.

Deep snowpack (opposite, top) lures winter trekkers who want to cross-country ski and camp.

Yellow-bellied marmots (opposite, bottom) are inquisitive creatures that sometimes like to investigate campers' gear.

phones – only the park service's satellite link. People leave doors unlocked so neighbors can always borrow coffee or books. The geography supplies most of the entertainment. "I noticed when a tree lost its leaves in the fall," wrote Wendy Walker, a teacher who spent two years in the Stehekin Valley. "I woke at night when rock slides clattered off nearby cliffs. I learned to tell winter temperatures by the sound of the river."

A good scenic stroll here is the **Chelan Lakeshore Trail**, which you can stretch into a 17-mile backpack to **Prince Creek**, almost halfway to Chelan. But **Agnes Gorge** is the quintessential Cascades hike. This five-mile round-trip is rightly celebrated for its showoff wildflowers – the orange-and-black tiger lily, the scarlet harsh paintbrush, the snow-white queen's cup, and trillium. This east slope forest is dark and dense, but a noticeably different biological world from the wetter woods across the passes. The dominating tree is the ponderosa pine instead of the Douglas fir, and moss and mushrooms are rare. (Stehekin gets only 34 inches of rain a year, less than Seattle.) Backpackers need to watch where they step; rattlesnakes thrive on this side.

But the forest isn't the star attraction of this trail. The nameless waterfall at its end is. The Pacific Northwest is promiscuous with waterfalls, but no other one offers such mesmerizing architecture. A pair of creeks tips over the south wall, marrying on the tumble, then strikes a bunch of rounded boulders and splays into silvery fans, like a crowd of veiled brides mingling in a misty park. The waterfall's final splashdown can't be seen – the gorge is 210 feet deep, its walls too vertical to risk peering down. It's another fitting introduction to the North Cascades, or a memory to hold in parting, a pantheon of noisy water and steepness and inscrutability.

TRAVEL TIPS

DETAILS

How to Get There

The Seattle airport is a three-hour drive from the park's North Cascades Visitor Center; rental cars are available at the airport. The Lake Chelan Boat Company (509-682-4584) provides service from Chelan to Stehekin. Chelan Airways (509-682-5555) offers floatplane service from Chelan to Stehekin. From mid-May to mid-October, bus service operates from Stehekin Landing into Stehekin Valley; call 360-856-5700, ext. 340, for information and reservations.

When to Go

The hiking season usually runs from April through October, though trails at the highest elevations can remain covered with snow into August. Most backcountry visitors come during the drier summer season, from mid-June through September. Peak visitation occurs in August; the fewest visitors come in January. Temperatures vary widely in summer from 95°F down to freezing, depending on location and elevation. Average annual rainfall on the park's west slopes is 80 inches; east slopes are dryer. Summer storms bring both rain and wind. Heavy snow and rain occur from fall through spring, when temperatures drop significantly.

What to Do

Hikers and backpackers have use of nearly 400 miles of trails and can explore the park off trail and on guided trips. Visitors also come to float and fish the lakes and rivers. Bicycles are not allowed on trails but may be used for touring the North Cascades Highway and the Mount Baker Scenic Byway. Mountain bikers are permitted to ride on side roads. The park is a popular destination for horseback riders, mountain climbers, cross-country skiers, and snowshoers.

Backcountry Permits

Permits are required for all overnight stays and are issued in person only, on the first day of a trip or the day before. They are available at the Wilderness Information Center and at various ranger stations; call 360-873-5700, extension 515, for locations.

Special Planning

When obtaining backcountry permits, visitors are encouraged to review their routes with a ranger. A "Wilderness Trip Planner" is available in advance from the park. Because the weather is unpredictable, travelers should carry dependable raingear and extra clothing. The park prefers that visitors use portable gas stoves rather than build campfires; fires are prohibited in some areas. All food and garbage must be stored in an animal-resistant canister or hung in a tree 15 feet aboveground and five feet from the trunk. Insect repellent and headnets are often necessary in July and August, peak time for biting insects. Winter visitors are advised to check with the park on road closures and avalanche conditions.

Car Camping

The park's campgrounds have some 400 sites available on a first-come, first-served basis. State and Forest Service campgrounds are located off State Route 20.

INFORMATION

North Cascades National Park Service Complex

2105 State Route 20, Sedro-Woolley, WA 98284; tel: 360-856-5700.

The complex includes other visitor centers: Golden West Visitor Center at Stehekin (tel: 360-856-5700, extension 340), Glacier Public Service Center in Glacier (tel: 360-599-2714), and North Cascades Visitor Center in Newhalem (tel: 206-386-4495). Most are open seasonally.

Northwest Interpretive Association

2105 State Route 20, Sedro-Woolley, WA 98284; tel: 360-856-5700, extension 291.

The association carries guidebooks (see Resource Directory) and maps of the national park.

LODGING

PRICE GUIDE – double occupancy

$ = up to $49 $$ = $50–$99

$$$ = $100–$149 $$$$ = $150+

A Cab in the Woods

9303 Dandy Place, Rockport, WA 98283; tel: 360-873-4106.

Set on five acres near the Skagit River are five cabins, each with a living room, bedroom, kitchen, and gas fireplace. $$

Cascade Corrals Log Cabins

P.O. Box 67, Stehekin, WA 98852; tel: 509-682-4677.

Two furnished cabins both have fully equipped kitchens. One sleeps five; the other sleeps nine. $$$

North Cascades Stehekin Lodge

P.O. Box 457, Chelan, WA 98816; tel: 509-682-4494.

Located at the headwaters of Lake Chelan, the lodge has 23 rooms, plus five cabins with kitchen facilities. It also has a restaurant. Guests can arrange hikes and bicycle tours and guided snowshoe walks. The lodge provides equipment and transportation to and from trails. $$–$$$

Ross Lake Resort

Rockport, WA 98285; tel: 206-386-4437.

Twelve cabins and three

bunkhouses sit on log floats along the Ross Lake shoreline. The cabins sleep one to five guests and have kitchens. The bunkhouses, accommodating six or more, have combined dining-sleeping-kitchen areas. The resort is reached by ferry. Guests and day users may rent canoes, kayaks, and motorboats, and have access to national park trails. $$–$$$

TOURS AND OUTFITTERS

Base Camp, Inc.

901 West Holly Street, Bellingham, WA 98225; tel: 360-733-5461.

During one- to five-day seminars, beginning mountain climbers learn skills such as using an ice ax and crampons, traveling in snow and on glaciers, and techniques of crevasse rescue. Instruction is offered from May through early August in the national park and Mount Baker Wilderness.

High Valley Llama Treks

7773 Pinelli Road, Sedro-Woolley, WA 98284; tel: 360-826-4133

From late May through September, llamas carry hikers' gear on treks of up to nine days. On longer trips, backcountry travelers can hike from Ross Lake to Lake Chelan, crossing several passes along the way. Shorter trips include hikes from Rainy Pass on the park's east side to Lake Chelan.

Redline River Adventures

P.O. Box 339, Darrington, WA 98241; tel: 360-436-0284 or 800-290-4500.

Visitors can take one-day float trips on the Skagit River beginning at Newhalem in the park. Trips lasting two to four days are offered on the Sauk River, part of the Skagit Wild and Scenic River System. Winter floats take wildlife watchers to see the bald eagles on the lower Skagit. Redline also provides shuttle services for backpackers and their vehicles.

Excursions

Crater Lake National Park

P.O. Box 7, Crater Lake, OR 97604; tel: 541-594-2211.

The collapse of a giant volcano created a basin that filled with 4.6 trillion gallons of rainwater and snowmelt to form a 1,932-foot-deep lake, the seventh deepest in the world. Crater Lake is the centerpiece of this 249-square-mile park with 90 miles of trails that include part of the Pacific Crest Trail. Backpackers hike through pine and hemlock forests and ascend peaks such as Mount Scott, the park's tallest. Cross-country skiers need never worry about the snowpack – the park receives more than 530 inches of snow each year.

Olympic National Park

600 East Park Avenue, Port Angeles, WA 98362; tel: 360-452-4501.

Backcountry travelers planning a trip to the Olympic Peninsula will soon realize why this national park is known as three parks in one. Of the 600 miles of trails, some take hikers through stands of temperate rain forest, and others head for glacier-capped mountains. Still other trails wander the 60-mile strip of Pacific Coast. Among the other backcountry choices, visitors may kayak offshore waters, cycle on park roads, and cross-country ski in winter.

Pacific Rim National Park

P.O. Box 280, Ucluelet, BC V0R 3A0; tel: 604-726-7721.

As its name reflects, this Canadian park is arrayed along the coast of British Columbia's Vancouver Island where old-growth rain forest meets the Pacific Ocean. Paddlers ply canoes and kayaks along the beaches and rocky shoreline and among the park's island clusters. Backpackers may experience the park on trails, including the West Coast Trail, a 45-mile route that makes a rewarding weeklong trek through old-growth cedar, spruce, and fir.

Gates of the Arctic National Park and Preserve *Alaska*

CHAPTER 22

At the crest of a ridge, two hikers pause. Four thousand feet below, the upper **John River** glints in the afternoon sun, its narrow valley hemmed in by steep slopes of tundra and jumbled talus. Ragged peaks of basalt pile off to the horizon. The air is so clear, the light so pure, that stone pinnacles 50 miles away seem close enough to touch. Time, like space, has become curiously fluid and transparent. Clock and compass explain little here. The eternal sun of the arctic summer circles the horizon, dipping low but never quite setting. ◆ **Gates of the Arctic National Park and Preserve** is off-the-charts huge: nearly eight million acres of wild, spectacular country where wolves and caribou roam, and scores of mountain peaks are still nameless. Headwaters and tributaries of four major Alaska rivers, the Kobuk, Noatak, Colville, and Koyukuk, drain this rugged Brooks Range heartland. With the exception of the gravel **Dalton Highway**, which brushes near the park's far eastern edge, there are no roads within hundreds of miles; besides isolated cabins and camps, the only permanent settlement inside park boundaries is the Eskimo village of **Anaktuvuk Pass**. Even by Alaskan standards, the sprawling park – more of a region, actually – is as remote as you can get. ◆ At the same time, it's surprisingly accessible, far more so than equally wild country elsewhere in the world. What's more, dozens of unguided summer trips are possible, from a few hours to two weeks in length, requiring only moderate back-country skills, solid equipment, a detailed map or two, and a sense of adventure. Or, if you'd rather depend on the services of an experienced

Forge a path over the tundra or let rivers carry you through this vast wilderness at the top of the world.

Dall sheep forage for plants in the upper elevations of the Brooks Range, where they are easy to spot against the rocky slopes.

An afternoon nap (left) is a fitting end to a day spent hiking over tussocks and scrambling up rocky slopes.

Bush planes (below) fly anglers to remote rivers and lakes that offer superb fishing for grayling, salmon, and Dolly Varden char.

outfitter, guided hiking and float trips are available to match any ability level.

The National Park Service has done something wise with Gates of the Arctic: left it alone. There are no hiking trails, mileposts, outhouses, picnic tables, or designated campsites. Once out in the country (as many Alaskans call the wilderness), you stand a better chance of encountering a wolverine than a park ranger. The freedom can be both intimidating and intoxicating. Which way you go or what happens next is truly up to you.

Robert Marshall's Peaks

How you arrive at your starting point is less a matter of choice. While it is possible to drive up the Dalton Highway from **Fairbanks** and walk into the eastern Gates, the only way to reach most areas is by small aircraft – scheduled passenger runs to one of several jumping-off points, combined with chartered bush planes. Flying services based in **Bettles**, **Ambler**, **Kotzebue**, and Fairbanks are generally very helpful and a good source of advice. Which service you choose depends on which part of the park you plan to visit. As a general rule, try to keep costly flying time to a minimum (you pay for the pilot's total time in the air, coming and going) and, whenever possible, end your trip at a settlement served by a regular air carrier.

A good place for the first-time visitor is the Inupiat village of Anaktuvuk Pass, just over an hour's scheduled flight from Fairbanks. Step off the small plane, walk to the edge of the runway, and the country begins: jumbled peaks and glacier-carved valleys seemingly without end. The Eskimos here call themselves Nunamiut, People of the Land. The village and much surrounding land are part of the local Native corporation's private inholdings. There is a National Park Service station here, a small but excellent cultural museum, and a place for visitors to camp. Just a half-day's stroll around town and onto the adjoining tundra under the craggy shadow of **Anaktiktok Mountain** gives you the feeling of having been somewhere far and away. For more ambitious

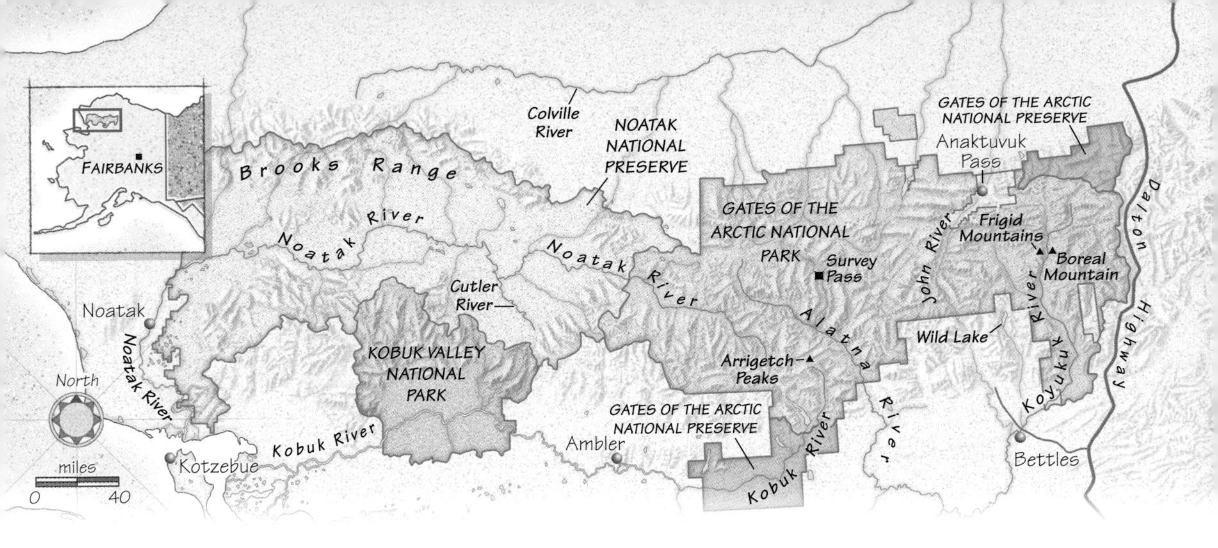

hikers, there are dozens of possible loops or one-way trips, from a few days to several weeks. Inquire at the ranger station for tips, information on private land, and matters of local etiquette.

A spectacular backpacking area is centered in the eastern park, near the **Frigid** and **Boreal Mountains**, the two peaks that outdoorsman Robert Marshall dubbed "Gates of the Arctic," a ringing phrase that became the name of this park. Extending in a band 40 miles north, the mountains are scenic and massive; some summits are above 7,000 feet, and near-vertical rock faces over 1,000 feet are common. Hike between the "Gates" and up the headwaters of the **Koyukuk River**, as Marshall did, or land at **Wild Lake** and spend a few days exploring out of a base camp. Fly into one of the lakes near **Survey Pass**, which sits astride the Continental Divide, and take one of several possible loop hikes in the area, from 10 to more than 50 miles.

Among the premier hiking destinations in all of Alaska is the **Arrigetch Peaks**. This cluster of abrupt granite spires, whose Eskimo name translates as "fingers outstretched," is accessible by air charter from Bettles and a hike from the **Alatna River** up any of several creeks that drain this 25-square-mile area of soaring, glacier-sculpted rock. Allow five to seven days; the sometimes strenuous trek is worth the visual spectacle.

Here, as with all other Gates trips, U.S. Geological Survey maps in 1:250,000 scale (1.5 inches equal to roughly five miles) are necessary for both planning and navigating. They're inexpensive and easily ordered from the USGS office in Fairbanks, preferably weeks in advance. Part of trip preparation should involve study – reading, researching, and careful poring over maps. This is more fun than work and will add tremendously to the richness of your experience.

If the thought of deciphering elevation contours on a foggy day up some nameless creek gives you the willies, take it as a sign that you should join a guided trip. This is big country, and finding your way can be difficult. Some backpackers, confident of their abilities honed on trails in Maine or Montana wildlands, find themselves in over their heads in the Gates of the Arctic, where the only trails are made by caribou.

Golden eagles raise one or two eaglets, which leave the nest 65 days after hatching.

Savoring the Land

Not only is this landscape without man-made reference points – it's also far rougher going than most folks are used to. Walking any distance in arctic Alaska means dealing with stretches of wet tundra, some of the most deceptive terrain on earth. From the air, it looks like manicured, rolling parkland; on the ground, it's another story. Imagine a foot-thick shag carpet, soaking wet and underlaid with half-inflated volleyballs and pockmarked with shin-deep holes. Dense bands of willow and alder – so thick you often have to wrestle through a step at a time – follow most streams. Then come waded crossings through cold, swift water. Higher up, slopes of crumbling rock demand care. A good day's trek for fit hikers with backpacks can be as few as five miles.

There are other hardships. On cloudy, windless summer days, swarms of mosquitoes require head nets, full-coverage clothing, slathered repellent, and a tight grip on sanity. The weather, too, is notorious in its extremes. Temperatures can rise or fall 30 degrees in less than an hour; rain may fall for days at a time. The traveling season, for hikers or boaters, is relatively short. Snow can lie deep in late May, and hard frosts can begin as early as mid-August. July is generally the safest month, for both conditions and stable weather.

The good news is that even if you don't hit a stretch of perfect conditions (which you just might), the country is stunning enough to make some inconvenience worthwhile. This is, after all, the Arctic. Part of your experience here involves stepping beyond the barriers we've erected between us and the natural world and embracing the challenges of each day.

Though the country makes demands, getting around on your own can be quite simple. Walking anywhere in the Gates means, for the most part, following river and creek valleys. As long as you pay attention to the direction of water and take frequent breaks to orient yourself, you stand little chance of getting lost. Study what lies ahead and behind, and make notes on your map.

Above all, relax. Rushing through the landscape without pausing makes little sense. There's nothing magical about miles covered, or about someplace you've marked as a goal. Find a good elevated vantage point where you can see for miles and travel with your eyes instead. Dig out binoculars and use them; make a conscious

The Arctic Winter

For a vastly different Gates of the Arctic experience, one much more true to the character of this spectacular landscape, consider a winter or spring visit. If you always wanted to walk on some distant planet, this is a good place to get the feel.

Human activity in the park falls off sharply after mid-September. The land becomes silent, wrapped in shrouds of ice fog and bathed in strange, slanted light. The sun hovers on the southern rim of the horizon. During the long arctic night – 20 hours of darkness at the winter solstice – the northern lights dance their pale green fire across the sky. Temperatures range from zero to –60°F, and much lower if you factor in wind chill.

Though extended trips require expedition skills, specialized equipment, and meticulous planning, a newcomer can still visit in winter. **Anaktuvuk Pass** is a good place to begin. You can make a day trip of it from Fairbanks, arriving on the earliest scheduled airline and leaving on the latest. Just the scenic flight in, over wild mountain country, is worth the entire trip. **Bettles**, south of the park, has a comfortable lodge, a National Park Service station, and an outfitter offering trips by dog sled. In both Anaktuvuk Pass and Bettles, cross-country skiers and snowshoers can use the network of snowmobile and dog-sled trails.

Remember to dress for serious cold – parka, coveralls, heavy mitts, and face mask, with layers of fleece, polypropylene, or wool underneath. Disposable chemical hand warmers are an excellent idea.

Though visiting in the depth of winter has its rewards, coming in late March through mid-April offers distinct advantages: There's still plenty of snow and cold, but the days are longer, brighter, and far more conducive to getting out and about.

Winter travel (above) is serious business in the Arctic, but newcomers can make short trips from Fairbanks to Bettles or Anaktuvuk Pass.

An outcropping in the Soakpak Mountains (opposite) affords a sweeping view of Anaktuvuk Pass and the surrounding valley.

effort to become part of the landscape. Try to think like a wolf or moose: your destination and your home are all around you.

It is at these times, when you're watching and listening, learning every bush and crease on a slope, that you're most likely to spot wildlife. Sharing the landscape with Dall sheep and grizzlies is one of the main attractions of the Gates. Given the remoteness, you expect to see animals behind every bush. The fact is, you may see little. This is cold, lean country, and wildlife is spread thin. On the other hand, you may have 10,000 caribou trot through camp. It's all a matter of local, often temporary abundance and blind chance.

If wildlife spotting or photography is your main aim, consult with park rangers, outfitters, or flying services for likely spots – often relatively small pockets where local conditions or seasonal migrations concentrate animals. The exact locations may change from year to year, and there are no guarantees, even though the western arctic caribou herd, the world's largest, numbers nearly half a million strong. As with all things in this country, it's a matter of feast or famine.

And yes, there are grizzlies out there. Enjoy them, but be respectful and use common sense. Constant ringing of bear bells and shouting are generally unnecessary and guarantee that you won't see any wildlife. Most local grizzlies are shy and retiring; they turn tail and run at the least whiff of human scent. Bluff charges, rare enough and unnerving, are just that. Pepper spray

is useful as a confidence builder. Hold your fire unless an animal is coming in fast, low, and hard at 20 paces or fewer. Never run. Standing your ground with your companions, bunched together and with jackets outstretched to make yourselves look bigger, is usually enough to send an inquisitive bear on its way.

Floating Through the Country

An alternate method of travel in the Gates is by canoe, kayak, or inflatable raft. Since a river carries your gear, longer, less strenuous trips are possible. Your camp of the day becomes a mobile base for unencumbered hikes. Also, wildlife congregates along waterways, and floating is a quiet, unobtrusive way to move through habitat. All of the major rivers draining the Gates of the Arctic – the **Colville**, **Koyukuk**, **Noatak**, and **Kobuk** – plus their major tributaries are easygoing for moderately experienced paddlers. The few rapids are easily bypassed. Be aware, though, that all these rivers rise and fall suddenly, and they can be deadly under flood conditions.

For river trips in the Gates, collapsible, compact craft are highly favored, since space in a bush plane is limited. Be sure that your chosen boat is expedition quality and that you have a complete repair kit, an extra paddle, life jackets, and so on. Studying a map and a good Alaska river guidebook will help you make a choice. Generally speaking, smaller tributary rivers are less traveled, more wild-feeling, and potentially more difficult.

If you're looking for a memorable trip, the upper **Noatak River** is hard to beat. Fox, caribou, and Dall sheep are often visible, the fishing for grayling and sea-run Dolly Varden char is good, and the river, under normal summer conditions, is transparent. The headwaters section between **Portage Creek** and the **Cutler River** is especially scenic. Fly out of **Bettles**, **Kotzebue**, or **Ambler**, and float 300 miles to **Noatak** village (10 to 14 days) or arrange for an air-charter pickup to shorten your trip. The Noatak, though remote and wild, is popular, and you may not be alone.

Even after extensive travel in the western and central reaches of the Gates of the Arctic, you will feel as if you've scarcely brushed the surface. Spreading out maps, you retrace where you've been and try to decide where you're headed next. Is that creek deep enough to float a canoe? How many walking miles between here and there? Even on the neatly scaled squares and contours of a topo map, the country rolls off toward some infinite vanishing point. As you look down on it all, take the flutter in your chest as a good sign. This is the reason you came here.

Northern lights (above) shimmer in the winter sky.

Boots (right) dry by a campfire after trekkers return from a wet tundra hike.

A young moose (opposite) can keep up with its mother a few days after birth.

TRAVEL TIPS

DETAILS

How to Get There

The closest airport is in Fairbanks. There are no roads in the park; the Dalton Highway from Fairbanks ends five miles outside the park's eastern boundary. The best access is by air taxis, which serve Anaktuvuk Pass, Bettles, and Coldfoot. Backcountry travelers can arrange flights by bush plane to remote locations.

When to Go

Most visitors come to the park in June, July, and August. The Gates of the Arctic experiences continuous daylight for at least 30 days at the height of summer, when temperatures at low elevations range from the mid-40s to the low 70s but are colder at higher altitudes. June through September is the rainiest period. Precipitation can reach 12 inches in some areas, and thunderstorms are common in June and July. Freezing temperatures can occur at any time of year and are common from mid-August on. July is usually the only month without snowfall. Winters last up to nine months, and temperatures reach lows of -30° to -40°F and rarely rise above zero.

What to Do

Hiking and backpacking, with or without a guide, are among the most popular activities in the park. Visitors also come to float the park's rivers, six of which are designated wild and scenic. Wintertime activities include cross-country skiing and dogsledding.

Backcountry Permits

A permit is not required for overnight stays in the park, but before entering the backcountry, visitors must attend an orientation at the Anaktuvuk or Bettles Ranger Stations or the Coldfoot Visitor Center, or must speak directly with a ranger if being taken in by plane.

Special Planning

Because the park has no established trails, backcountry users need to feel confident about their wilderness skills and be prepared to be self-sufficient. Bear-resistant food canisters, available at the Bettles Ranger Station, must be used to store food, and portable gas stoves should be used in lieu of campfires. Visitors traveling by bush plane should discuss their plans thoroughly with air-taxi operators. They are advised to bring extra food and allow for alternate itineraries if weather prevents pilots from making scheduled pickups.

Camping

The park does not have automobile access or developed campgrounds. A campground run by the Bureau of Land Management, open from June through mid-September, is located five miles north of Coldfoot at milepost 180. Call 907-678-5209 for information. Camping is allowed in a designated area in the village of Anaktuvuk Pass; call 907-661-3026 for details.

INFORMATION

Gates of the Arctic National Park and Preserve

201 First Avenue, Dogon Building, Fairbanks, AK 99701; tel: 907-456-0281.

Anaktuvuk Pass Ranger Station

P.O. Box 21102, Anaktuvuk Pass, AK 99721; tel: 907-661-3520.

Bettles Ranger Station

P.O. Box 26030, Bettles, AK 99726; tel: 907-692-5494.

Marion Creek Ranger Station/Coldfoot Visitor Center

P.O. Box 9072, Coldfoot, AK 99701; tel: 907-678-5209.

Alaska Public Lands Information Center

250 Cushman Street, Suite 1A, Fairbanks, AK 99701; tel: 907-456-0527.

The office provides a range of travel information and advice and also carries books about Gates of the Arctic (see Resource Directory) and other federal and state parks, as well as USGS topo maps.

AIR TAXIS

Bettles Air Service

P.O. Box 26027, Bettles, AK 99726; tel: 907-692-5111.

Brooks Range Aviation

P.O. Box 26010, Bettles, AK 99726; tel: 907-692-5444.

Frontier Flying Service

3820 University Avenue, Fairbanks, AK 99708; tel: 907-474-0014.

Wright's Flying Service

East Ramp International Airport, Fairbanks, AK 99708; tel: 907-474-0502.

LODGING

PRICE GUIDE – double occupancy

$ = up to $49 | $$ = $50–$99

$$$ = $100–$149 | $$$$ = $150+

Bettles Lodge

P.O. Box 27, Bettles, AK 99726; tel: 907-692-5111.

Open year-round, the lodge has a bunkhouse, apartments, and suites, as well as a restaurant. $$–$$$

Holly Hollow Cabins

P.O. Box 26066, Bettles, AK 99726; tel: 907-692-5252.

Two cabins both have a living area, kitchen, and sleeping loft. Guests use a central bathhouse facility. Accommodations are also available in a bunkhouse. $$

Nunamiut Camp

Nunamiut Corporation, P.O. Box 21009, Anaktuvuk Pass, AK 99721; tel: 907-661-3026.

This small camp has 14 beds in six rooms, plus a kitchen and dining room. Prices are per person and include three meals. $$$$

Slate Creek Inn

Coldfoot Services, P.O. Box 9041, Coldfoot, AK 99701; tel: 907-678-5224.

Open from March through October, the inn has 50 rooms, each with a private bath. Coldfoot Services also operates a cafe. $$$

TOURS AND OUTFITTERS

Arctic Treks

P.O. Box 73452, Fairbanks, AK 99707; tel: 907-455-6502.

Guiding in Gates of the Arctic from June through August, Arctic Treks offers seven-day trips in which travelers fly into a base camp and explore the area on day hikes. Backpacking excursions and raft trips on park rivers can also be arranged.

Bettles Lodge

P.O. Box 27, Bettles, AK 99726; tel: 907-692-5111.

This year-round outfitter offers multiday guided float trips and backpacking trips, with or without guides, in Gates of the Arctic. In winter, travelers lead their own dogs on guided dogsled trips up to 12 days long. Visitors may also explore the park by snowmobile and on cross-country skis.

Sourdough Outfitters

P.O. Box 26066, Bettles, AK 99726; tel: 907-692-5252.

Travelers choose from a variety of multiday guided trips including backpacking, canoeing, rafting, and wildlife viewing. Sourdough offers dogsledding and snowmobiling trips in winter.

Excursions

Denali National Park and Preserve

P.O. Box 9, Denali Park, AK 99755; tel: 907-683-2294.

The majestic, snow-covered Alaska Range, sweeping expanses of tundra, and legendary wildlife – grizzly bears, caribou, moose, Dall sheep, and wolves – make Denali an irresistible destination for back-country travelers. In the absence of extensive marked trails, hikers traverse the easily negotiated terrain and camp in the backcountry. Visitors may also arrange guided river floats, tours of Mount McKinley, and dogsledding and skiing trips.

Lake Clark National Park and Preserve

4230 University Drive, Suite 311, Anchorage, AK 99508; tel: 907-271-3751.

Containing mountain ranges, glaciers, volcanoes, wide-open tundra, pristine lakes, countless waterfalls, and coastal rain forests, this park is an Alaskan sampler. Grizzly bears, caribou, moose, Dall sheep, and other Alaskan wildlife are also found here. The only way to reach these roadless four million acres is by bush plane, and most of the hiking is cross-country. Guides and outfitters take visitors on extended backpacking, kayaking, mountain climbing, fishing, and wildlife-watching trips.

Misty Fiords National Monument

3031 Tongass Avenue, Ketchikan, AK 99901; tel: 907-225-2148.

At 2.3 million acres, this park is only one of the two national monuments and 12 wilderness areas in the Tongass National Forest, the largest in the United States. Here, in Alaska's southeastern panhandle, traveling by kayak and boat is the best way to see misty fjords and coves, precipitous mountains covered with lush forest, and waterfalls tumbling from the highlands. Marine mammals such as orca whales and Dall porpoises are common sightings. Tides can be dramatic. Paddlers can find safe, accessible campsites or stay in Forest Service cabins.

SECTION THREE

Resource Directory

FURTHER READING

Backcountry Skills

If you're new to backcountry travel, the best way to learn outdoor skills is to take a class from an outfitter, equipment retailer, or other organization. Using the books below, you can refresh your knowledge or explore topics such as navigation, wilderness first aid, canoe travel, and leave-no-trace camping in depth.

Avalanche Aware: Safe Travel in Avalanche Terrain, by John Moynier (Falcon Publishing, 1998).

The Backcountry Kitchen: Camp Cooking for Canoeists, Hikers and Anglers, by Teresa Marrone (Bookmen, 1996).

The Basic Essentials of Map and Compass, by Cliff Jacobson (Globe Pequot Press, 1999).

Be Expert with Map and Compass: The Complete Orienteering Handbook, by Bjorn Kjellstrom (IDG Books, 1994).

Bear Aware: Hiking and Camping in Bear Country, by Bill Schneider (Falcon Publishing, 1996).

Camping's Top Secrets: A Lexicon of Camping Tips Only the Experts Know, by Cliff Jacobson (Globe Pequot Press, 1998).

Canoe Camping: An Introductory Guide, by Cecil Kuhne (Lyons Press, 1997).

Canoe Country Camping: Wilderness Skills for the Boundary Waters and Quetico, by Michael Furtman (Pfeifer-Hamilton, 1992).

The Complete Walker III: The Joys and Techniques of Hiking and Backpacking, by Colin Fletcher (Random House, 1984).

The Complete Wilderness Paddler, by James West Davidson and John Rugge (Vintage Books, 1983).

Desert Survival Handbook: How To Prevent and Handle Emergency Situations, by Diane M. Fessler and Charles A. Lehman (Primer Publications, 1998).

A Hiker's Companion: 12,000 Miles of Trail-Tested Wisdom, by Cindy Ross and Todd Gladfelter (Mountaineers Books, 1993).

Kayak Touring and Camping, by Cecil Kuhne (Stackpole Books, 1999).

Land Navigation Handbook: The Sierra Club Guide to Map and Compass, by William S. Kals (Sierra Club Books, 1983).

Leave No Trace: Minimum Impact Outdoor Recreation, by the American Hiking Society (Falcon Publishing, 1997).

NOLS Cookery, by Claudia Pearson and the National Outdoor Leadership School (Stackpole Books, 1997).

Orienteering, by Steven Boga (Stackpole Books, 1997).

The Outward Bound Canoeing Handbook, by Paul Landry and Matty L. McNair (Lyons Press, 1992).

The Outward Bound Map & Compass Handbook, by Glenn Randall (Lyons Press, 1998).

The Outward Bound Wilderness First-Aid Handbook, by Jeffrey Isaac (Lyons Press, 1998).

The 2 Oz. Backpacker: A Problem Solving Manual for Use in the Wilds, by Robert S. Wood (Ten Speed Press, 1982).

The Ultimate Guide to Backcountry Travel, by Michael Lanza (Appalachian Mountain Club Books, 1999).

Walking Softly in the Wilderness: The Sierra Club Guide to Backpacking, by John Hart (Sierra Club Books, 1994).

Wilderness Cuisine: How to Prepare and Enjoy Fine Food on the Trail and in Camp, by Carole Latimer (Wilderness Press, 1991).

Wilderness First Aid: Emergency Care for Remote Locations, by the National Safety Council and Wilderness Medical Society (Jones and Bartlett, 1998).

Wilderness Navigation: Finding Your Way Using Map, Compass, Altimeter, and GPS, by Bob Burns et al. (Mountaineers Books, 1999).

Wilderness 911: A Step-by-Step Guide for Medical Emergencies and Improvised Care in the Backcountry, by Eric A. Weiss (Mountaineers Books, 1999).

Winter Camping, by Stephen Gorman (Appalachian Mountain Club Books, 1999).

Regional Guidebooks – East

If you're going to a destination east of the Mississippi River, you'll want to consult these guides as you plan your trip. You'll also find books describing the natural history of the area you'll be visiting.

Adirondack Canoe Waters: North Flow, by Paul Jamieson and Donald Morris (Adirondack Mountain Club, 1993).

Adirondack Canoe Waters: South and West Flow, by Alec Proskine (Adirondack Mountain Club, 1993).

An Adirondack Sampler II: Backpacking Trips for All Seasons, by Bruce Wadsworth (Adirondack Mountain Club, 1995).

Adventure Guide to Canada's Atlantic Provinces, by Barbara Radcliffe Rogers (Hunter Publications, 1999).

Backcountry Skiing Adventures: Classic Ski and Snowboard

Tours in Maine and New Hampshire, by David Goodman (Appalachian Mountain Club Books, 1998).

Big Cypress Swamp and the Ten Thousand Islands: Eastern America's Last Great Wilderness, by Jeff Ripple (University of South Carolina Press, 1992).

Boat and Canoe Camping in the Everglades Backcountry, by Dennis Kalma (Florida Flair Books, 1988).

Canyons, Coves and Coastal Waters: Choice Canoe and Kayak Routes of Newfoundland and Labrador, by Kevin Redmond et al. (Breakaway Books, 1996).

Discover the Adirondack High Peaks, by Barbara McMartin et al. (Lake View Press, 1993).

Everglades: The Park Story, by William B. Robertson (Florida National Parks and Monument Association, 1989).

Fun on Flatwater: An Introduction to Adirondack Canoeing, by Barbara McMartin (North Country Books, 1995).

The Geological Story of Isle Royale National Park, by N. King Huber (Isle Royale Natural History Association, 1983).

Geology of the Adirondack High Peaks Region: A Hiker's Guide, by Howard and Elizabeth Jaffe (Adirondack Mountain Club, 1986).

Great Smoky Mountain National Park, by Rose Houk (Houghton Mifflin, 1993).

A Guide to the Wilderness Waterway of Everglades National Park, by William Truesdell (University of Miami Press, 1985).

Hiking Guide to Newfoundland, by Barbara Naryniak (Goose Lane Editions, 1994).

Hiking Trails of the Smokies, Don DeFoe, ed. (Great Smoky Mountains Natural History Association, 1994).

Isle Royale National Park: Foot Trails and Water Routes, by Jim DuFresne (Mountaineers Books, 1984).

Meditations at 10,000 Feet: A Natural History of the Appalachians, by James Trefil (Macmillan, 1987).

Monongahela National Forest Hiking Guide, by Allen De Hart and Bruce Sundquist (West Virginia Highlands Conservancy, 1993).

Nova Scotia and the Maritimes by Bike, by Walter Sienko (Mountaineers Books, 1995).

Sea Kayaking Florida and the Georgia Sea Islands, by James Bannon (Out There Press, 1998).

Southwest Florida's Wetland Wilderness, by Jeff Ripple and Clyde Butcher (University Press of Florida, 1996).

Strangers in High Places: The Story of the Great Smoky Mountains, by Michael Frome (University of Tennessee Press, 1993).

Superior Wilderness: Isle Royale National Park, by Napier Shelton (Isle Royale Natural History Association, 1997).

Trees of the Smokies, by Steve Kemp (Great Smoky Mountains Natural History Association, 1993).

Walking the Appalachian Trail, by Larry Luxenberg (Stackpole, 1994).

West Virginia Hiking Trails: Hiking the Mountain State, by Allen De Hart (Appalachian Mountain Club Books, 1997).

White Mountain Guide, Gene Daniell and Jon Burroughs, eds. (Appalachian Mountain Club Books, 1998).

The Wildflowers of Isle Royale, by Robert Janke (Isle Royale Natural History Association, 1996).

Wildflowers of the Smokies, by Peter White (Great Smoky Mountains Natural History Association, 1996).

Wonderous Worlds of the Mangrove Swamps, by Katherine Orr (Florida Flair Books, 1989).

Regional Guidebooks – West

Here are some resources to explore if you're traveling to a destination in the West, whether the far north of Alaska or the deserts of the Southwest.

Adventuring in Alaska: The Ultimate Travel Guide to the Great Land, by Peggy Wayburn (Sierra Club Books, 1999)

Adventuring in the California Desert, by Lynne Foster (Sierra Club Books, 1999).

Adventuring in the Rockies, by Jeremy Schmidt (Sierra Club Books, 1997).

Alaska, by Nick Jans and Art Wolfe (Sasquatch Books, 2000).

Alaska Paddling Guide, by Jack Mosby and David Dapkus (J&R Enterprises, 1992).

Along the Arizona Trail, by Jerry Sieve and John M. Fayhee (Westcliffe, 1998).

Arches and Canyonlands, by Nicky Leach (Sierra Press, 1997).

Arkansas Hiking Trails, by Tim Ernst (Wilderness Visions Press, 1998).

Canyoneering III: Loop Hikes in Utah's Escalante, by Steve Allen (University of Utah Press, 1997).

Cascade-Olympic Natural History: A Trailside Reference, by Daniel Mathews (Raven Editions, 1988).

Colorado's Continental Divide Trail: The Official Guide, by Tom Lorang Jones (Westcliffe, 1997).

Don't Waste Your Time in the North Cascades, by Kathy and Craig Copeland (Wilderness Press, 1996).

Exploring Arizona's Wild Areas: A Guide for Hikers, Backpackers, Climbers, X-C Skiers, and Paddlers, by Scott S. Warren (Mountaineers Books, 1996).

Exploring the Black Hills and Badlands, by Hiram Rogers (Johnson Books, 1993).

On Foot in Joshua Tree, by Patty Furbush (M. I. Adventure Publications, 1995).

Geology of Arizona, by Dale J. Nations (Kendall/Hunt, 1996).

Geological Story of the Great Plains, by Donald E. Trimble (Theodore Roosevelt Nature and History Association, 1990).

The Guide to the National Parks of the Southwest, by Nicky Leach (Southwest Parks and Monuments Association, 1992).

The High Sierra: Peaks, Passes, and Trails, by R. J. Secor (Mountaineers Books, 1999).

Hiking Big Bend National Park, by Big Bend Natural History Association (Falcon Publishing, 1993).

Hiking the Bob Marshall Country, by Eric Molvar (Falcon Publishing, 1998).

Hiking the Escalante, by Rudi Lambrechtse (Wasatch Publications, 1985).

Hiking Grand Staircase-Escalante and the Glen Canyon Region, by Ron Adkison (Falcon Publishing, 1998).

Hiking North Cascades National Park, by Eric Molvar (Falcon Publishing, 1998).

Hiking Trails of Southwestern Colorado, by Paul Pixler (Pruett Publishing, 1992).

Impressions of the North Cascades: Essays about a Northwest Landscape, by John C. Miles (Mountaineers Books, 1996).

Joshua Tree Rock Climbing Guide, by John Harlin (Chockstone Press, 1996).

Mountain Biking Colorado, by Gregg Bromka (Falcon Publishing, 1998).

Naturalist's Big Bend, by Roland H. Wauer (Texas A&M University Press, 1992).

100 Hikes in Washington's North Cascades National Park Region, by Ira Spring (Mountaineers Books, 1994).

Ouachita Trail Guide, by Tim Ernst (Wilderness Visions Press, 1996).

Ouray Hiking Guide, by Kevin B. Kent (Wayfinder Press, 1993).

A Place Beyond: Finding Home in Arctic Alaska, by Nick Jans (Graphic Arts Publishing, 1996).

River Guides to the Rio Grande, Vols 1-3, John Pearson, ed. (Big Bend Natural History Association, 1993).

Road Guide to the Backcountry Dirt Roads of Big Bend National Park, John Pearson, ed. (Big Bend Natural History Association, 1993).

Road Guide to Paved and Improved Dirt Roads of Big Bend National Park (Big Bend Natural History Association, 1993).

Roadlog Guide for the North and South Units of Theodore Roosevelt National Park, by Edward Murphy et al. (Theodore Roosevelt Nature and History Association, 1999).

Rock Climbing Colorado, by Stewart Green (Falcon Publishing, 1995).

75 Great Hikes in and near Palm Springs and the Coachella Valley, by Philip Ferranti (Kendall/Hunt, 1995).

Sierra South: 100 Backcountry Trips in California's Sierra, by Thomas Winnett et al. (Wilderness Press, 1993.

Snowshoeing Colorado, by Claire Walter (Fulcrum Press, 1998).

Telluride Hiking Guide, by Susan Kees (Wayfinder Press, 1992).

Theodore Roosevelt National Park: The Story Behind the Scenery, by Bruce Kaye and Henry Schoch (K. C. Publications, 1993).

Trail Guide to Bob Marshall Country, by Eric Molvar (Falcon Publishing, 1994).

25 Bicycle Tours in the Texas Hill Country and West Texas: Adventure Rides for Road and Mountain Bikes, by Norman D. Ford (Countrymen Press, 1995).

Walking in Wildness: A Backpacking Guide to the Weminuche Wilderness, by B. J. Boucher (Durango Herald Press, 1998).

History, Nature, and Conservation

From classics by John Muir, Rachel Carson, Mary Austin, and other authors to observations by contemporary naturalists and conservationists, these books make great armchair reading. If you find a lightweight paperback edition, you can tuck it into your backpack.

Alaska Wilderness: Exploring the Central Brooks Range, by Robert Marshall (University of California Press, 1970).

American Nature Writing, John Murray, ed. (Sierra Club Books, 1998).

Arctic Dreams: Imagination and Desire in a Northern Landscape, by Barry H. Lopez (Bantam Books, 1988).

Arctic Village: A 1930s Portrait of Wiseman, Alaska, by Robert Marshall (University of Alaska Press, 1991).

Basin and Range, by John McPhee (Farrar, Strauss & Giroux, 1981).

Cadillac Desert: The American West and Its Disappearing Water, by Marc P. Reisner (Viking, 1993).

Cross Creek, by Marjorie Kinnan Rawlings (Collier Books, 1987).

The Desert, by John C. Van Dyke (Gibbs Smith, 1980).

Desert Solitaire: A Season in the Wilderness, by Edward Abbey (Ballantine, 1985).

The Diversity of Life, by Edward O. Wilson (Harvard University Press, 1992).

The Essential Theodore Roosevelt, John Gabriel Hunt, ed. (Random House, 1994).

Everglades: River of Grass, by Marjory Stoneman Douglas (Pineapple Press, 1997).

The Final Forest: The Battle for the Last Great Trees of the Pacific Northwest, by William Dietrich (Viking Penguin, 1992).

The Immense Journey, by Loren S. Eiseley (Random House, 1959).

In Suspect Terrain, by John McPhee (Farrar, Straus & Giroux, 1984).

Isle Royale: A Photographic History, by Thomas P. Gale and Kendra Gale (Isle Royale Natural History Association, 1995).

The Klamath Knot, by David Rains Wallace (Random House, 1984).

The Land of Journey's Ending, by Mary Austin (University of Arizona Press, 1983).

The Land of Little Rain, by Mary Austin (University of New Mexico Press, 1974).

The Last Light Breaking: Living Among Alaska's Inupiat Eskimos, by Nick Jans (Graphic Arts Publishing, 1995).

My First Summer in the Sierra, by John Muir (Sierra Club Books, 1990).

Never Cry Wolf, by Farley Mowat (Thorndike Press, 1982).

Of Men and Mountains, by William O. Douglas (Chronicle Books, 1990).

Of Wolves and Men, by Barry H. Lopez (Macmillan, 1979).

Pilgrim at Tinker Creek, by Annie Dillard (Harper Collins, 1998).

A Place in the Woods, by Helen Hoover (Knopf, 1969).

Reflections from the North Country, by Sigurd F. Olson (University of Minnesota Press, 1998).

Run, River, Run: A Naturalist's Journey Down One of the Great Rivers of the West, by Ann Zwinger (University of Arizona Press, 1984).

A Sand County Almanac with Essays on Conservation from Round River, by Aldo Leopold (Oxford University Press, 1960).

The Sea Around Us, by Rachel Carson (Oxford University Press, 1961).

Silent Spring, by Rachel Carson (Houghton Mifflin, 1988).

The Solace of Open Spaces, by Gretel Ehrlich (Viking Penguin, 1986).

Tracks of the Unseen: Meditations on Alaskan Landscape, Photography, and Wildlife, by Nick Jans (Fulcrum Press, 2000).

Travels, by William Bartram (Viking Penguin, 1986).

Travels in Alaska, by John Muir (Houghton Mifflin, 1998).

True Tales of the Everglades, by Stuart McIver (Florida Flair Books, 1989).

Two in the Far North, by Margaret Murie (Graphic Art Center, 1997).

Walden, by Henry David Thoreau (Oxford University Press, 1999).

A Walk in the Woods, by Bill Bryson (Broadway Books, 1998).

Wind in the Rock: The Canyonlands of Southeastern Utah, by Ann Zwinger (University of Arizona Press, 1986).

The Wolves of Isle Royale National Park: A Broken Balance, by Rolf O. Peterson (Willow Creek Press, 1995).

The Worst Weather on Earth: A History of the Mount Washington Observatory, by William Lowell Putnam (American Alpine Club, 1993).

Magazines

Check out these periodicals for information on the newest outdoor equipment, backcountry activities such as kayaking and climbing, and national parks and other destinations in the United States and Canada.

Alaska
619 East Ship Creek Avenue, Suite 329, Anchorage, AK 99501; tel: 800-288-5892.

Audubon
700 Broadway, New York, NY 10003; tel: 800-274-4201.

Backpacker
33 East Minor Street, Emmaus, PA 18098; tel: 800-666-3434.

Birder's World
P.O. Box 1612, Waukesha, WI 53187; tel: 800-533-6644.

Canadian Geographic
39 McArthur Avenue, Vanier, ON KIL 8L7; tel: 800-267-0824 or 613-745-4629.

Canoe Journal
P.O. Box 3418, Kirkland, WA 98083; tel: 800-692-2663.

Canoe & Kayak
P.O. Box 420235, Palm Coast, FL 32142; tel: 800-829-3340.

National Parks
1776 Massachusetts Avenue, N.W., Washington, D.C. 20036; tel: 800-628-7275.

National Wildlife
8925 Leesburg Pike, Vienna, VA 22184; tel: 815-734-1160.

Nature Canada
1 Nicholas Street, Suite 606, Ottawa, ON K1N 7B7; tel: 800-267-4088.

Outside
400 Market Street, Santa Fe, NM 87501; tel: 800-678-1131.

Paddler
P.O. Box 775450, Steamboat Springs, CO 80477; tel: 970-879-1450.

Sea Kayaker
P.O. Box 17170, Seattle, WA 98107; tel: 206-789-9536.

Sierra
Sierra Club, 85 Second Street, San Francisco, CA 94105; tel: 415-977-5653.

ORGANIZATIONS

Through the organizations listed here – and their websites – you can pursue your interest in conservation, obtain topographical maps, and find orienteering and hiking clubs in your community. Some, such as the Sierra Club and Boulder Outdoor Survival School, sponsor backcountry trips and teach outdoor skills.

American Canoe Association
7432 Alban Station Boulevard, Suite B-232, Springfield, VA 22150; tel: 703-451-0141; www.aca-paddler.com.

American Hiking Society
1422 Fenwick Lane, Silver Springs, MD 20910; tel: 301-565-6704; www.americanhiking.org.

Bob Marshall Foundation
P.O. Box 1052, Kalispell, MT 59903; tel: 406-758-5237; www.cyberport.net/russ/bmf.

Boulder Outdoor Survival School
P.O. Box 1590, Boulder, CO 80306; tel: 800-335-7404 or 303-444-9779; www.boss-inc.com.

Bureau of Land Management
1849 C Street, N.W., Washington, DC 20241; tel: 202-452-7780; www.blm.gov.

Canada Map Office
615 Booth Street, Ottawa, ON K1A 0E9; tel: 800-465-6277; www.nrcan.gc.ca.

Canadian Nature Federation
1 Nicholas Street, Suite 606, Ottawa, ON K1N 7B7; tel: 613-562-3447; www.cnf.ca.

Canadian Orienteering Federation
Box 62052, Covent Glen Post Office, Orleans, ON KIC 2R9; tel: 613-830-1147; www.orienteering.ca.

Friends of the Earth
1025 Vermont Avenue, N.W., Suite 300, Washington, DC 20005; tel: 202-783-7400; www.foe.org.

National Audubon Society
700 Broadway, New York, NY 10003; tel: 212-832-3000; www.audubon.org.

National Fish and Wildlife Foundation
1120 Connecticut Avenue, N.W., Suite 900, Washington, DC 20036; tel: 202-857-0166, www.nfwf.org.

National Outdoor Leadership School
P.O. Box 997, Boulder, CO 80306; tel: 800-332-4100; www.lnt.org.

National Parks and Conservation Association
1776 Massachusetts Avenue, N.W., Washington, DC 20036; tel: 800-628-7275; www.npca.org.

National Parks Foundation
1101 17th Street, N.W., Suite 1102, Washington, DC 20036; tel: 202-785-4500; www.nationalparks.org

National Wildlife Federation
8925 Leesburg Pike, Vienna, VA 22184; tel: 703-790-4000; www.nwf.org.

The Nature Conservancy
4245 North Fairfax Drive, Suite 100, Arlington, VA 22203; tel: 703-841-5300; www.tnc.org.

Sierra Club
85 Second Street, San Francisco, CA 94105; tel: 415-923-5630; www.sierraclub.org.

Trails Illustrated
P.O. Box 3610, Evergreen, CO 80439; tel: 303-670-3457.

U.S. Fish and Wildlife Service
4401 North Fairfax Drive, Arlington, VA 22203; tel: 800-344-9453 or 202-857-0166; www.fws.gov.

U.S. Orienteering Federation
P.O. Box 1444, Forest Park, GA 30298; www.us.orienteering.org.

USGS Information Services
Box 25286, Denver, CO 80225; tel: 888-275-8747; www.usgs.gov.

Wilderness Information Network
Wilderness Institute, University of Montana School of Forestry, Missoula, MT 59812; tel: 406-243-6933; www.wilderness.net.

Wilderness Society
900 17th Street, N.W., Washington, DC 20006; tel: 202-833-2300; www.wilderness.org.

PHOTO AND ILLUSTRATION CREDITS

AlaskaStock Images 39T

Daniel H. Bailey 5B, 18B, 31B, 49, 152, 153T, 157B

Matt Bradley 104, 106L, 106M, 107, 108B

Robin Brandt 209

Dugald Bremner 34B, 43, 67T, 150, 151T, 157M, 197, 212-213

Dominique Braud/Tom Stack and Associates 125T, 199B

Arvilla Brewer 160

Skip Brown 46T, 64, 82, 83T, 83B, back cover top

Luigi Ciuffetelli 41B

Carr Clifton 131B, 161B, 187T

Michael Collier 169B, 171T, 171B

Richard Cummins/Photophile 181

Kevin Downey 47T

John and Susan Drew/ImageArtist 145T, 153B

Susan Gibler Drew/ImageArtist 142T

Richard Durnan/DB Studio 174, 178L

Joel B. Dyer/Photophile 2-3, 4, 51

David Edwards 30T, 52-53, 169T

John Elk III 106R, 108T, 135B, 161T, 184

Patrick J. Endres/Wide Angle Productions 208T

Jeff Foott/Jeff Foott Productions 9B, 46-47, 73T, 98B, 132B, 162B, 177B, 178R, 180T, 183B, 189

Winston Fraser 59B

Lynn Gerig/Tom Stack and Associates 75T

John Gerlach/Tom Stack and Associates 170

Ray Hafen/Ken Graham Agency 204T

A. C. Haralson/Arkansas Dept. of Parks and Tourism 109B

Bill Hatcher 6-7, 20-21, 27B, 48B, 50T, 151B, 163, 168, back cover bottom

Kim Heacox/Ken Graham Agency 211B

Christian Heeb/Gnass Photo Images 16

Joe Mac Hudspeth, Jr. 100B

George H. H. Huey 173T

Henry Huntington/AlaskaStock Images 206

David J. Job/Ken Graham Agency 14-15

Gary Johnson/Adstock Photos 166

Wolfgang Kaehler 59T, 61T, 103B, 157T, 195T

James Kay 27T

Layne Kennedy 32B, 42T, 74T, 112, 119T, 119B

Thomas Kitchin/Tom Stack and Associates 61M, 79T, 186, 211T

Lee Kline 162T

Bill Lea 91T (bear), 103M

Tom and Pat Leeson 154T

Library of Congress 198

Chlaus Lotscher 207

Chlaus Lotscher/AlaskaStock Images 204B

Joanne Lotter/Tom Stack and Associates 18T, 24, 31T

John and Ann Mahan 114, 115T, 115B, 116T, 116B, 117B, 119M

Alan Majchrowicz 192

Stephen Matera 10-11, 19, 41T, 195B, 196T, 196B, 199T

Buddy Mays/Travel Stock Photography 61B, 201T

John McGrail 54, 56-57, 58B

Bruce Montagne 117T

National Park Service 124T

Mark Newman/Tom Stack and Associates 100T

Jack Olson 127T, 165T, 165B, 191T

Laurence Parent 1, 62, 87B, 111T, 127M, 158, 165M, 179T, 183M

Larry Prosor 9T, 25T, 25B, 35, 40, 147M

Paul Rezendes 57T, 65T, 65B, 69T, 69M, 69B, 73B, 75B, 77, 79B, 90, 92B, 95M, 95B, 98T, 101

Larry Rice 99

Sam Roberts 180B, 187B

Ronald Roman 91B, 92T, 93T, 93B, 173M

Cheyenne Rouse/Photophile 176

Rex Rystedt 8T, 34T

Carl R. Sams III 91T (fox)

Jeff Schultz/AlaskaStock Images 42B

Stephen J. Shaluta, Jr. 80, 84T, 84B, 85

John Shaw/Tom Stack and Associates 5T

Bill Sherwonit 202, 211M

Scott Spiker 8L, 12-13, 28, 30B, 33, 36, 38, 44, 48T, 50B, 72, 131T, front cover

Spencer Swanger/Tom Stack and Associates 148, 154B

Tom Till 70, 76, 79M, 87M, 88, 95T, 103T, 111M, 111B, 124M, 127B, 137T, 137B, 138, 141B, 142B, 144B, 145B, 147T, 155, 191B, 201B

Stephen Trimble 140, 141T, 143, 147B, 177T, 179B

Larry Ulrich 67B, 122, 123B, 125B, 183T, 191M

Wiley/Wales 22, 144T, 188T

Steve Warble 58T

The Wilderness Society 133

Warren Williams 109T

Art Wolfe 32T, 87T, 123T, 124B, 134, 173B, 201M, 205

George Wuerthner 39B, 66, 74B, 96, 120, 128, 130, 132T, 135T, 137M, 188B, 208B

Maps by Karen Minot

Design by Mary Kay Garttmeier

Layout by Ingrid Hansen-Lynch

Indexing by Elizabeth Cook

T-top, B-bottom, M-middle, R-right, L-left

INDEX

Note: page numbers in italics refer to illustrations

A

Achenbach Trail, ND 123-5
Adirondack Loj, NY 73-6, 78
Adirondack Mountains, NY 25, 71-9
Adirondack Scenic Railway, NY 79
Adirondack State Park, NY 24, *70*, 71-9
agave (century plant) *161*, 161-2, *170*
Agnes Gorge, WA 199
air travel 103, *204*
Alaska *14-15*, 42, 49, 203-11
Alatna River, AK 205
Albright, Horace 92
Algonquin Provincial Park, ON 79
Allagash Wilderness Waterway, ME 69
Allegheny Front 81, 84, 85
Allegheny River Islands Wilderness, PA 79
alligators *98*, 101, 103
Alpine Lakes Wilderness, WA *19*
alpine terrain *18*, *19*, 57, 69, 147, 152-4, 157, 186, 191-201
wildflowers 84-5, 151-4, *155*, 173, 188-9, 191, 192, *196*, 199
wildlife 56, 129, 132-3, 147, 157, 191, 194, 197-8, *199*
altitude problems 40-41
Ambler, AK 204, 208
American Discovery Trail 85
American Forests 92
Anaktuvuk Pass, AK 203, 204, *206*, 207
Anasazi peoples 145, 157
Anasazi State Park, UT 145
angling, *see* **fishing**
Animas River, CO 150
Anza-Borrego Desert State Park, CA 183
Appalachian Mountain Club 67, 68, 69
Appalachian Mountains 61, 63-9, 81-7
Appalachian Trail 27, 61, 64, 65, 67, 69, 87
archaeology 111, 117, 140, 144-5, *145*, 157, 179-80
Arches National Park, UT *18*
Arctic 56, *202*, 203-11
Arizona *6-7*, *52-3*, *166*, 167-73
Arizona Trail 168
Arkansas 25, *104*, 105-11
armadillos 103
Arrigetch Peaks, AK 205
Assateague Island National Seashore, MD 87
Austin, Mary 175, 178, 179
avalanches 194, 195, 196

B

backcountry dos and don'ts 26
backpacking 26, *28*, 29-34, *34*
badlands 25, 121-7, 157, 183
Badlands National Park, SD 127
bald eagles 61, 69, 133
balds 90-93
Bandelier National Monument, NM 157
Banff National Park, AB *27*
Barnhardt Trail, AZ 168, 173
bats 95, 111, 165, 179
Baxter State Park, ME 24, 69
Bay of Fundy, NB 61
beaches 59, 87, 103, 191, 201
bear dos and don'ts 34, 42, *43*, 57, 162, *see also Travel Tips*
bears, *see* **black bears**; **grizzlies**
beaver 72, *73*, 79, 111, 119
dams and ponds 66, 74, 75, 81, 113, 116
Bettles, AK 204, 205, 207, 208
Big Bend National Park, TX 25, *158*, 159-65
Big Cypress National Preserve, FL 100
Big Cypress Watershed, FL 98
bighorns 125, 127, 133, 144, 151, 157, 176, 178, 179, 183
Big Salmon Lake Trail, MT 135
biking *5*, *12-13*, *25*, 26, *44*, 47-9, *52-3*, *64*, 82-4, 149, 151, *152*
birds 90, 95, 99, *100*, 101, 108, 133, 143, 147, 189
birding 25, 59, 61, 87, 103, 161-2
birds of prey 61, 69, 125, 133, 143, 144, 161, 163, 169, 189, *205*
desert birds 161, *162*, 163, 165, 173, 178, 179, 183
bison 121, *123*, 124, 127, 137
black bears 85, *91*, 93, 107, 132, 189, 197
in excursion areas 61, 69, 103, 111, 119, 173
Black Fork Mountain, AR 108, 109
Black Hills National Forest, SD 127
blueberries 72, 79, *85*, 91, *115*
Blue Lakes, CO 152-4
Blue Ridge Mountains, VA 87
bobcats 83, 111, *134*, 169, 179, 183
Bob Marshall Wilderness, MT *128*, 129-37
Boot Canyon, TX 160-61
boots *30*, 167, *208*
Boquillas Canyon, TX 163
Boulder, UT 142, 145
bouldering 46
Boundary Waters Canoe Area Wilderness, MN 49, 119
Bridger Wilderness, WY 137
Brooks Range, AK *202*, 203
Bryce Canyon National Park, UT 139
Buckeye Trail, AR 106
buffalo, *see* **bison**
Buffalo National River, AR 111
Burr Trail, UT *140*, 142
butterflies *65*, *120*

C

cacti *142*, 163, 165, 167, 173, *178*, 179, 183
Cades Cove, TN *88*, 90, *93*
California 25, *50*, *174*, 175-91
California Riding and Hiking Trail 175, 178
campfires 26, *171*, *208*
camping *18*, *22*, 26, *30*, *31*, 42, *73*, *98*, *109*, *116*
car camping, *see Travel Tips*
cooking *32*
equipment *32*, 32-4, 42
winter 38, *48*, 69, 79, 157
Canaan Mountain Backcountry, WV 84-5
Canada 24, *27*, *32*, 42, *50*, *54*, 55-61, 79, 81, 119, 131, 201
Canaveral National Seashore, FL 103
Caney Creek Wilderness, AR 106-8
canoeing 26, 38, 49, 72, *74*, 97-103, *112*, *116*, 163, 208, *see also* **whitewater**
Canyonlands National Park, UT *20-21*, *30*
canyons *2*, *6*, *22*, *51*, *52*, 111, 137, *138*, 140-61, *162*, *163*, 167, 173, 183, 187

Cape Breton Highlands National Park, NS 61
Cap Gaspé,QC 61
Capitan Reef, TX 165
Capitol Reef National Park, UT 139, 142
car camping, *see Travel Tips*
caribou 117, 203, 205, 207, 208, 111
Carlsbad Caverns National Park, NM 47, 165
car shuttle 154
Carson, Rachel 18
Cascade Range 191, 193
caves and caving 46-7, *47*, 87, 111, 157, 165
cell phones 41
century plant (agave) *161*, 161-2, *170*
Champlain, Samuel de 72
Chelan Lakeshore Trail, WA 199
chiggers 107-8
Chihuahuan Desert 159, *161*, 162-5, 173
Chincoteague National Wildlife Refuge, MD 87
chipmunks 92
Chisos Mountains, TX 159-65
cliff dwellings 157
cliffs 75, 142, 143, *144*, 163
Clifty Wilderness, KY 87
climbing, *see* **ice climbing**; **rock climbing**
clothing 31-2, 38, 48, 206, 207
coatimundis 173
code of conduct 26
Cohutta Wilderness, GA 95
Colima warbler 161
Colorado *2-3*, *4*, *22*, *27*, *31*, *51*, *148*, 149-57
Colorado Desert, CA 25, 177-8, 183
Colorado River *27*, 49, 173
Congaree Swamp National Monument, SC 95
Consasauga River, GA 95
Continental Divide 130, 131, 132, 149, 205
Continental Divide National Scenic Trail, MT 134
Copper Creek Trail, CA 188
Coronado National Forest, AZ 173
cougar 198
courses 37-8, *see also Travel Tips*
coyotes 72, 125, 127, 144
crampons 38, 50, 67, 134
Cranberry River, WV 82-3
Crater Lake National Park, OR 201
creosote bushes 178, 179-80
cross-country travel 26, *see also* **skiing**; **snowshoeing**
Cruiser Lake Trail, MN 119
cryptobiotic soil 143
Cumberland Island National Seashore, GA 103
Current River, MO 111
cycling, *see* **biking**

D

Dall porpoises 211
Dall sheep *202*, 207, 208, 211
Daniel Boone National Forest, KY 87
Death Valley National Park, CA 183
deer 83, 92, 129, 144, 151
Coues 160, 173
mule 125, 132, 162, 176, 178
white-tailed 103, *109*, 111, 116, 123, 132, 162
dehydration 38, 48
Del Norte Coast State Preserve, CA 191
Denali National Park and Preserve, AK 211
deserts 25, 159-83
wildlife 165, *169*, 173, 178-83, 189
Divide Trail, AZ 171
dogsledding *46-7*, 50, 79, 207, 211
Dolly Sods Wilderness, WV *85*
Douglas, William O. *198*
dunes 87, 103, 173, 183
Durango-Silverton Narrow Gauge Railroad, CO 150

E

Eleven Point Scenic River, MO 111
elk 124, 127, 129, *132*, 133, 151, 157
El Malpais National Monument, NM 157
epiphytes 92, 100
equipment 26, *28*, 29-34, *39*, *41*, *42*, 48, 207
Escalante River, UT 139, *141*, 141-4, *144*
Eskimos 203, 204
Everglades National Park, FL *96*, 97

F

Fairbanks, AK 204, 205, 207
Finger Lakes National Forest, NY 79
first aid 38, 39-40, *42*
fishers 132, 189
fishing 114, *115*, 137, 150, 186, *204*, 208, 211
fly-fishing 27, *82*, 87, 95, *104*, 147, *188*
see also **trout**
fjords 55, 211
float trips, *see* **canoeing**; **kayaking**; **rafting**
Florida 26, *96*, 97-103
footwear *30*, 167, *208*
Forillon National Park, QC 61
Fort Niobrara Wildlife Refuge, NE 127
fossils 122, 131, 140, 162, 165
four-wheel-drive 82, 85, 147, 151, 154, 157, 165, 173, 183
foxes *91*, 113, 173, 208
Frank Church River of No Return Wilderness, ID 24, 137
Franklin, Benjamin 113
Frijoles Canyon, NM 157
Fundy National Park, NB 61

G

Gabes Mountain Trail, NC 91, 93
Gates of the Arctic National Park, AK 203-11
General Sherman Tree, CA 185
geology 25, 59, 95, 108, 109, 122, 127, 140, 147, 183, 194
Georgia 95, 103
geysers 137
ghost town *141*
Giant Forest, CA 185
Gila National Forest, NM 165
glaciers 137, 193, *195*, 196, 201, 211
Glen Canyon, UT 139, 142
global positioning systems (GPS) *41*
golden eagles 125, 143, 162, 169, 189, *205*
gorges 87, 95, 198, 199, *see also* **canyons**
GPS receivers *41*
Grand Canyon National Park, AZ *6-7*, *27*, *48*, 173
Grand Staircase, UT *144*
Grand Staircase-Escalante National Monument, UT 25, *16*, *138*, 139-47

Great Basin Desert, CA 183
Great Bear Wilderness Area, MT 130
Great Forest 89
Great Lakes 47, 49, *112*, 113-18
Great Smoky Mountains National Park 25, *88*, 89-95
Great Western Divide, CA 186
Green Gardens Trail, NF 58-9
Green Mountain National Forest, VT 69
Greenstone Ridge Trail, MI *115*, 116
Gregory Bald, TN 90
grizzlies 42, 129, 132, 137, 197-8, 207-8, 211
Gros Morne National Park, NF *54*, 55-61
Guadalupe Mountains National Park, TX 165
guided treks 27, 38, *see also Travel Tips*

H

Headquarters Creek Pass Trail, MT 135
heat problems 40
high altitude problems 40-41
High Peaks, NY 72-6
High Sierra Trail, CA 186-8
High Uintas Wilderness, UT 147
hiking 26, *40*
Hitchcock, C. H. 66
horses *25*, 82, 90, 131, *132*, 134, 151, *161*, *166*, 167-73
  packing 26, 95, *132*, 137, 140, *142*, 178, 191
  see also Travel Tips
Hoyt, Minerva 180
huckleberries 81, 85, 107
hummingbirds 161, 173, 178
hypothermia 39-40

I

ice axes 34, 38, 50, 67, 134, 194
iceberg viewing *59*
ice climbing *49*, 50, *151*, *197*
Idaho 24, 137
Indian Pass Trail, NY 74-6
insect repellents 41-2, *42*
instruction 37-8, *see also Travel Tips*
Interlocken National Recreation Trail, NY 79
Isle Royale National Park, MI *112*, 113-19

J

Jacks Ford River, MO 111
Jarbridge Wilderness, NV *25*, 147
javelinas 169, 173
Jedediah Smith State Preserve, CA 191
John Muir Trail, CA *188*, 191
Joshua Tree National Park, CA 25, *174*, 175-83
Joshua trees 175, *177*
Joyce Kilmer-Slickrock Wilderness 95
Junction Cave, NM 157

K

Kabetogama Peninsula, MN 119
Kaiparowits Plateau, UT 141
kangaroo rats 144, 178
kayaking *14*, 26, 38, *46*, 49, 79, 87, 95, 111, *162*, 163, 208, 211
  sea kayaking 49, 61, 99-103, 114, 201, 211
  see also **whitewater**
Kennison Mountain Trail, WV 82
Kentucky 47, 87
Kern River Canyon, CA 186
key exchange 154
Keys, Bill 177
Kilkenny Ridge Trail, NH 65
Kings Canyon National Park, CA 185-91
Kotzebue, AK 204, 208v
Laguna Meadow Trail, TX 160
Lake Chelan National Recreation Area, WA 194
Lake Clark National Park and Preserve, AK 211
Lake Ouachita, AR *107*
lakes, records 116, 198, 201
Lassen Volcanic National Park, CA 191
Leopold, Aldo 18, 165
lightning 41
Little Missouri Falls, AR 108-9
Little Missouri National Grasslands, ND 121
Little Missouri River *104*, 108-9, *109*, 121, 123
Little Missouri Trail, AR 108
lizards *169*, 175, 178, 179, 183
llama packing 26, 87, 95, 137, 140-41, 147, 151, 173, 191, 201
lodging, *see Travel Tips*
logging 72, 82, 85, 92, 195
  trails 26, 82, 84, 152
Long Range Mountains, Nfld 55-9
loons 69, 79, 116, 117
Lyme disease 42
lynx 67, 129, 132

M

MacIntyre Trail, NY 76
Maddron Bald Trail 91-3
Mahoosuc Range, NH 64
Maine 24, 64, 69
Mammoth Cave, KY 47
mangroves 98-9, *100*, *101*
maps 26, 38, 39, 41, 57, 205
  topographical *41*, 57, 208
marine life 59, 61, 98-103, 191, 211
Mariscal Canyon, TX *162*, 163
Mark Twain National Forest, MO 111
marmots 133, 189, *199*
Marshall, Bob 18, *133*, 205
Maryland 87
Mazatzal Divide Trail, AZ 168-71
Mazatzal Wilderness, AZ *166*, 167-73
Merced Wild and Scenic River, CA 191
mescal 170
Mexico 173
Michigan *112*, 113-19
middens, desert pack rat 179-80
mining 113, 117, 170, 180, 183, 195
  trails 26, 151, 152, 180
Minnesota 49, 119
Missouri 111
Misty Fiords National Monument, AK 211
Moab, UT 48, 152
Mojave Desert, CA 25, 175-7, 183
Mojave National Preserve, CA 183
Monarch Divide, CA 188-9
Monongahela National Forest, WV *80*, 81-7
Montana *44*, *128*, 129-37
moose *57*, 72, 113, 116, *117*, 133, *209*
  in excursion areas 61, 69, 79, 119, 157, 211
mosqitoes 41-2, *42*, 107-8, 133, 140, 194, 206
mountain biking, *see* **biking**
mountaineering 45-6, *50*, 198, 211, *see also* **rock climbing**
mountain goats 133, 151, *154*
mountain lions 129, 132, 144, 157, 162, 169, 189
Mount Algonquin, NY 71, 76

Mount Baker Wilderness, WA *195*
Mount Lassen, CA 191
Mount McKinley, AK 211
Mount Marcy, NY 71, 76
Mount Shuksan, WA *195*
Mount Sneffels, CO 152-4
Mount Stuart, WA *19*
Mount Washington, NH *65*, *66*, 66-7, 69
Mount Whitney, CA 186-7
Muir, John 17-18, *124*
mules 27, 137, 167, 169, 173, 194
Murray, William H. H. 74
mushrooms *75*
muskrats 79

N

national parks system 18, 24-6, 124
Native Americans 71-2, 170, 180
navigation 26, 38, 39, 41, 57
Nebraska 127
Nevada *25*, 147
New Brunswick 61
Newfoundland 55-61
New Hampshire *62*, 63-9
New Mexico 27, 47, 157, 165
New York 24, 71-9
Niobrara National Scenic River, NE 127
Noatak River, AK 208
North Absaroka Wilderness, WY 24
North Carolina 89-95
North Cascades National Park, WA *10-11*, *192*, 193-201
North Dakota 25, *120*, 121-7
northern lights *208*
Nova Scotia 61

O

oases 179, 183
Ochopee Prairie, FL 100
off-road vehicles 82, *see also* **four-wheel-drive**
Okefenokee Wilderness, GA 103
Oklahoma 108
old-growth forests *88*, 89-95, 185-91, 201
Olympic National Park, WA *18*, *24*, 201
Ontario 79
opossums 95
Oregon 201
osprey 69, 133
otters 93, 119, 169
Ouachita National Forest, AR 25, *104*, 105-11
Ouachita National Recreation Trail, AR 108, 109, 111
outdoor ethics 26
outfitters 27, *see also Travel Tips*
owls 133, 161, 189
Ozark Mountains, AR 105-6, 111
Ozark National Scenic Riverways, MO 111
Ozark Trail, MO 111

P

Pacific Crest Trail 187, 191, 201
Pacific Rim National Park, BC 201
paddling 26, 38, 49, *96*, *see also* **canoeing**; **kayaking**; **rafting**; **whitewater**
Pajarito Plateau, NM 157
Paleo-Indians 111, 113, 117, 144-5, 170
palms, fan *179*, 183
parks and preserves system 18, 24-6, 124
peccary 162, 163
Pennsylvania 79
peregrine falcons 133, 143, 163, 169
permits, *see Travel Tips*
Petrified Forest Loop Trail, ND 123-5
Phipps Arch, UT 144
pikas 133, *186*, 189, 197
Pinacate and Grand Desert Biosphere Preserve, Mexico 173
pine martens 67, 132
Pinnacle Mountain State Park, AR 109
Pinnacles Trail, TX 160
Pisgah National Forest, NC 95
planning 23-7, *see also Travel Tips*
Pocahontas Trail, WV 82
Powell, John Wesley 139
Prairie Creek State Preserve, CA 191
prairie dogs 125
prairies 100, 111, 121-7, 191
preparations 23-7, *31*
pronghorn antelope *124*, 127, 173
Props Run, WV 83-4
Puebloan peoples 157

Q

Quebec 61
Quetico Provincial Park 119

raccoons 99, 103
Rae Lakes route, CA *187*, 187-8
rafting 26, 27, 49, 87, 134, *135*, *144*, 150, 163, *168*, 208
railroads 79, 150
Rainbow Falls, WA 198
rappelling *48*, 50, 183
records
gorges 198
lakes 116, 198, 201
low temperatures 132
trees 92
winds 66
Red River Gorge, KY 87
Redwood National Park, CA 191
reef formations *131*, 139, 142, 165
Rio Grande, CO/TX 149-50, 159-65
Rio Grande National Forest, CO 150
River of No Return, ID 24, 137
rivers *46*, 49, *76*, *77*, *82*, *151*
crossing *36*, *39*, *161*
wild and scenic 24, 111, 119, 191, 201
roadrunners *180*
rock art 144-5, *145*, 157, 180
rock climbing *2*, *4*, *6*, *20*, 45, *48*, *51*, *80*, *95*, *153*, *174*, *178*, 183, 191
rock glaciers 108, 109
Rocky Harbour, NF 57
Rocky Mountain Front, MT 130-31, 132
Rocky Mountain National Park, CO 157
Roosevelt, Franklin D. 180
Roosevelt, Theodore 18, 121, *124*, 125, 149
Ross Lake National Recreation Area, WA 194
Ruess, Everett 145

S

safety 37-42, 57
Sage Creek Wilderness, SD 127
Sahale Arm Trail, WA 193, 195-8
St. Croix National Scenic Riverway, WI 119
St. Regis Canoe Area, NY 74, 79
salamanders 90, 108
Salmon River, ID 24, 137
sandstone formations 142, *144*, 147, 183
San Juan Mountains, CO *148*, 149-57

scuba diving 47, 114
sea kayaking 49, 61, 99-103, 114, 201, 211
seasons 25-6, *see also Travel Tips*
Sequoia National Park, CA 185-91
Shenandoah National Park, VA 87
Sierra Nevada *185*, 185-91
signal devices 38, 57
Siskiwit Lake, MI 116
Skagit Wild and Scenic River, WA 201
skiing 50, 67, *84*, 84-5, 150, 194, 207, *see also Travel Tips*
skijoring 50
skills training 37-8, *see also Travel Tips*
sleeping bags *31*, 32-3
Snake Den Ridge Trail, NC 91, 93
snakes 42, 178, 183, 199
snow camping 38, *48*, 69, 79, 157, *199*
snowshoeing 48, 50, 69, *72*, 137, 150, 157, 165, 194, 207
Sonoran Desert 173, 183
South Dakota 127
Stanleyville, NF 58
Stehekin, WA 198-9
survival aids 38-9
survival skills 37-42, *see also Travel Tips*
swimming 108, 111

T

Tablelands, ND 58-9
Talimena Scenic Byway *108*
Talimena State Park, OK 109
Tea Creek Recreation Area, WV 83
Telluride, CO 152
temperatures, low 132, 207
Tennessee *88*, 89-95
Ten Thousand Islands, FL 26, *96*, 97-103
tents 33-4, *35*, *67*
Texas 25, *47*, *158*, 159-65
Theodore Roosevelt National Park, ND 25, *120*, 121-7
Thoreau, Henry David 66
thunderstorms 41, 134
ticks 42, 107-8
tides 61, 97-8, 211
Tongass National Forest, AK 211
Tonto National Forest, AZ 168, 173
tour boats 55, 59
tours 27, *see also Travel Tips*
training courses 37-8, *see also Travel Tips*
transmitters 57
tree frogs *179*
trees *98*, 107-8, 109, *125*, *150*, 159, 185
juniper *140*, *145*, *187*
old-growth 89-95, 185, 196-9
pines 106, 159, 185
record size *92*, 185, *189*
trout 83, 114, 133, 137, 137, 150, 188, *see also* **fishing**
tundra 69, 153-4, 157, 203-11
Tunnel Brook Trail, NH 65-6
Tuolumne Wild and Scenic River, CA 191
turkey vultures 144
turtles 92, 99

U, V

Uintas Mountains, UT 147
Uncompahgre National Forest, CO 150
Upper Buffalo Wilderness, AR 111
Utah *16*, *18*, *20-21*, 25, 26, *30*, 48, *138*, 139-47
Vancouver Island, BC 201
Van Hoevenberg Trail, NY 76
Verde River, AZ *168*, *171*, 173
Verde River Trail, AZ 171, 173
Vermilion Cliffs, UT 143, *144*
Vermont 69
Vikings 56
Virginia 87
volcanic formations 114, *115*, 152, 157, 173, 183, 191, 201, 211
Voyageurs National Park, MN 119

W

Washington *10-11*, *18*, *19*, *24*, *192*, 193-201
waste disposal 26
waterfalls 50, 67, 108-9, 111, 187, 193, 194, 197, 198, 199, 211
water supplies *38*, 38-9, 40, 122, 177
weather 27, 39-40, 41, 66-7, *see also Travel Tips*
Weminuche Wilderness, CO 149, 157
West Coast Trail 201
West Virginia *80*, 81-7
whales 59, 61, 191, 211
White Mountain National Forest, NH *62*, 63-9
whitewater *46*, 49, 69, 134, 137, 163, 173
wild boars 91
wildcats, *see* **bobcats**; **mountain lions**
wilderness areas 17-18, 24
Wilderness Society 133
wilderness survival skills 37-42, *see also Travel Tips*
wilderness transmitters 57
Wilderness Waterway, FL 97
wildflowers *5*, *58*, 87, 95, *106*, 107, 108, *122*, 143, 147, 149, 157
alpine *18*, 57, 69, 84-5, 151-4, *155*, 173, 188-9, 191, 192, *196*, 199
desert *161*, 161-2, 163, 165, 167-8, 170, 173, *180*, 183, *see also* **cacti**
old-growth forest 90-91, 93, 186
wild horses 87, 124
wildlife *57*, *65*, 72, *73*, 83, 87, 95, 111, 140, 147
alpine 56, 129, 132-3, 147, 157, 191, 194, 197-8, *199*
arctic 56, 203-11
badlands/prairies *120*, *123*, 124, 125, 127
desert 165, *169*, 173, 178-83, 189
wild turkeys 83, 105
Wind River Range, WY 137
wind speeds 66, 67
winter trips *48*, 49-50, *67*, 69, *72*, 79, 84-5, *91*, *299*, *207*
Wisconsin 119
wolverines 129, 204
wolves 113, *117*, 119, 129, 132-3, 137, 203, 211
woodpeckers 95
Wyoming 24, 26, 27, 137

Y, Z

Yellowstone National Park, WY 26, 137
Yosemite National Park, CA *50*, 191
yuccas 25, 177, 178
Zion National Park, UT 147